THE POETICS OF CONVERSION IN EARLY MODERN ENGLISH LITERATURE

D1556902

Christians in post-Reformation England inhabited a culture of conversion. Required to choose among rival forms of worship, many would cross – and often recross – the boundary between Protestantism and Catholicism. This study considers the poetry written by such converts, from the reign of Elizabeth I to that of James II, concentrating on four figures: John Donne, William Alabaster, Richard Crashaw, and John Dryden. Murray offers a context for each poet's conversion within the era's polemical and controversial literature. She also elaborates on the formal features of the poems themselves, demonstrating how the language of poetry could express both spiritual and ecclesiastical change with particular vividness and power. Proposing conversion as a catalyst for some of the most innovative devotional poetry of the period, both canonical and uncanonical, this study will be of interest to all specialists in early modern English literature.

MOLLY MURRAY is Assistant Professor of English and Comparative Literature at Columbia University. She has published articles on medieval and Renaissance literature and culture in *English Literary History*, *Studies in English Literature*, and a variety of edited collections, including *Catholic Culture in Early Modern England*, edited by Ronald Corthell, Frances Dolan, Christopher Highley, and Arthur Marotti (2007).

THE POETICS OF CONVERSION IN EARLY MODERN ENGLISH LITERATURE

Verse and Change from Donne to Dryden

MOLLY MURRAY

Columbia University

CAMBRIDGE
UNIVERSITY PRESS

CAMBRIDGE UNIVERSITY PRESS
Cambridge, New York, Melbourne, Madrid, Cape Town,
Singapore, São Paulo, Delhi, Tokyo, Mexico City

Cambridge University Press
The Edinburgh Building, Cambridge CB2 8RU, UK

Published in the United States of America by Cambridge University Press, New York

www.cambridge.org
Information on this title: www.cambridge.org/9781107402829

First published 2009
First paperback edition 2011

A catalogue record for this publication is available from the British Library

ISBN 978-0-521-11387-8 Hardback
ISBN 978-1-107-40282-9 Paperback

for E. L. M. and J. H. M.

Contents

Acknowledgments

All first monographs, even ones as brief as this, necessarily cast a long shadow of indebtedness behind them. I must first thank those institutions whose generosity permitted many years of reading and writing. A Kellett Fellowship from Columbia University funded two years of pastoral postgrad life at Clare College, Cambridge. At Yale, where this book took shape as a doctoral dissertation, I was the grateful recipient of a William Wimsatt scholarship and grants from the Yale Center for British Art, the Beinecke Library, and the Mrs. Giles Whiting Foundation. A graduate fellowship at Yale's Whitney Humanities Center provided a cozy office in which to finish the dissertation, and lively lunch companions who helped me understand what it was saying. I found time to rethink and revise thanks to a Chamberlain Fellowship from Columbia University, and grants from the Huntington Library and Columbia's junior faculty development program. I am also much obliged to the patient and expert staff of the Beinecke, British, Butler, Houghton, and Sterling Libraries, as well as the UK National Archives and the archives of Lambeth Palace, St. Mary's College Oscott, and the Venerable English College in Rome.

As an undergraduate at Columbia, I learned about reading and writing from Andrew Delbanco, Kathy Eden, Michael Rosenthal, and especially Edward Tayler. At Cambridge, I found my way into early modern intellectual history guided by Brendan Bradshaw, Mark Goldie, John Morrill, Quentin Skinner, and Richard Tuck. At Yale, I aspired to the scholarly examples of David Bromwich, John Hollander, Lawrence Manley, David Quint, and John Rogers. Returning to Columbia, I have been fortunate in my colleagues, especially the mighty Renaissance quintumvirate of Julie Crawford, Jean Howard, David Kastan, Jim Shapiro, and Alan Stewart. Michael Golston has made me a better reader and teacher of poems (and drinker of margaritas). He, Amanda Claybaugh, Sarah Cole, Tricia Dailey, Nick Dames, Jenny Davidson, Erik Gray, and Ezra Tawil have been models of collegial sanity and solicitude. Our students at Columbia have sharpened my sense of what matters in a work of literature, especially Fred Bengtsson, Jon Blitzer, Musa Gurnis, Jason Kim, David Nee, Britt Peterson, Chris Russell, Julian Smith-Newman, and Matt Zarnowiecki. Bryan Lowrance gave invaluable eleventh-hour research assistance. I am also grateful for the bracing scholarly insights of many non-Columbian colleagues over the years: Jeff Dolven, Thomas Fulton, Heather Hirschfeld, Jim Kearney, Arthur Marotti, Steven Pincus, Richard Rambuss, Alison Shell, Nigel Smith, Adam Smyth, Abe Stoll, Richard Strier, and especially Ramie Targoff. The anonymous readers at Cambridge University Press offered many helpful suggestions, and Ray Ryan provided much-needed editorial confidence. Christina Sarigiannidou and Caroline Howlett somehow made the final stages of book production a pleasure.

The indefatigable Annabel Patterson deserves her own paragraph of thanks. As a counselor, interlocutor, and mentor, she has supported this project (and its author) at every stage. Her style of intellectual tough love is deservedly legendary, and every page of this book has been improved by it.

I wish I could give each of the following people their own paragraphs, but instead I will ask them to imagine the particulars of my gratitude, and to expect its more lavish expression in person: Tim Baker, Jane Benson, Molly Breen, Neal Brennan, Lara Cohen, the Conde-Burkes, James Covert, The Drapes, Brent Edwards, Herschel Farbman, Alan Fishbone, the family Golston, Caroline Goodson, Ben Greenman, Scott Korb, Sasha Koren, David Kurnick, Molly Larkey, John Leibovitz, Maya Lester, Seth Lobis, Victoria Sancho Lobis, Stefanie Markovits, Tim Martin, Mark Miodownik, Heather and Lily Lux O'Donnell, George Pendle, Matthew Pincus, Alex Robertson Textor, Kelefa Sanneh, Linnaea Saunders, Allison Schiller, Michael Schmelling, Stefanie Sobelle, Rebecca Stanton, Alexandra Stara, Jessamin Swearingen, Charlotte Taylor, Craig Taylor, Nick and Danny Waplington, Benj Widiss, and Emily Wilson.

Finally, without Thomas McElligott I wouldn't be someone who cares about poetry, and without Jim, Beth, Megan, Matt, and Meredith Rita Murray I wouldn't be anything at all.

Note on the text

In quotations from primary sources I have silently modernized i/j and u/v, as well as superscripts and subscripts, but have otherwise preserved original spelling.
I have used the following abbreviations throughout:

BL: British Library
ELH: *English Literary History*
HJ: *Historical Journal*
JEH: *Journal of Ecclesiastical History*
MLQ: *Modern Language Quarterly*
MP: *Modern Philology*
PMLA: *Proceedings of the Modern Language Association*
PQ: *Philological Quarterly*
RH: *Recusant History*
SEL: *Studies in English Literature*

I have used the following editions of poetry, with line numbers quoted in the text:

Alabaster, William, *The Sonnets*, ed. G. M. Story and H. Gardner (Oxford University Press, 1959).

Crashaw, Richard, *The Complete Poetry*, ed. G. W. Williams (New York: Norton, 1974).

Donne, John, *The Complete English Poems*, ed. C. A. Patrides (London: Everyman, 1994).

Dryden, John, *Works*, ed. H. T. Swedenberg (Berkeley: University of California Press, 1956–2000).

Eliot, T. S., *Collected Poems, 1909–1962* (New York: Harcourt Brace Jovanovich, 1970).

Southwell, Robert, *The Collected Poems*, ed. P. Davidson and A. Sweeney (Manchester: Carcanet, 2007).

Spenser, Edmund, *The Faerie Queene*, ed. A. C. Hamilton (New York: Longman, 1977).

Spenser, Edmund, *The Yale Edition of the Shorter Poems*, ed. W. A. Oram (New Haven: Yale University Press, 1989).

Unless otherwise noted, I have used the Authorized Version for all Biblical quotations.

Introduction: toward a poetics of conversion

> Oh, to vex me, contraryes meet in one:
> Inconstancie unnaturally hath begott
> A constant habit: that when I would not
> I change in vowes and in devotione.
>
> (John Donne, Holy Sonnet 19)

The troubled speaker of Donne's quatrain could be early modern England itself: a nation with a "constant habit" of religious change. From the first emergence of Tudor Protestantism to the last years of the Stuart monarchy, England would officially "change in vowes and in devotione" numerous times according to the religion of its successive rulers, and often seemed poised on the verge of further national conversions. No matter what creed was imposed from above, early modern English Christianity stubbornly comprised various "contraryes [met] in one": ceremonialist and iconoclast, recusant and orthodox, Anglican and Puritan, and especially the constantly evolving "contraryes" of Catholic and Reformed. The work of revisionist historians, most notably John Bossy, Christopher Haigh, and Eamon Duffy, has effectively dismantled the longstanding Whiggish account of the nation's relatively rapid and ultimately triumphant Protestantization.[1] More recently, a new generation of "post-revisionists" has depicted England's long Reformation as a matter of myriad complex and contested allegiances, and provisional or partial redefinitions of terms.[2] It is now no longer possible to imagine sixteenth- and seventeenth-century English

---

[1] J. Bossy, *The English Catholic Community, 1570–1850* (London: Longman, 1975); C. Haigh, *English Reformations: Religion, Politics and Society Under the Tudors* (Oxford: Clarendon, 1993); E. Duffy, *The Stripping of the Altars: Traditional Religion in England c. 1400–1580* (New Haven: Yale University Press, 1992).

[2] For an overview of the "post-revisionist" move in Reformation scholarship, see the introduction to E. Shagan (ed.), *Catholics and the "Protestant Nation": Religious Politics and Identity in Early Modern England* (Manchester University Press, 2005), 8–18. Notable works in this vein are P. Lake, *Anglicans and Puritans? Presbyterian and Reformist Thought from Whitgift to Hooker* (London: Allen and Unwin, 1988); A. Milton, *Catholic and Reformed: The Roman and Protestant Churches in English Protestant*

religious culture as dominated by a single struggle between two monolithic churches, one destined to defeat the other. Instead, we have come to accept that Christianity in early modern England was much more "vexed" and various than once was thought, and remained so for much longer.

Even as it maps this varied confessional terrain in ever more precise detail, moreover, much recent work in Reformation history has also emphasized how often Christians in early modern England moved across any borders that we, or they, might have drawn. As an example of this movement we might consider the Baptist Susanna Parr, who joined a separatist conventicle in the mid-seventeenth century, and justified her apostasy with an *Apology Against the Elders* (1659); here, she describes one of her brethren who "had formerly been an Anabaptist, then a Seeker, next (as I was informed) a Papist … then turning to prelacy, and the Book of Common Prayer, and afterward an Independent."[3] After decades of sectarian proliferation within Christianity, such a miscellaneous confessional résumé was hardly unusual. The work of Michael Questier and Caroline Hibbard has particularly demonstrated how even the most dramatic instances of individual Christian conversion – conversion to or from Roman Catholicism – occurred with remarkable frequency throughout the long seventeenth century, independently of England's official changes of religion.[4] Parr's account suggests that early modern people understood conversion as something that could occur between sects as well as between churches; an Anabaptist turned Seeker would be as much a convert as a papist turned Puritan.[5] But if conversions from Catholicism to Protestantism (or vice versa) were not unique in kind, they nevertheless provide the most striking evidence both of the perceived reality of Christian confessional boundaries, and of their porousness. It is this kind of conversion that most preoccupied men and women in early modern England, and it is this preoccupation, in turn, that most vividly illustrates the instability of the period's religious culture, and of individual identities within it.

Thought 1600–1640 (Cambridge University Press, 1995); A. Walsham, *Church Papists: Catholicism, Conformity, and Confessional Polemic in Early Modern England* (Woodbridge: Boydell, 1993); L. Wooding, *Rethinking Catholicism in Reformation England* (Oxford University Press, 2000); E. Shagan, *Popular Politics and the English Reformation* (Cambridge University Press, 2002); and P. Marshall, *Religious Identities in Henry VIII's England* (London: Ashgate, 2006).

[3] *Susanna's Apology Against the Elders: Or, a Vindication of Susanna Parr* (Oxford, 1659), 9.
[4] M. Questier, *Conversion, Politics and Religion in England, 1580–1625* (Cambridge University Press, 1996); C. Hibbard, *Charles I and the Popish Plot* (Chapel Hill: University of North Carolina Press, 1983).
[5] See, for instance, Peter Fairlambe, *The Recantation of a Brownist, or A Reformed Puritan* (London, 1606), in which a sectarian Protestant describes his reconversion to the Church of England.

This monograph focuses on cases of conversion to and from Catholicism in England, in the period between the excommunication of Elizabeth I and the deposing of James II. As my title and epigraph imply, however, it will do so by focusing on a kind of text that does not cross the desks of many historians: the devotional poem. Scholars of the English Reformation have been surprisingly reluctant to engage with the poetry of the period, even as they have become increasingly attuned to the importance of imaginative literature in reconstructing early modern *mentalités*. To take one striking example, Peter Lake subtitles a recent collection of essays "Protestants, Papists, *and Players* in Post-Reformation England," and in many of these essays offers suggestive new interpretations of Shakespeare and Jonson in terms of religious conflict.[6] But in its 731 pages, the book contains no mention of the poetry of Southwell, Donne, Spenser, Herbert, or Milton, literature that addresses such issues at least as effectively as any of Shakespeare's plays. How can we account for this omission? One possibility might be that poetry, even compared to other literary genres, seems to take a particularly imprecise or oblique approach to its subject, so that its conceptual content is finally, fatally occluded by merely literary concerns, by *style*.[7] We can see such suspicion toward the literary in Questier's groundbreaking study of Catholic/Protestant conversions between 1580 and 1625. Throughout this book, Questier attends sensitively to the polemical literature developed around the subject, and presents in fascinating detail its strategies for representing change. Yet he dismisses the particular formal characteristics of this writing as "word-games and literary sleight of hand," verbal superfluities that not only "did not contain the essence of conversion," but can obscure the more important spiritual, ecclesiastical, or political realities that caused and shaped it.[8] Such skepticism, I would suggest, is deeply inimical to an understanding of one of the most prominent Jacobean converts, John Donne, or indeed of any poet I will discuss in

---

[6] P. Lake, with M. Questier, *The Anti-Christ's Lewd Hat: Protestants, Papists and Players in Post-Reformation England* (New Haven: Yale University Press, 2002). The Catholic poet Robert Southwell is mentioned once, as the author of the prose work *An Humble Supplication*. Donne appears as the author of the prose tract *Pseudo-Martyr* and a Protestant friend of the Catholic convert Sir Toby Matthew. Milton receives one mention (as a polemicist, and in a footnote), Herbert and Spenser none at all.

[7] Wooding suggests that the composition of religious verse in the late sixteenth century was, like the writing of hagiography, part of a more general cultural turn to "outward displays of loyalty and piety"; such a formulation suggests an interest in poetry purely as evidence of confessional identification, and not as an object of aesthetic analysis *per se*. Wooding, *Rethinking Catholicism*, 262.

[8] Questier, *Conversion, Politics and Religion*, 37.

the pages that follow.[9] Poetry, and especially the metaphysical poetry of Donne and Crashaw, is perhaps the most ostentatiously "stylish" writing produced in the period, characterized precisely by what we might call "word-games and literary sleight of hand." The dense "literariness" of such poetry, however, does not indicate a lack of intense or sustained engagement with religious controversy and conflict. This study will propose, in fact, that the complex formal strategies used by these poets demonstrate precisely such an engagement. The poetry written by converts like Donne and Crashaw thus invites us to think more subtly and flexibly about the relationship between literary form and historical context, in addition to thinking more skeptically about the division between Catholic and Protestant aesthetics in the early modern period.

This latter invitation has been largely unheeded by scholars of English literature, despite the so-called "religious turn" in recent early modern literary studies.[10] In fact, the renewed critical attention to matters of belief in Renaissance literature has often, and unfortunately, assumed early modern devotional categories to be absolute. This is not to deny that many critics have explored the complexity of these categories. Complementing Louis Martz's account of the Jesuit "poetry of meditation," for instance, we now have the work of, among others, Arthur Marotti, Ceri Sullivan, and Alison Shell, showing the breadth and vitality of English Catholic writing.[11] Complicating Barbara Lewalski's account of a unified "Protestant poetics,"[12] we now have Debora Shuger's and Jeanne Shami's studies of literature and conformity, Ramie Targoff's discussion of prayerbook poetry, Nigel Smith's exploration of radical sectarian writing, and Brian Cummings's magisterial

---

[9]   Donne's name is notably absent from Questier's exhaustive bibliography of Elizabethan and Jacobean converts and controversialists; the book's one mention of Donne asserts that he was "loftily detached in his religious opinions until he finally took orders in the Church of England" (56). In Chapter 2, I suggest that Donne's devotional poetry belies the neatness of this formulation.

[10] For a survey of this turn, and its response to the secularizing tendencies of much new historicist criticism, see K. Jackson and A. Marotti, "The Turn to Religion in Early Modern English Studies," *Criticism* 4.1 (2004), 167–90.

[11] L. Martz, *The Poetry of Meditation* (New Haven: Yale University Press, 1954, rev. edn. 1962). In *Catholicism, Controversy and the English Literary Imagination, 1558–1660* (Cambridge University Press, 1999), A. Shell attacks the persistent anti-Catholic bias in early modern literary studies, and surveys Catholic literature of exile, loyalism, and martyrdom. A. Marotti takes a similar stance in *Religious Ideology and Cultural Fantasy: Catholic and Anti-Catholic Discourses in Early Modern England* (University of Notre Dame Press, 2005). Other notable studies of Catholic writing include A. D. Cousins, *The Catholic Religious Poets from Southwell to Crashaw* (London: Sheed and Ward, 1991); C. Sullivan, *Dismembered Rhetoric: English Recusant Writing 1580–1603* (London: Associated University Presses, 1995); and F. Dolan, *Whores of Babylon: Catholicism, Gender, and Seventeenth-Century Print Culture* (Ithaca, NY: Cornell University Press, 1999).

[12] B. Lewalski, *Protestant Poetics and the Seventeenth-Century Religious Lyric* (Princeton University Press, 1979).

account of the English Reformation's various engagements with language and text, to name only a few important recent critical works.[13] But, again, the project of diversifying the map can also lead us to neglect the permeability of its borders. Any taxonomy of confessional categories, no matter how subtle, can implicitly minimize the importance of changes *between* those categories in the religious literature of early modern England. They can blind us to the ways in which denominational change *itself* might have influenced the work of Thomas Lodge, Henry Constable, Ben Jonson, William Alabaster, John Donne, Toby Matthew, Richard Crashaw, Walter Montague, William Davenant, Andrew Marvell, John Dryden, and other poets who moved between Catholic and Reformed positions – sometimes more than once – over the course of their writing lives.

This book proposes that conversion, understood in its early modern sense as movement between churches and not solely as a progression toward grace, profoundly influenced the English literary imagination. More specifically, it proposes that such conversion influenced poetic style. And more specifically still, it proposes that some early modern poets understood their changes in devotional form and their experiments in literary form to be both analogous and symbiotic. Considered etymologically, the terms "verse" and "trope" signal poetry's intrinsic affiliation with turning, with movement, with change.[14] In early modern English poetic theory, descriptions of poetic language can sound almost uncannily like descriptions of apostasy. Thomas Wilson, for example, defines "trope" as "an alteration of a word or sentence from the proper signification to that which is not proper."[15] "Proper signification," here, bears a double meaning: it is both the meaning that adheres to a social consensus about what a word should signify ("proper" as "appropriate"), and it is also the meaning appropriate to the word itself (cognate to the French *propre*). In violating these two kinds of propriety, the poet both separates himself from a community of speakers and converts language itself into something new and essentially, improperly "altered."

---

[13] J. Shami, *John Donne and Conformity in Crisis in the Late Jacobean Pulpit* (Woodbridge: Brewer, 2003); D. Shuger, *Habits of Thought in the English Renaissance: Religion, Politics and the Dominant Culture* (Berkeley: University of California Press, 1990); R. Targoff, *Common Prayer: The Language of Public Devotion in Early Modern England* (University of Chicago Press, 2001); N. Smith, *Perfection Proclaimed: Language and Literature in English Radical Religion, 1640–1660* (Oxford: Clarendon, 1989); B. Cummings, *The Literary Culture of the Reformation: Grammar and Grace* (Oxford University Press, 2002).

[14] For a discussion of "dialogic" movement in secular lyric, see P. Phillippy, *Love's Remedies: Recantation and Renaissance Lyric Poetry* (Lewisburg, PA: Bucknell University Press, 1995).

[15] Thomas Wilson, *The Art of Rhetoric (1560)*, ed. P. Medine (University Park, PA: Pennsylvania State University Press, 1994), 197.

George Puttenham puts it even more provocatively in *The Art of English Poesy* (1589): "As figures be the instruments of ornament in every language, so be they also in a sorte abuses or rather trespasses in speech, because they passe the ordinary limits of common utterance ... drawing it from plainnesse and simplicitie to a certain doublenesse, whereby our talke is the more guilefull and abusing, for what els is your *Metaphor* but an inversion of sence by transport?"[16] In Puttenham's playful account, metaphor transports language across an accepted boundary or definitional "limit," thus rendering it altered, doubled or inverted in a way that resembles other kinds of transgression.[17] As an act of verbal "abuse, cross-naming, new naming, change of name," metaphor is always close to the outright scandal of catachresis.[18] Puttenham offers a particularly potent contemporary analogy to such a dramatic, scandalous "change of name"; without vigilant attention to the rules of decorum, he warns, poetic utterances can become "trespasses in speech" which, he notes, "are called, and not without cause ... *heresies of language.*"[19]

Puttenham's connection between poetry and heterodoxy is, itself, only a metaphor, and a lighthearted one at that – but it is nevertheless suggestive. In the ensuing chapters, I will follow some of the implications of this metaphor of verbal "heresy," exploring the ways in which early modern convert-poets do more than merely describe or justify their "change in vowes and in devotione," but actively seek to perform or enact versions of that change of name in and through poetic language. The four chapters of this book center on four figures whose careers span a century of religious instability: Donne, Alabaster, Crashaw, and Dryden. For these poets, I will argue, the composition of verse offers neither an escape from, nor a solution to, the heated "contraryes" of confessional conflict. Instead, it acts as a mechanism for actively transforming the terms of this conflict, and thus the terms through which identity is defined and maintained.[20] Throughout their extremely diverse devotional poetry, each of these four poets invokes a voluminous and vociferous polemical literature on the subject of conversion.

[16] George Puttenham, *The Art of English Poesy*, ed. F. Whigham and W. Rebhorn (1589; Ithaca, NY: Cornell University Press, 2007), 238.
[17] The pioneering account of the connection between rhetorical and ethical theory is D. Javitch, *Poetry and Courtliness in Renaissance England* (Princeton University Press, 1978). See F. Whigham, *Ambition and Privilege: The Social Tropes of Elizabethan Courtesy Theory* (Berkeley: University of California Press, 1984), 138–42 for an account of the ethics of figuration in Puttenham particularly.
[18] Puttenham, *Art*, 262.   [19] *Ibid.*, 239.
[20] Frank Burch Brown discusses the theological implications of metaphor in *Transfigurations: Poetic Metaphor and the Languages of Religious Belief* (Chapel Hill: University of North Carolina Press, 1983); he does not, however, discuss the literary effects of denominational conversion.

Each does so, however, precisely in order to think beyond the definitive claims of the polemicists, whether Catholic or Protestant. Refusing to versify simple creeds or credos, each of these writers instead practices a variation of what I will call an early modern *poetics of conversion*, in which the particular formal qualities of poetry – its schemes and tropes, its distinctive styles of signifying – are used to confront the unsettling phenomenon of religious change. In the rest of this chapter, I will offer a preliminary account of what such a phenomenon, and such a poetics, might involve.

TURNING CHRISTIAN

What do Christians mean by "conversion"? It is a question that takes us to the beginning of the Christian tradition, when the evangelists first proposed individual transformation as an index of holiness. From its earliest mentions in the Gospels, however, this transformation has been defined in two distinct ways: as a change of church and as a change of soul. Pagans and Jews become Christians by undergoing a ritual, baptismal induction into a new community, but also through *metanoia*, a word that literally indicates a change in spirit or mind, and is often translated into English as "repentance" or "penitence." So, in Matthew, John announces "I indeed baptize you with water unto repentance" (Mt. 3:11) [*ego men umas baptizo en udati eis metanoian*]; Mark terms this same activity "a baptism of repentance for the remission of sins" (Mk. 1:4) [*baptisma metanoias eis aphesin hamartion*]. These phrases, describing a single event in two very different registers – the ritual and the spiritual – indicate how paradoxical, even at its origin, the concept of conversion might be. To trace the subsequent discourse of conversion is to see generations of Christian writers elaborating upon this paradox and discovering others. Conversion can be a deliberate, voluntary action, and the passive receipt of the grace of God. It can be incremental and painfully protracted, and it can be instantaneous and cataclysmic. It can be a matter of refusal and rejection, and a matter of intensifying commitments that already exist. It can bolster individual and communal identities, and it can destroy and refashion them.[21]

---

[21] For a classic sociological account of the paradigms and paradoxes of Christian conversion, see William James, *The Varieties of Religious Experience*, ed. R. Niebuhr (New York: Touchstone, 1997). For a classic historical account of their origin, see A. D. Nock, *Conversion: The Old and the New in Religion from Alexander the Great to Augustine of Hippo* (Oxford: Clarendon, 1933).

Many of these paradoxes can be found in the paradigmatic story of Christian conversion, the story of the Jewish Pharisee Saul, "breathing out threatenings and slaughter against the disciples of the Lord" en route to Damascus.[22]

> Suddenly, there shined round about him a light from heaven: and he fell to the earth, and heard a voice saying unto him, Saul, Saul, why persecutest thou me? And he said, Who art thou Lord? And the Lord said I am Jesus whom thou persecutest: it is hard for thee to kick against the pricks. And he trembling and astonished said, Lord, what wilt thou have me to do? (Acts 9:3–6)

This episode centers on a crisis of self-definition. Saul's question, "Who art thou?," although aimed at the mysterious voice from heaven, ultimately ricochets back toward its speaker. Called upon to re-examine his actions and attitudes, Saul has *already* undergone a sudden inward change, signaled by his instinctive address of Jesus as "Lord." *Metanoia*, however, is not the end of the story. From the first, conversion is not just a matter of what Saul believes, but what he is to do: he must reject his old earthly communities and commitments in favor of his new ones, and dedicate his life to the project of evangelism.[23] His story thus emphasizes both the dramatic action of God upon him, and his own deliberate action in consequence: as soon as his vision was restored, the new convert "arose, and was baptized" as a Christian, "preached Christ in the synagogues," and finally "assayed to join himself to the disciples" (Acts 9:18–26). Saul the persecutor becomes Paul the proselytizer, a convert whose life's work will be to convert others. The conversions he encourages, again, will combine the turning of the soul with the transformation of action in the world. He urges unbelievers to "repent and turn to God, and do works meet for repentance" [*Metanoein kai epistrephein epi ton theon, axia tes metanoias erga prassontas*] (Acts 26:20). Paul's entreaty combines the inward and outward registers of conversion; to become a Christian involves both *metanoia*, repentance, and *erga*, works.

---

[22] See H. G. Wood, "The Conversion of Paul: Its Nature, Antecedents, and Consequences," *New Testament Studies* 1 (1955), 276–82. Alan Segal points out that, *pace* Luke, Paul's conversion is "not typical of the first generations of Christians," as it does not come from Jesus's teachings, but rather from a direct divine revelation, and is thus continuous with certain aspects of Jewish apocalyptic thought. Segal, *Paul the Convert: The Apostasy and Apostolate of Saul the Pharisee* (New Haven: Yale University Press, 1990), 2 and *passim*. Segal offers a useful survey of the meaning of conversion in diasporic Judaism (72–114). More recently, Julia Reinhard Lupton has reconsidered Paul's relationship to Judaism, and the relevance of this relationship to ideas of political affiliation in early modern England. Lupton, *Citizen-Saints: Shakespeare and Political Theology* (University of Chicago Press, 2005), 21–48.

[23] For the Pauline idea of "separation" see G. Agamben, *The Time that Remains: A Commentary on the Letter to the Romans*, trans. P. Dailey (Stanford University Press, 2005), 44–58.

Turning to Christianity, Paul also turns to writing. His evangelical mission consists in composing letters, "both to the Greeks and to the Barbarians; both to the wise and to the unwise" (Rom. 1:14–15), which will effect further conversions on his own model. This strategy of epistolary conversion centers on a kind of transformative empathy, which he describes in 1 Corinthians: "unto the Jews I became as a Jew, that I might gain the Jews; to them that are under the law, as under the law, that I might gain them that are under the law" and so forth (1 Cor. 9:20). Paul "becomes as" his audience, in other words, precisely in order to effect the opposite transformation. "Be as I am," he writes, "for I am as ye are" (Gal. 4:12) – and to "be as [Paul is]" requires conversion in both inner and outer senses. Describing in rich detail his membership in another devotional community, "circumcised on the eighth day, of the stock of Israel, of the tribe of Benjamin, an Hebrew of the Hebrews; as touching the law a Pharisee," Paul the convert asks other unbelievers to "be followers together of me" in his new Christian way of life (Phil. 3:5, 17). Such conversion is not merely a matter of the heart, but also a matter of refashioning outward identity, of becoming a recognizable member of a new church. Paul aims not only to turn sinners into godly men, but also to turn Corinthians, Thessalonians, Romans, and Hebrews into Christians.

Paul's ministry gained many converts, none more important for the subsequent literature of conversion than St. Augustine. In the *Confessions*, Augustine demonstrates how thoroughly he has "become as" his predecessor by recapitulating key features of the Pauline narrative, with a few significant differences. Like Saul the Pharisee, Augustine the Manichee undergoes a miraculous "reorientation of the soul." Augustine's conversion to Christianity may have been more protracted than Paul's (he reads and investigates scripture long before he believes it), but its culminative moment, as he recounts it in Book 8, is similarly rapid, and triggered by divine coincidences: first the overhearing of the child's chant – "*tolle lege*," take and read – in the garden, and then the lucky game of scriptural *sortes* that led him to Paul's Letter to the Romans, at which point faith arrived and "all the shadows of doubt were dispelled."[24] Like Paul, Augustine also emphasizes two necessary phases of conversion: first, the mysterious instant of spiritual transformation, and then its necessary expression in earthly, practical terms. For Augustine, conversion centers on the receipt of a divine

---

[24] St. Augustine, *The Confessions*, ed. and trans. H. Chadwick (1991; paperback edn. Oxford University Press, 1998), 153. Further quotations will be from this edition, and parenthetical page numbers will be given in the text.

light that dispels doubt, illuminating the convert's past sins as well as his future actions in the world. The first thing this light reveals, however, is the way into a new devotional community, signaled by Augustine's conversion of his best friend Alypius, and reunion with his Christian mother Monica. In *The Confessions*, becoming a Christian requires not just the receipt of grace, but also a renegotiation of relationships with friends, family, and teachers. Augustine's narrative as a whole presents two inextricable turns: a radical reorientation of mind, and a radical redirection of life, signaled by a crossing of church borders.

Augustine refracts both registers of conversion – the inward and the outward – through an increasingly intense engagement with text. Indeed, *The Confessions* as a whole reframes the story of Paul's conversion in explicitly textual terms. So, where Paul persecutes Christians, Augustine parses Christian exegetical writings. Where Paul is cast to the ground, Augustine's eyes are cast upon scripture. Where Paul hears the voice of God in the heavens, Augustine reads the Word, and more particularly the words of Paul himself, on the page of a codex. The moment of epiphanic reading that Augustine narrates in Book 8 animates the dead letter of scripture – a private hermeneutic quickening that would inspire generations of Christian theologians. But Augustine is converted as a writer as well as a reader. The exegetic unfolding of Genesis in the final books of the *Confessions* is not just an exercise in solitary *lectio divina*, but Augustine's public performance of his new Christian identity. This textual performance of conversion extends to the *Confessions* as a whole: a text meant both to demonstrate its author's new life, and to urge similar transformations in its readers. Throughout the narrative, Augustine describes a number of other text-based conversions, placing his own moment of transformation along-side the readerly conversions of Antony and Ambrose, Ponticianus, Simplicianus, and Alypius; this chain of exemplars implicitly extends to the latest person turning the pages of the *Confessions*.[25]

---

[25] I will return to a discussion of the *Confessions* in Chapter 1 below. The most sustained discussion of Augustine's textual engagements is B. Stock, *Augustine the Reader: Meditation, Self-Knowledge, and the Ethics of Interpretation* (Cambridge, MA: Harvard University Press, 1996), ch. 3 and *passim*. For broader and more theoretically inflected discussions of conversion, mimesis, and exegesis in Augustine, see B. Stock, *After Augustine: The Meditative Reader and the Text* (Philadelphia: University of Pennsylvania Press, 2001), as well as G. G. Harpham, *The Ascetic Imperative in Culture and Criticism* (University of Chicago Press, 1987), 91–134; L. Freinkel, *Reading Shakespeare's Will: The Theology of the Figure from St. Augustine to the Sonnets* (New York: Columbia University Press, 2002), 1–45; and especially K. Morrison, *Conversion and Text* (Charlottesville: University of Virginia Press, 1992), 1–38.

CHRISTIAN TURNING

In these two seminal accounts of Christian conversion, a change of soul involves a change in devotional community – and both of these transformations are inseparable from changes in reading and writing. As Christianity gained institutional strength, however, its prevailing definitions of conversion evolved. While efforts to convert non-Christians, by sermon or sword, would persist through the middle ages and beyond, the idea of *conversio* that would dominate medieval theology did not signify a turn to Christianity by a pagan, Muslim, or Jew.[26] Instead, it simply indicated a Christian's turn to the deeper piety of monasticism: the *conversio morum*, or change of living, described by St. Benedict's rule.[27] By the twelfth century, Bernard of Clairvaux could use the term more generally still, to describe the ethics of the *imitatio Christi*. In a sermon known as *De Conversione*, Bernard insists that "our true life is to be found only through conversion, and there is no other way to enter upon it (1 Tim. 6:19)."[28] Bernard does not mean to encourage a change of churches, as his audience was comprised of Christian clerics, nor does he mean to urge them all to enter strict regular orders.[29] By *conversio*, Bernard simply indicates the soul's turn to repentance, inaugurated by God's call: "[t]he voice of magnificence and power (Ps. 28:4) rolling through the desert (Ps. 28:8) … shaking souls free of sluggishness."[30] For Bernard, as for Paul and Augustine, conversion involves self-scrutiny, atonement for past sins, and preparation for a culminative union with God. This process may be complex in itself, as Caroline Walker Bynum's work on hybridity and metamorphosis has amply demonstrated.[31] But it nevertheless modifies earlier definitions of conversion in a number of important ways. First, it eliminates the need for an individual

---

[26] K. Morrison, *Understanding Conversion* (Charlottesville: University of Virginia Press, 1992), 3–23.

[27] See P. Delatte, *Commentary on the Rule of St. Benedict*, trans J. McCann (London. Burns, Oates, and Washburn, 1921), 389–90.

[28] Bernard of Clairvaux, "On Conversion," in *Selected Works*, ed. G. R. Evans (New York: Paulist Press, 1987), 66 (*vera nobis vita nonnisi in conversione est, nec aliter ad eam patet ingressus*). Bernard also invokes Matthew 18:30: "the Lord says 'Unless you are converted and become like little children, you will not enter the kingdom of heaven' [*nisi conversi fueritis et efficiamini sicut parvuli, non intrabitis in regnum caelorum*]."

[29] Although, according to one of Bernard's early biographers, Geoffrey of Auxerre, the sermon caused three men to be converted (*conversi*) "from vain studies to the worship of true wisdom," at which point they did take monastic orders. See Bernard of Clairvaux, *Sermons on Conversion*, ed. and trans. M.-B. Saïd (Kalamazoo, MI: Cistercian Publications, 1981), 13–14.

[30] Bernard, "On Conversion," 67.

[31] Bynum explores the doubleness and hybridity implicit in *De Conversione*, which she sees as an expression of Bernard's ambivalent attitude toward body and soul. She argues that for Bernard, conversion is not a resolution of this opposition, but rather the construction of "a radically disjunctive

change of soul to be registered through an institutional change of a Pauline or Augustinian kind. Conversion, on this model, is resolutely inward and upward; rather than a choice among competing human institutions, it is an interior journey to God made by every Christian soul. Second, it effectively minimizes the importance of textuality in this process. While such a conversion could inspire imaginative literature (Dante's *Commedia* being the most obvious example), it need not be based on reading or productive of writing.

These elements of confessional specificity and essential textuality would return to prominence in sixteenth-century Germany, with the conversion – and the conversion narrative – of the Augustinian monk Martin Luther. Luther describes his transformative *Türmerlebnis*, or "tower-experience," in the preface to the 1545 edition of his Latin works. This brief autobiographical account, like Book 8 of the *Confessions*, represents conversion as a hermeneutic crisis following an encounter with the writings of St. Paul.[32] The difference, of course, is that in Luther's account the crisis befalls a man who is already nominally a believing Christian, and indeed is already subject to the discipline of the monastery. "Though I lived as a monk without reproach," Luther writes, "I felt that I was a sinner before God with an extremely disturbed conscience. I could not believe that [God] was placated by my satisfaction." The monastic *conversio morum*, in other words, had failed to provide Luther with adequate assurance of the presence of God's grace. "Thus," he continues, "I raged with a fierce and troubled conscience," and in this state turned to a text: the letters of Paul, patron saint of converts, and particularly Paul's account of salvation and grace:

I beat importunately upon Paul at that place ... At last, by the mercy of God, meditating day and night, I gave heed to the context of the words, namely "In it the righteousness of God is revealed, as it is written, 'He who through faith is righteous shall live.'" There I began to understand that the righteousness of God is that by which the righteous lives by a gift of God, namely by faith ... Here I felt that I was altogether born again, and had entered paradise itself through open gates.[33]

---

self," or "a *unitas* that is forever two." Bynum, *Metamorphosis and Identity* (New York: Zone, 2005), 131, 150. This ambivalence, nevertheless, is located primarily in the individual's definition of self, and has little to do with the claims of rival churches on earth. See also G. R. Evans, "A Change of Mind in Some Scholars of the Eleventh and Twelfth Centuries," *Studies in Church History* 15 (1978), 27–38, and *Bernard of Clairvaux* (Oxford University Press, 2000), 23–6.

[32] Martin Luther, "Preface," trans. Lewis W. Spitz, in Luther, *Complete Works*, ed. Helmut Lehmann, vol. xxxiv (Philadelphia: Muhlenberg Press, 1960), 328. For Luther's debt to Augustinian hermeneutics, see Cummings, *Literary Culture*, 60–101.

[33] Luther, *Works*, vol. xxxiv, 337.

Luther's readerly epiphany forms the kernel of his theology of conversion, elaborated in his further commentaries on Paul. This theology has been described in terms of its intense individualism, particularly its increasing emphasis on spiritual justification through the "gift of ... faith" alone, mediated through intense individual engagements with scripture.[34] But Luther's more important contribution to the conceptual history of conversion, for my purposes here, is precisely his rejection of a *purely* spiritual definition of being "born again." Brian Cummings has suggested that "[Luther's] conversion consists in nothing less than a new understanding of conversion," and while it may have been new to Luther himself, his indictment of "the pillagings, traffickings, and endless impostures of Roman rascals" in fact revives an older definition of the concept, recoupling two strands of conversion that had long been separated: a radical reorientation of the soul and a radical change of outward confessional identity.[35] For Luther, the invisible conversion of the heart, however crucial, implies a visible conversion of the church, however difficult – in Donne's words, a "change in vowes *and* in devotione."[36]

As Luther's schism widened, this restored emphasis on outward re-affiliation as a corollary of inward regeneration intensified. In Geneva, John Calvin's theology would surpass Luther's in its stress on the futility of human effort in the achievement of grace. But even as Calvin emphasized the universal Christian need for a divinely bestowed conversion of the soul, he also strengthened the implicit link between spiritual transformation and confessional reidentification. Extending Luther's description of the "Babylonian captivity" of the church, Calvin reverses the chronology of the Reformation, making Catholics into heretical innovators; "having bidden farewell to the prophets and apostles, and neglecting the ancient Church, they want their revolt from the Gospel to be regarded as the consent of the catholic Church."[37] Reformed Christians like himself, by contrast, become ideally "repentant"

---

[34] While the scholarship on related concepts in Luther's thought, particularly his theology of justification, is extensive, Marilyn Harran provides the only sustained study of his theology of conversion *per se*. Harran, *Luther on Conversion: The Early Years* (Ithaca, NY: Cornell University Press, 1983).

[35] Cummings, *Literary Culture*, 62; Luther, *Works*, vol. XXXIV, 330.

[36] Lisa Freinkel, subtly analyzing Luther's attitude toward *figura*, points out the impossibility of this demand: "Luther's church is an ambivalent union of visibility and disembodiment. Coextensive with its earthly institution, the Church nevertheless fails to embody God's Word." Freinkel, *Reading Shakespeare's Will*, 320, n. 18. In this, she follows Heiko Oberman, who argues that Luther, unlike Wyclif and Hus, took a generally pessimistic attitude toward the possibility of church reform on earth, even as he advocated efforts toward it. Oberman, *Luther: Man between God and the Devil*, trans. Eileen Walliser-Schwarzbart (New Haven: Yale University Press, 1989), 56–7.

[37] Commentary on Colossians, in John Calvin, *New Testament Commentaries*, vol. X: *Epistles of Paul the Apostle to the Galatians, Ephesians, Philippians and Colossians*, ed. David and Thomas Torrance, and trans. T. H. L. Parker (Edinburgh: Oliver and Boyd, 1965), 316.

converts. Bidding his readers to "return to the apostles and their preaching," Calvin means to encourage not just a turn away from worldly things, but a return to a Pauline conception of conversion as a separation from the ungodly. This is clearer still in his gloss on 1 Thessalonians, an epistle in which Paul encourages his pagan readers to embrace Christianity. Asserting that "the aim of true conversion" is an inward turning to God enabled by divine grace, Calvin admits that "we see many abandoning their superstitions, only to fall into a worse condition when they have taken this step, because they fail to advance in Godliness."[38] Calvin here seems to privilege spiritual transformation over mere confessional change. But implicit in this account is the assumption that "true conversion" requires both turning to God *and* turning away from the "super-stitions" of improper devotional practice. Calvin echoes Paul in emphasizing conversion's confessional register, neatly mapping the division between elect and reprobate onto the division between true and false churches.[39] In contrast to Paul, who proposed outward conversion as a necessary *consequence* of inward change, however, Calvin proposes church-conversion as a *prerequisite* for advancing in holiness, a "step" in the gradual process of sanctification. His English contemporaries and successors would continue to debate the proper relationship between inward and outward conversion, and would do so in an increasingly crowded polemical arena.

CLAIMING CONVERSION IN THE ENGLISH REFORMATION

Recent historical scholarship has cautioned against reading a robustly Protestant theology into the earliest writings of the English Reformation. Criticizing such anachronism, Ethan Shagan suggests that "the whole meta-narrative of conversion which historians have used to conceptualize the Reformation has impeded our ability to ask a different set of questions, to see the Reformation not in globalising terms, but as a more piecemeal process."[40] Shagan's work, as well as that of Lucy Wooding, persuasively argues that Catholic and Reformed positions in the early Tudor period in fact exhibited more continuities than immediate or obvious antagonisms.[41]

[38] John Calvin, *New Testament Commentaries*, vol. VIII: *The Epistles of Paul the Apostle to the Romans and Thessalonians*, ed. David and Thomas Torrance, and trans. Ross MacKenzie (Edinburgh: Oliver and Boyd, 1960), 338.
[39] For Calvin's abiding interest in boundaries and binaries see W. Bouwsma, *John Calvin: A Sixteenth-Century Portrait* (Oxford University Press, 1988), 35–7.
[40] Shagan, *Popular Politics*, 7.
[41] Wooding suggests that a humanistic, Reformist strain of Christianity united Catholic and Protestant thought in the early Tudor period, when "religious identities were being reworked and reformed." Wooding, *Rethinking Catholicism*, 15.

Ironically, however, one of the most important of these continuities was a shared investment in precisely "the whole meta-narrative of conversion." Like their predecessors in the medieval period and earlier, sixteenth-century English Christians – no matter what their confessional orientation – saw conversion as a crucially defining element of a sanctified life. The increasing availability of print, meanwhile, meant that its paradigms could be ever more insistently urged, and its paradoxes could be ever more exhaustively elaborated.[42] In the preface to his 1534 vernacular New Testament, for example, the English reformer William Tyndale offers this ambiguous definition:

Concerning this word repentance, or (as they used) penance, the Hebrew hath in the Old Testament generally *sob* [*shub*] – turn, or be converted. For which the translation that we take for Saint Jerome's hath most part *converti* – to turn, or be converted, and sometime yet, *agere paenitentiam*. And the Greek in the New Testament hath perpetually *metanoeo* – to turn in the heart and mind, and to come to the right knowledge, and to a man's right wit again.[43]

Tyndale's definition, here, seems to stress the inward definition of grace as the penitential *metanoia* that brings man from sin to salvation. He goes on, however, to specify four aspects of this penitential turning: confession to God, contrition, faith, and, finally, satisfaction, which he glosses as "amends-making ... and submitting of a man's self unto the congregation of the church of Christ, and to the officers of the same, to have his life corrected and governed henceforth of them, according to the true doctrine of the church of Christ." Here, a spiritual "turn to God" is reflected not only in ethical action ("amends-making"), but also in submission to the proper institutional authorities on earth ("the congregation ... and officers"). The relationship between the two kinds of turning remains imprecise, but their coexistence is nevertheless imperative.

   In the first wave of true Protestant propaganda, accounts of conversion began to take a still more explicitly polemical stance, measuring the sincerity of spiritual change according to the thoroughness of confessional change, and thus marshaling *metanoia* to the task of denominational differentiation.[44]

---

[42] Surveying some of this early literature, Peter Marshall argues that the idea of conversion "was perhaps the most significant factor giving shape to an emergent 'Protestantism,' in the years before that phenomenon found either institutional structures or an agreed set of descriptive labels." Marshall, *Religious Identities*, 41.

[43] "William Tyndale unto the Reader," in *New Testament* (1534).

[44] For a fascinating case study of one pre-Elizabethan convert to Protestantism, see T. Holien, "A Conversion and its Consequences in the Life and Letters of Nicholas Sheterden," in M. McClendon, J. P. Ward, and M. MacDonald (eds.), *Protestant Identities: Religion, Society, and Self-Fashioning in Post-Reformation England* (Stanford University Press, 1999), 43–62.

Throughout the *Acts and Monuments*, for instance, John Foxe equates the turn to God with the turn away from Catholicism. In one of many such conversion stories, Foxe describes the life of Hugh Latimer, once as "obstinate a papist as any was in England," until the evangelical Thomas Bilney led him to "smell the word of God, and forsake the school-doctors and such fooleries."[45] John Bale, in a preface to his edition of the first trial transcript of another Protestant martyr, Anne Askew, refers to the "terryble turmoylynges of our tyme" in matters of religion. "As Esaye reporteth, though the posteryte of Jacob be as the see sande (innumerable) yet shall but a remnaunt of them convert than unto their lorde God, Esaie 10." This converted "remnaunt," according to Bale, included "good Wyllyam Tyndale, Robert Barnes, and soche other more, whome Antichristes violence hath sent hens in fyre to heaven," as well as Askew herself, who gave "dylygent hede ... to [God's] worde when it was ones taught without superstycyon, and wolde no longer be a false worshypper or ydolatour after the wycked scole of Antichrist."[46] Foxe and Bale rehearse the familiar idea of conversion as a process of repentance inspired by reading. And they insistently define this repentance in terms of separation, particularly from "ydolatrous" Popish practices. Paul's Romans have become Foxe's Romanists, their acceptance of God's grace linked to their rejection of their church's error.

Protestants were not the only ones who exploited the idea of conversion in the early Tudor period, however. If reforming ministers associated the scriptural call to "repentance" with the escape from the "Babylonian captivity" of Rome, Catholics used that same concept to describe the "return" of Reformed apostates. Nicholas Harpsfield's 1557 life of Sir Thomas More, for instance, describes the numerous conversions of More's son-in-law, William Roper. "This saide Master William Roper," Harpsfield writes,

at what time he maried with mistris Margarete More, was a mervailous zealous Protestant, and so fervent, and withal so well and properly liked of himself and his divine learning, that he tooke the bridle into the teeth, and ranne forth like a headstronge horse, harde to be plucked backe againe ... yea, for the burning zeale he bare to the furtherance and advauncement of Luthers newe broched religion, and for the pretie lyking he hadd of himselfe, he longed so sore to be pulpited, that

[45] John Foxe, *Acts and Monuments*, ed. G. Townsend, 8 vols. (New York: AMS Press, 1965), vol. IV, 646; cf. 620, 651.

[46] John Bale, epistle dedicatory to *The First Examynacyon of Anne Askewe* (1546), in E. Beilin (ed.), *The Examinations of Anne Askew* (Oxford University Press, 1990), 4–5, 9.

to have satisfied his madd affection and desire, he could have beene content to have forgone a good portion of his landes.[47]

Harpsfield's account of Roper's first conversion to Protestantism rehearses a number of familiar Augustinian details: it centers on reading, and produces a dramatic shift in affiliation, as Roper abandons "ceremonies and Sacramentes" in order to "company … with divers of his own sect" (86). But Harpsfield finally suggests that Roper's turn should not be considered a proper conversion at all, because the "licentious lessons" of "Luthers newe broached religion" derive their power less from theological truth than from zealotry and conceit ("the pretie lyking he hadd of himself"), preying on Roper's "corrupt affections."

Meanwhile More, having "reasoned and argued" in vain with Roper, declares that he will "clean give him over, and gett me another while to God and praye for him" (87). This silent prayer, and the complementary force of the "great mercy of God," finally brings Roper back into the fold: "[h]e perceived his owne ignorance, oversight, malice and folie, and turned him againe to the Catholike fayth" (88). Harpsfield presents the reining-in of the "headstronge horse" Roper, again, with language borrowed from pre-Reformation accounts of conversion as both repentance and correction, as an instantaneous change of heart triggered by the work of God's grace, but expressed in terms of earthly communities. He explicitly likens the newly reconverted Catholic Roper to "the great, virtuous Clarke, St. Austen [Augustine], who, after he had continued nyne yeres a detestable Maniche … was at length, by the fervent devoute prayers and teares of his good mother Monica, reduced to the true Catholike fayth" (88). Harpsfield's account implies an analogy between Roper's individual reconversion to Rome and the recent Catholic reconversion of England as a whole under Mary Tudor; in both cases, the unmistakable sign of "repentance" is confessional change.[48]

EQUIVOCAL CONVERSION: ELIZABETH AND AFTER

The centrality of conversion in the early decades of the English Reformation is unsurprising: the national changes of religion legislated by the early

---

[47] N. Harpsfield, *The Life and Death of Sir Thomas Moore, Knight, sometimes Lord High Chancellor of England, written in the time of Queene Marie*, ed. E. V. Hitchcock (Oxford University Press, 1932), 84–5. Further references will be given by page number in the text. For further discussion of Roper, see R. Marius, *Thomas More* (New York: Knopf, 1985), 314–16.

[48] Roper, Harpsfield tells us, "is a goodly faire president for many other of our time, being of muche lesse witt, vertue, and learning, to reforme themselves [and to conforme themselves] to the Catholike faith of their mother, the holy Church" (*Life and Death of Sir Thomas Moore*, 89).

Tudors allowed English Christians to recall or anticipate confessional alternatives as they sought to lead holy lives. But conversions to and from Rome
continued, and continued to inspire a copious and contentious polemical
literature, even after England's official Reformation would seem to have
been definitively achieved.[49] By the last two decades of the sixteenth century
Elizabeth I had been excommunicated by papal encyclical, the oaths of
supremacy and uniformity had been repeatedly strengthened, penalties
against recusancy had been stiffened, and the last plausible Catholic claim-
ant to the English throne had been executed. In practice, however, England
remained a country of multiple churches, all of them using centuries of
theological writing to insist that a true conversion of the soul was both
necessary for all Christians and impossible without the correct outward
performance of devotion. Men and women continued to believe, in the
words of one anonymous seventeenth-century convert, "how necesarie it is
in these unhappie times of division for men desirous of their salvation to
know the truth, which being pretended by different professions, can be
retained but by one."[50] They continued to wonder, in the titular words of
one representative tract on the subject, "which religion ought to be
embraced?"[51]

By the 1580s, representatives of the two major "professions" confronted a
new generation of English Christians who had grown up asking precisely
that question. Patrick Collinson and Peter Lake, among others, have
demonstrated that Elizabethan Protestants were not content to rely on
pursuivants and penal codes to enforce conformity, but instead redoubled
their proselytizing efforts to earn true conversions from Catholicism.[52]
Meanwhile the new English Jesuit mission worked not only to confirm
the faith of recusants and "schismatics" (Catholics who outwardly conformed to the Protestant church), but also, for the first time, to convert

[49] Questier begins his study of conversion in 1580, but admits that "in one sense, of course, the issue was
decided" by the end of that decade, when England's Catholics "started to accept minority status"; see
Conversion, Politics and Religion, 4. In this, he follows Bossy, who sees the 1580s as the turning point in
his story of "the fall of a church and the rise of a sect." Bossy, *The English Catholic Community*, 11 and
chs. 1–3 *passim*.
[50] BL Lansdowne MS 7876, "Justification and Apology of some Person abjuring the Protestant and
embracing the Roman Catholic Religion" (n.d.) fo. 1r.
[51] Leonardus Lessius, *Quae Religio Sit Capessenda* (Paris, 1609). This Catholic guide to choice among
churches was translated as *A Consultation What Faith and Religion is Best to be Imbraced*, 2nd edn. (St.
Omer, 1621). I will discuss Lessius, and other contributors to this genre, in Chapter 2 below.
[52] See especially P. Collinson, *The Religion of Protestants* (Oxford: Clarendon, 1982); P. Lake, *Moderate
Puritans and the Elizabethan Church* (Cambridge University Press, 1982); and the essays collected in
Lake and Questier, *The Anti-Christ's Lewd Hat*. See also P. Milward's annotated bibliography,
Religious Controversies of the Elizabethan Age (Lincoln: University of Nebraska Press, 1977), and its
Jacobean sequel (London: Scolar, 1978).

those English men and women who had been Protestant since birth.[53] In 1581, Robert Persons offered this survey of recent ecclesiastical history:

In the beginning of heresie, when first the banner of sedition was raysed agaynst the Church, great multitudes of people revolted together (as in al commotions is wonte to happe, by some generall false suggestion of the principal rebels): yet afterward, the heate being past, and more calmer consideration coming in place, men have staied them selves, and harkened to the cause, and divers also returned, which in the first furie ranne out with the rest.[54]

Persons suggests that the very success of the Elizabethan settlement enabled former Catholics to reconsider their "first fury" and return to their mother church. But by acknowledging that some Protestants had only recently "harkened to the cause," Persons also indicates one of the central premises of the Jesuit Mission he spearheaded: that after several decades of reformation, Roman Catholicism had become a religion to which many English men and women might *turn*, and not just *re*turn.[55] New arrivals from the English seminaries at Rome and Douai were instructed "firstly, to preserve … and to advance in the faith and in our Catholic religion, all who are found to be Catholics in England; and secondly, to bring back to it whoever may have strayed from it."[56] Despite the conservative tone of these instructions, however, the work of priests like John Gerard and William Weston was substantially evangelical. Gerard's memoir of the early 1590s describes his interactions with born-and-bred heretics, as well as recusants and schismatics, and recounts his efforts to bring new recruits to Rome. Although he admits that "it is easy to make many converts" in places "where a large number of people are Catholics and nearly all have leanings toward Catholicism," Gerard's mission nevertheless involved radically altering the beliefs of many of the men and women he encountered.[57]

[53] The problem of Catholic "schismatics" has been elegantly surveyed in Walsham, *Church Papists*; see also E. Rose, *Cases of Conscience: Alternatives Open to Recusants and Puritans under Elizabeth I and James I* (Cambridge University Press, 1975), and P. Zagorin, *Ways of Lying* (Cambridge, MA: Harvard University Press, 1990).

[54] Robert Persons, *Discouerie of I. [John] Nicols minister, Misreported a Jesuit, Lately Recanted in the Tower* (1581), 3–4.

[55] E. E. Reynolds, *Campion and Parsons: The Jesuit Mission of 1580–1* (London: Sheed and Ward, 1980), 29–30. Bossy has argued that 1568, the year of the founding of the English seminary at Douai, can be said to signal English Catholicism's transformation (*The English Catholic Community*, 4, 25–31).

[56] Reynolds, *Campion and Parsons*, 60–1.

[57] John Gerard, *The Autobiography of a Hunted Priest*, trans. P. Caraman (New York: Image Books, 1955), 59. Questier surveys Jesuit evangelical tactics in "'Like Locusts all over the World': Conversion, Indoctrination, and the Society of Jesus in Late Elizabethan and Jacobean England," in T. McCoog, SJ (ed.), *The Reckoned Expense: Edmund Campion and the Early English Jesuits* (Woodbridge: Boydell, 1996), 265–84. For a contemporary, slanderous account of Catholic evangelism, see Edwin Sandys, *A View or Survey of the State of Religion in the Western Parts of the World* (1599, rpt. 1632), 34–7.

Even if the large-scale history of English denominational conflict awards the victory to the Protestant side, then, both Catholics and Protestants sought and gained converts throughout the early modern period. Questier's study of English conversion ends in 1625, but the religious instability he so eloquently describes would continue well beyond the death of James I. On the level of national religion, fears (or hopes) for the reconversion of England were reanimated with the accession of each Stuart king. James's Danish wife, Anna, had converted to Catholicism before 1603, and many Protestants feared that she would use her influence to return England to the Catholic fold.[58] The accession of her son Charles, and his French Catholic wife Henrietta Maria, only exacerbated these fears. The open recusancy of the queen, and the perceived frequency of Catholic conversions among Caroline courtiers and ladies in waiting, added to a growing popular sense of English Protestantism under threat; the coming of civil war was, at least in part, fueled by a desire to forestall the threat of a national return to Catholicism.[59] If the Restoration indicated England's equal mistrust of sectarian Protestantism, it is nevertheless the case that Catholic conversion would return to its central position in the English national consciousness during the reign of Charles II. Like his father, Charles took the throne with a Catholic queen and a religious position that struck many as disturbingly unfixed. His younger brother James, by contrast, made his own conversion to Catholicism public, along with that of his first wife Anne Hyde – to the delight of English and European Catholics, and to the horror of staunch Anglicans such as Anne's father, the Earl of Clarendon. The codes, crises, and plots characteristic of the 1670s and 1680s may have indicated new fears of "popery and arbitrary government," but they also drew on a popular fear of royal conversion that had begun nearly a century before.

Even as they speculated about the religion of their kings and queens, many English men and women would have experienced the phenomenon of conversion closer to home. At the English Catholic College in Flanders, Peter Guilday tells us, "the favorite drama [was that of] a loyal Catholic son and an apostate father, who later is the cause of the son's death."[60] This

---

[58]   The evidence surrounding Anna's conversion is surveyed by J. L. Barroll, *Anna of Denmark, Queen of England: A Cultural Biography* (Philadelphia: University of Pennsylvania Press, 2001), 166–8.

[59]   For Henrietta Maria's French Catholicism, and its effect on the Caroline court, see G. Albion, *Charles I and the Court of Rome: A Study in 17th-Century Diplomacy* (Louvain: Bureaux du Recueil, Bibliothèque de l'Université, 1935), and especially Hibbard, *Charles I and the Popish Plot*. I will discuss this period further in Chapter 3, below.

[60]   P. Guilday, introduction to *The English Catholic Refugees on the Continent, 1558–1795*, vol. 1: *The English Colleges and Convents in the Catholic Low Countries* (London: Longmans, 1914), n.p. The play is in the Vatican Library, MS Vaticana Lat. t.8263, f. 389. P. Davidson notes that in 1615, students at

melodramatic scenario nevertheless recalls the many true stories of English families riven by the conversions of parents, spouses, siblings, or children.[61] The Rainolds brothers, John and William, for example, were gifted evangelists on opposite sides of the Reformation divide – so gifted, in fact, that they were rumored to have converted each other to their respective religions during a particularly energetic debate.[62] In the Gage family, Francis and George became Jesuit priests, while their brother Thomas abandoned his vocation as a Dominican missionary to become a Protestant advisor to Cromwell.[63] The nephew of the Jesuit missionaries Jasper and Ellis Heywood, Henry Donne, died in prison for harboring a Catholic priest; his brother John would become Dean of St. Paul's. One of John Donne's friends, the Catholic convert Sir Toby Matthew, was the son of the violently anti-Jesuit Archbishop of York, Tobias Matthew. Similarly, the Catholic converts Richard Crashaw and Walter Montague were sons of prominent figures in the established religion: William Crashaw wrote copiously against the missionary Jesuits, while Montague's father, the Earl of Manchester, published a response to his son's Catholic conversion with a supplementary letter by Lucius Cary, Lord Falkland.[64] Cary, in turn, was the son of the Catholic convert and playwright Elizabeth Cary, who defied her Protestant husband and successfully converted several of her other children to Rome.[65] If conversions could fracture Christian households, meanwhile, the surprisingly common phenomenon of serial conversion suggests that such fracturing could characterize the lives of individual Christians. Examples

Valladolid performed a play called *Psyche et filii eius*, which he describes as "an allegory of a family divided by political and religious faction." Davidson, *The Universal Baroque* (Manchester University Press, 2007), 50.

[61] See A. Shell, "Furor Juvenilis: Post-Reformation English Catholicism and Exemplary Youthful Behaviour," in Shagan (ed.), *Catholics and the 'Protestant Nation'*, 185–206.

[62] I will discuss the Rainolds brothers, and William Alabaster's poetic commemoration of them, in Chapter 1 below.

[63] Thomas Gage's recantation sermon was published as *The Tyranny of Satan Discovered in the Tears of a Converted Sinner* (1642). See also the introduction to A. P. Newton's edition of Gage's *The English-American: A New Survey of the West Indies, 1648* (London: Routledge, 1928), and E. Burton (ed.), *Douai Diaries* (London: Publications of the Catholic Record Society, 1911), vol. ii, Appendix 3, 571–3.

[64] William Crashaw's controversial works include *Falsificationum Romanarum* (1606), *The Bespotted Jesuit* (1641), and, most intriguingly given his son's future career, a verse parody of Counter-Reformation devotional handbooks entitled *The Jesuites Gospel* (1610). Cf. Walter Montague, *The Coppy of a Letter by Mr. Walter Mountagu to his father the Lord Privie Seale, with his answer therunto, also a Second Answer to the Same Letter by the Lord Faukland* (1641).

[65] The posthumous biography of Cary written by her daughter provides a fascinating account of the heterodoxy of the Cary household. Elizabeth Cary, *The Tragedy of Mariam, The Fair Queen of Jewry, with The Lady Falkland, her Life, by One of Her Daughters*, ed. B. Weller and M. Ferguson (Berkeley: University of California Press, 1994). See also M. W. Davies, "'To Have Her Children With Her': Elizabeth Cary and Familial Influence," in H. Wolfe (ed.), *The Literary Career and Legacy of Elizabeth Cary* (New York: Palgrave, 2007), 223–41.

of men who converted at least twice between Catholicism and Protestantism include not only Nicholas Harpsfield, but William Alabaster, Anthony Tyrrell, John Nichols, Theophilus Higgons, Ben Jonson, Benjamin Carier, Richard Carpenter, and the "Dalmatian apostate" Marc'Antonio de Dominis.[66]

Changes of religion in this period were inevitably inspired and influenced by a variety of factors, from the political to the spiritual to the familial to the aesthetic. They took place in divergent cultural and historical circumstances; a Catholic conversion under Elizabeth I differed from one under James II. The following chapters will discuss some of the particular justifications and contexts for conversion in greater detail. Here, I wish merely to reiterate how persistent the subject was throughout seventeenth-century English Christian culture, and how persistently vexing. In the contentious climate of early modern England, conversion was an experience that most Christians desired and dreaded in equal measure, depending on how it was defined. The sermons and devotions of Archbishop William Laud, for example, continually emphasize the necessity of inward *poenitentia*, and the corresponding necessity of correct outward devotional practice. For Laud, this meant encouraging conversions to the Reformed way; as he put it in his debate with the Jesuit John Fisher, "there is peril, great peril ... by living and dying in the Roman faith, tainted with so many superstitions as it now is."[67] In his diary, however, Laud imagines conversion as a terrible, unexpected accident:

March 3 (1626/7): I came to London. The night following I dreamt that I was reconciled to the Church of Rome. This troubled me much; and I wondered exceedingly, how it should happen. Nor was I aggrieved with myself only by reason of the errors of that church, but also upon account of the scandal, which from that my fall would be cast upon many eminent and learned men of the church of England. So being troubled at my dream, I said with myself, that I would go immediately, and, confessing my fault, would beg pardon of the Church of

---

[66] For Alabaster, see Chapter 1 below. See C. Devlin, "An Unwilling Apostate: The Case of Anthony Tyrrell," *The Month* 6 (1951), 346–58; W. B. Patterson, "The Peregrinations of Marco Antonio de Dominis, 1616–24," *Studies in Church History* 15 (1978), 241–66, and N. Malcolm, *De Dominis (1560–1624)* (London: Strickland and Scott, 1984) (cf. John Sweet, *Monsignor Fate'Voi. Or: a Discovery of the Dalmatian Apostata, M. Antonius de Dominis* (1617) and Richard Neile, *M. Ant. De Dnis. Archbishop of Spalato, his Shiftings in Religion* (1624)); M. Questier, "Crypto-Catholicism, Anti-Calvinism and Conversion at the Jacobean Court: The Enigma of Benjamin Carier," *JEH* 47 (1996), 45–64. For Carpenter, see A. Shell, "Multiple Conversions and the Menippean Self," in A. Marotti (ed.), *Catholicism and Anti-Catholicism in Early Modern English Texts* (New York: St. Martin's Press, 1999), 154–97.

[67] *A Relation of the Conference between William Laud ... and Mr. Fisher the Jesuit* (1624), in William Laud, *Works*, ed. J. Bliss and W. Scott, 7 vols. (Oxford: J. H. Parker, 1847–60), vol. II, 332.

England. Going with this resolution, a certain priest met me, and would have stopped me. But moved with indignation, I went on my way. And while I wearied myself with these troublesome thoughts, I awoke.[68]

Inward forces ("I wondered exceedingly, how it should happen") have legible outward consequences ("errors" and "scandal"). All of these seem to overpower the conscious will of the dreamer, who vainly struggles to recant ("confessing my fault"), and ends up more "troubled" and "wearied" than ever. This nightmarish conversion is as dramatically transformative as Augustine's experience in the garden or Luther's in the tower. But the experience does not confirm, but rather undermines both the soul's peace and the church's community. If Laud the minister encourages conversion as a reasonable choice, Laud the dreamer imagines conversion as a mysterious trauma.

TELLING STORIES OF THE END OF CHANGE

The polemical accounts of conversion streaming from the presses in the period, then, can be read as efforts to dispel the persistent penumbra of uncertainty, contention, and "trouble" surrounding the question of devotional allegiance. Controversialists from both sides attempted to underscore the differences between Catholic and Reformed, making legible, categorical claims for the conclusive truth of their respective positions. Starting in the reign of Mary, Catholic writers supplemented the work of confessors and priests with printed devotional manuals and guides to faith.[69] In one of the earliest and most popular of these, Edward Campion's *Rationes Decem* (1570), the Catholic martyr offered ten reasons for which he was willing to die rather than abandon his faith. But as the catalogues edited by Peter Milward, Anthony Allison, and D. M. Rogers attest, "Campion's Brag" was only one of innumerable Catholic "articles," "reasons," and "motives," often written by recent converts, that began to appear in the last decades of the sixteenth century, and would continue to appear throughout the

---

[68] *The Autobiography of Dr. William Laud, Collected from his Remains* (Oxford: J. H. Parker, 1839), 88–9.
[69] Sullivan, *Dismembered Rhetoric*, esp. 26–40, 87–123. For an account of the secret press, see also Reynolds, *Campion and Parsons*, 84–96; N. P. Brown, "Paperchase: The Dissemination of Catholic Texts in Elizabethan England," *English Manuscript Studies 1100–1700* 1 (1989), 120–43; and H. Thurston, "Catholic Writers and Elizabethan Readers," *The Month* 82 (1894), 457–76; and 83 (1895) 231–45. For a discussion of the bibliographical problems that attend the cataloguing of these clandestine books, see T. A. Birrell, "English Counter-Reformation Book Culture," *RH* 22 (1994), 113–21.

seventeenth.[70] Meanwhile, Protestants made use of cheap print in efforts to convert England's remaining recusants to the Reformed way, adding tracts specifically on conversion to the more familiar genres of prayerbooks, scriptural translations, homilies, and broadsides.[71]

If such schematic accounts of religious choice and change did not accurately reflect the more fluid and provisional reality of Christian spiritual experience, this was precisely their point. These texts instead had a palliative effect, offering early modern Catholics and Protestants alike a rubric for understanding and regulating the mysterious workings of God's grace. If "[r]egeneration through grace could be aligned with peregrination between Churches," as Questier phrases it, then conversion could be seen as intelligible and definitive rather than terrifyingly arbitrary. The binary structure proposed by these writings also created a reassuring sense of a single confessional conflict, overriding the ongoing divisions *within* Catholic and Protestant churches.[72] Anthony Milton, discussing the role of polemic in consolidating distinct Catholic and Reformed positions, offers an anecdote of the Venetian Ambassador to the Jacobean court, who "reported the existence of twelve different religious parties in England" ranging from papist to Puritan.[73] Given this apparent proliferation of confessional options, we can imagine that English people would have been relieved to

---

[70] As Shell discusses in her introduction to *Catholicism, Controversy*, the Short Title Catalogues edited by Pollard and Redgrave and by Wing omit an enormous amount of early modern English Catholic writing. The most significant attempt to redress this bibliographical bias is A. Allison and D. M. Rogers, *The Contemporary Printed Literature of the English Counter-Reformation Between 1558 and 1640*, 2 vols. (Aldershot: Scolar, 1989–94). See also R. Miola, *Early Modern Catholicism: An Anthology of Primary Sources* (Oxford University Press, 2007).

[71] The scholarship on Protestant popular literature is nearly as copious as that literature itself. Among the most important studies are J. King, *English Reformation Literature: The Tudor Origins of the Protestant Tradition* (Princeton University Press, 1982); T. Watt, *Cheap Print and Popular Piety 1550–1640* (Cambridge University Press, 1991); R. Whiting, *The Blind Devotion of the People: Popular Religion and the English Reformation* (Cambridge University Press, 1989); and, more recently, J. Lander, *Inventing Polemic: Religion, Print and Literary Culture in Early Modern England* (Cambridge University Press, 2006).

[72] Historians have offered numerous accounts of Protestant sectarianism, but fewer studies exist of factions within early modern English Catholicism, possibly because recusant historians have been unwilling to imply that Catholic thought was "incoherent" (see Haigh's excellent bibliographical essay at the end of *English Reformations*, 335–42). J. H. Pollen discusses one particular intra-Catholic debate in "The Politics of the English Catholics during the Reign of Queen Elizabeth," *The Month* 100 (1902), 176–83; for the Archpriest controversy see Bossy, *The English Catholic Community*, Chapter 2. Michael Questier's study of aristocratic households reveals the subtle political, theological, and cultural shadings within early modern English Catholicism. *Catholicism and Community in Early Modern England: Politics, Aristocratic Patronage, and Religion, c.1550–1640* (Cambridge University Press, 2006).

[73] Milton, *Catholic and Reformed*, 7.

understand religious conflict and choice in terms of a simple binary opposition.

Of course, Catholics and Protestants genuinely differed in their under-standing of the sacrament, and of the efficacy of human works in achieving sanctification. They differed in their attitudes toward the status of the visible church, the existence of purgatory, and the veneration of saints. Polemicists seeking to gain converts would lay out these legitimate differ-ences with what Questier describes as "absolutely bigoted clarity ... The whole course of the Reformation, readers were told, could be understood by referring to the diametrically opposed Roman and Protestant doctrines of faith, assurance, perseverance, election and predestination, and the Church, underwritten by disagreement about the relative weight of authority in Scripture, and in the Church's tradition."[74] But if we look at these texts in terms of their formal characteristics and argumentative strategies, rather than concentrating exclusively on their doctrinal content, they can appear surprisingly uniform. Catholics and Protestants contributed equally to the same polemical genres – from first-person accounts of motive for conversion and answers to third-person letters of advice and guides for waverers. In these writings, they drew on the same intellectual inheritance, each invok-ing the same scriptural and patristic sources, particularly Paul and Augustine.[75] To make matters still more confusing, they also borrowed and adapted contemporary texts on conversion written by their opponents. So, the Jesuit Robert Persons's *Christian Directory*, adapted by Edmund Bunny, became a popular devotional manual among Protestants. After the Catholic convert Toby Matthew translated St. Augustine's *Confessions* into English in 1620, Matthew Sutcliffe dismissed it as a work of "masse-mongering," but this did not prevent William Watts from plagiarizing it for a Protestant readership a decade later.[76]

Despite the fierceness of their argumentative postures, then, polemics about conversion in this period did not fall neatly into two aesthetically or

---

[74] Questier, *Conversion, Politics and Religion*, 12.
[75] So one convert notes that "I had often heard and read St. Augustine alleadged, both by Catholikes and Protestants, for a faithfull witnesse of antiquitie and a shining light in the church of God," BL Lansdowne MS 7876, fo. 13r. See R. Dodaro and M. Questier, "Strategies in Jacobean Polemic: The Use and Abuse of St. Augustine in English Theological Controversy," *JEH* 44.3 (July 1993), 432–49.
[76] Toby Matthew (trans.), *The Confessions of the Incomparable Doctour S. Augustine* (1620, second edn. 1623); M. Sutcliffe, *The Unmasking of a Masse-monger, who in the counterfeit habit of S. Augustine hath cunningly crept into the closets of many English ladies. Or, the Vindication of Saint Augustines Confessions, from the calumniations of a late noted Apostate* (1626). William Watts claims to answer the "marginall notes" of the "former popish translation" but leaves Matthew's English text virtually intact. Watts, *Saint Augustines Confessions translated: and with some marginall notes illustrated. Wherein, Diuers Antiquities are explayned; and the marginall notes of a former Popish Translation, answered* (1631).

intellectually distinct categories on either side of the Reformation divide. In fact, Catholic and Protestant antagonists could become harder to distinguish the more furiously they inveighed against each other, a situation comically illustrated by a dialogue in doggerel by Samuel Hieron. Hieron introduces a "late runnagate" from the Protestant church, who slanders his former faith in clumsy couplets:

> Many sundry sects appeare
> Now in the world farre and neere
> The Calvinist, the Protestant
> The Zwinglian, the Puritant
> And Brownist and the Family of Love
> And many more which I can prove …
> And every one confesse IESU
> Saying that their faith is true;
> But among these, tell me how
> The Trueth from fayned lyes to know.[77]

This accusation of sectarian division was a commonplace of anti-Reformed polemic. The "runnagate"'s Protestant interlocutor is, unsurprisingly, ready with a retort:

> But now what sects you papists have,
> I doe but thy owne witnesse crave:
> Some Capucines, some Franciscanes
> And some be called Dominicanes
> Some Iesuites, some Seculars
> Some grey, some black, some white Friars,
> And that your store may not be spent
> New Locusts still from hell are sent.
> Thou sayst, thou wouldst the Church find out
> So that I see thou art in doubt:
> And so indeed Uncertainty
> Is still the fruite of Popery.

This is not a defense, properly speaking, but an imitative counter-accusation, made more striking by the identical verse form. The process of argumentative echoing continues on a variety of topics throughout the dialogue, confirming but not clarifying the basic conflict between Catholic and Protestant positions. The papist and the Protestant seem to argue not primarily because they believe different things, but because each claims the same basic justifications for his church, in the same language. Moreover,

---

[77] Samuel Hieron, *Answer to a Popish Ryme, lately scattered abroad in the West Parts, and much Relyed upon by some simply-seduced* (1608).

even as the poem insists on denominational difference, it also demonstrates the lability of individual identity; each speaker promises to "be converted soone" if the other makes his case.

Hieron's doggerel verses indicate two paradoxes intrinsic to the early modern controversial literature of conversion, paradoxes to which other, better poets will respond. The first paradox is, again, that polemical discussions of conversion could undermine on a stylistic and generic level the very boundary that they sought to underscore on the level of argument. Catholics and Protestants maintained distinct theologies, but they also shared a repertoire of tropes and figures, allusions and rhetorical tactics. This rhetorical mirroring around the subject of conversion facilitated the forgery of texts by members of one side wishing to "claim" a member of the other, ensuring that all such texts were read with a certain suspicion.[78] It also facilitated the rapid-fire production of boilerplate "answers," "replies," and "counter-replies" to any offering from the other side.[79] By the 1680s, after decades of this kind of textual accumulation, we find such dizzying titles as *Papists Protesting against Protestant-Popery, in Answer to a Discussion Entituled, A Papist not Mis-Represented by Protestants: Being a Vindication of the Papist Mis-Represented and Represented, and the Reflections on the Answer* (1686). We also find instances of near-comic formal exhaustion, as in the polemical tract simply entitled: *I. Question: Why are you a Catholic? (The answer follows) II. Question: But why are you a Protestant? (An answer attempted)* (1686). Although this tract ultimately gives Catholics the upper hand, its title makes the two positions seem, in the end, neatly interchangeable. In this sense, the anxiety experienced by Christians seeking God's true church on earth might have been intensified by the very polemic that purported to allay it.

The second paradox in the controversial literature of conversion is that it generally minimizes or avoids any discussion of conversion itself. Catholic and Protestant polemicists shared a goal: to gain new members for their respective churches. This goal necessarily implies the mutability of even the most firmly held religious convictions. And yet, on both sides, writers most frequently ground their arguments for conversion on principles that are

---

[78] See, for instance, the late sixteenth-century forged conversion narratives of "Malachias Malone," and "Samuel Mason" (BL Additional MS 4791), discussed in T. E. Bridgett, *Blunders and Forgeries* (London, 1890). Daniel Johnson discusses this kind of forgery in "Apostates Who Never Were: The Social Construction of Absque Facto Apostate Narratives," in D. Bromley (ed.), *The Politics of Religious Apostasy* (Westport, CT: Praeger, 1998), 115–30.

[79] Cummings discusses an earlier example of such a "bewildering" proliferation of reasons and answers, inaugurated by "Campion's Brag," in *The Literary Culture of the Reformation*, 382–3.

precisely opposed to the idea of change; each claims his church's superior stability, unanimity, antiquity, and universality. First-person narratives of conversion, meanwhile, generally follow a neat structure of before-and-after, in which the inadequacy of one church is juxtaposed with the persuasiveness of the other. In seeking to contrast their current convictions with their former errors, authors of such accounts generally do not represent the indecision, ambivalence, terror, and doubt that might have accompanied any shift from one system of belief, and one community of believers, to another. The inherent teleology of narrative underscores this idealized notion of conversion as singular and conclusive: I was blind, but now I see. Even serial converts like de Dominis and Tyrrell wrote apologies and justifications in which they portrayed themselves as souls liberated from what one convert calls "evasion or further tergiversation," transformed entirely and for ever.[80]

A SENSE OF UPENDING: TOWARD A POETICS OF CONVERSION

I have suggested that conversion between Catholic and Reformed churches was one of the most common topics of controversial writing throughout the early modern period, and that most of this polemical writing actively seeks to deny the potential complexity and trouble of religious change. Imaginative literature, by contrast, provides some more candid representations of this difficulty. In the drama, for example, the idealized concept of conversion as a singular achievement of redemption or repentance is frequently belied by stagings of such change as insincere or inconclusive. This is perhaps clearest in plays that represent the conversions of non-Christians. Daniel Vitkus, for example, has described the vexed Muslim conversions in the "Turk plays" of Greene and Massinger, while James Shapiro has discussed the ambivalent representations of Jewish conversions on the early modern stage, most notably, but not exclusively, in *The Merchant of Venice*.[81] When depicting conversion *within* Christianity, early modern playwrights could ironize the process by associating it with performance

---

[80] BL Lansdowne MS 7876, fo. 43r.

[81] Vitkus edits Greene's *Selimus* (1594) and Massinger's *The Renegado* (1623), along with Robert Daborne's *A Christian Turned Turk* (1612), as *Three Turk Plays from Early Modern England* (New York: Columbia University Press, 2000). Shapiro describes conversion and crypto-conversion in *Shakespeare and the Jews* (New York: Columbia University Press, 1996), esp. 131–66. More specifically, in "'We all expect a gentle answer, Jew': *The Merchant of Venice* and the Psychotheology of Conversion," *ELH* 73.1 (Spring 2006), 61–81, Heather Hirschfeld uses psychoanalytic theory to explore the play's "contradictory desires that Shylock convert and that he not convert" (63).

itself, implicitly designating such apostasy as a mere change of costume or props. In *The Staple of News* (1625), Ben Jonson makes explicit this analogy between conversion and performance. Thomas Barber, asked for "Newes of the Stage," responds

> O! yes.
> There is a *Legacy* left to the *Kings Players,*
> Both for their various shifting of their *Scene,*
> And dext'rous change o'their persons to all shapes,
> And all disguises: by the right reverend
> *Archbishop of Spalato.* (III.2.200–5)[82]

The joke here is in Barber's association of the "disguises" of stage actors with the serial conversions of the "Dalmatian apostata" de Dominis. If this point wasn't clear enough, Jonson immediately follows it with a reference to the Spanish Catholic agent Gondomar, sore after "cleansing his posterior" with "the poore English-play, was written of him" (209–11). This "English-play," Thomas Middleton's *Game at Chesse* (1624), mocked Catholic conversions at the Stuart court by presenting thinly veiled versions of Gondomar, de Dominis, and other contemporaries who either underwent or encouraged such conversions. In Middleton, as in Jonson, Catholic and Protestant positions might be black and white, but there is always the possibility of changing one's color.[83]

Some dramatists were willing to acknowledge what most religious apologists denied: that conversions were not always faithful and not always final. But to represent conversion satirically or ironically is to misrepresent it in a different way. If conversion could be a frightening index of religious instability, it could also provide the convert with a sense, however temporary, of greater religious *certainty*. It is an experience that could call the permanence and sincerity of all religious convictions into question, but at the same time an experience that could lend a convert's convictions new force. Conversion both challenges *and* confirms the importance of outward forms to interior spiritual life; if the receipt of God's grace transcends the

---

[82] Jonson, *The Staple of News*, in *Works*, ed. C. H. Herford, P. Simpson, and E. Simpson, 11 vols. (Oxford: Clarendon, 1925–52), vol. VI, 271–382.

[83] Ian Donaldson suggests that "duplicity lies at the very heart of Jonson's drama, and of his social vision." Donaldson, *Jonson's Magic Houses: Essays in Interpretation* (Oxford: Clarendon, 1997), 48. I have discussed how Jonson's first collaboration with Queen Anna of Denmark uses color to describe the mutability of devotional identity, particularly that of women, in "Performing Devotion in *The Masque of Blacknesse,*" *SEL* 49.2 (Spring 2007), 427–49. For a discussion of conversion and later plays, see A. Brunning, "'Thou art damn'd for altering thy religion': The Double Coding of Conversion in City Comedy," in D. Mehl (ed.), *Plotting Early Modern London: New Essays on Jacobean City Comedy* (London: Ashgate, 2004), 145–62.

boundaries of particular churches, most early modern people nevertheless remained convinced that receiving God's grace required an adherence to one particular church. Finally, and perhaps most fundamentally, conversion both confirms *and* denies the stability of the self in time; the convert both is, and is not, the same person before and after his change. For all these reasons, some early modern converts (as opposed to those who wished simply to depict or direct them) might have developed a kind of parallax view, a way of understanding individual identity as both conclusive and contingent, a way of understanding beliefs as both passionate and provisional. This book will propose that John Donne, William Alabaster, Richard Crashaw, and John Dryden – all converts either to or from Rome – possessed such a parallax view, and that they saw English poetry as the best way, or perhaps the only way, to give it voice.

Considered in sequence, the careers of each of these four poets illuminate distinct moments in a century of acute anxiety about confessional instability, from the launch of the Jesuit Mission in the 1580s to the end of Stuart monarchy in the 1680s. I begin with William Alabaster, whose turn to Catholicism in the last decade of the sixteenth century reflects a newly invigorated culture and discourse of conversion in the late Elizabethan period. By tracing Alabaster's religious biography, my first chapter surveys some of the foundational battles waged between Protestant divines and Catholic priests over high-profile converts, battles that would be remembered and refought in decades to come. In my second chapter, I discuss Donne's turn to Protestantism in the context of Jacobean religious culture, a culture deeply concerned with issues of publicity and silence, interpretability and dissimulation. My third chapter contrasts this culture of suspicion and disguise with the more overt theological antagonisms of the Caroline court. The Catholic turn of the courtier poet Richard Crashaw gestures toward one particularly pressing mid-century issue: the conversions of noblewomen surrounding the Catholic Queen Henrietta Maria in the 1630s and 1640s. In their causes and consequences, such conversions can tell us much about the increasingly polarized religious culture on the eve of civil war. My fourth chapter resists the scholarly tendency to separate early Stuart culture from late, and explores this polarization as it persists into the Restoration. By considering the Catholic conversion of John Dryden in the mid-1680s, I show how the cultural preoccupation with religious change both endures and evolves toward the end of the seventeenth century, particularly in the years preceding and following the accession of the Catholic James II. These case studies of conversion present four distinct phases within early modern religious history, then, but they also indicate deep continuities within that history.

The second underlying structure of my argument has to do with literary history, and more precisely with the history of polemical genres. Each of the poets I consider engages in a deep and productive dialogue with specific sub-genres of early modern controversial literature, using these sub-genres as both sources and foils for poetic experiment. In each chapter, I read the poetry of conversion against what we might call its particular "counter-genre," demonstrating how each poet explicitly draws on its conventions and commonplaces in order to modify or challenge their usual implications. For Alabaster, the crucial counter-genre is the prose conversion narrative, as exemplified by Augustine's *Confessions*, and as composed by new converts at the English College at Rome, including Alabaster himself. For Donne, it is the declaration of theological motives for conversion, often published along with methodical guides to choosing the true church, and composed by Catholics and Protestants alike. Crashaw's counter-genres are two: the familiar letter of spiritual advice directed specifically to women in the throes of ecclesiological doubt, and the hagiographical account of female conversion and martyrdom. Finally, Dryden's deepest engagement is with popular religious satire, particularly the comic dialogue and the "transversal" in which religious change is mocked and disparaged. Each chapter, then, reveals a similar dynamic at work: a poet transmuting – or, better, convert-ing – the polemical material that he would have encountered in the process of reconsidering his own religious identity.

But how does this transmuting work? This question can be phrased another way: what, exactly, do I mean by the "*poetics* of conversion" in early modern England? In a sense, the readings throughout the rest of this book comprise my fuller answer to this question. At this point, I will simply state my thesis in basic terms: the poetry of Alabaster, Donne, Crashaw, and Dryden, while it reflects varied aspects of the early modern history and discourse of conversion, also demonstrates a shared commitment to a deeper poetic project, to harness-ing what Puttenham calls figurative "heresies" in order to emphasize how radically minds can move. Resisting the static and strident credos of polemic, each of these poets seeks to represent change between positions, and each, in order to do so, makes virtuosic use of the formal capacities of English poetry. Alabaster, for instance, having attempted to describe his conversion in auto-biographical prose, finally turns to a different medium: the English sonnet. Here, he is able to register his own spiritual dynamism not only in vividly figurative language, but in poetic schemes that vividly indicate interruption, revision, and reversal: the sonnet's internal stanzaic divisions, particularly its *volta* between octave and sestet, as well as its characteristic line breaks and caesuras. If Alabaster's poetics of conversion has primarily to do with figures of speech, Donne's centers primarily on figures of thought. My second chapter revisits the concept of the "metaphysical conceit," or extravagantly extended metaphorical structure, so familiar to readers of Donne. In the devotional poetry, Donne's use of figures that are at once ostentatious and opaque provides a formal corollary to his understanding of conversion as a paradox, an act of simultaneous self-declaration and self-concealment.

In their close analyses of poetic scheme and trope, my first two chapters set up some basic analytical paradigms for the latter two. In these chapters, I suggest that Crashaw and Dryden employ some of the same figures of speech and thought prominent in the poetry of Alabaster and Donne. At first glance, Crashaw's impassioned hymns would seem to have little in common with Dryden's neo-classical couplets. Both, however, exhibit some signal techniques of the poetics of conversion – from the chiastic line to the unexpected, extended, or serialized metaphor (whether it be Crashaw's figuring of the Magdalene's tears in "The Weeper" or Dryden's representation of churches as beasts in *The Hind and the Panther*). But these two poets also make their own distinctive contributions to the early modern poetics of conversion. Crashaw, for instance, experiments with the possibilities of poetic *voice*. Through manipulations of syntax and shadings of tone, Crashaw depicts the lability of religious identity by fusing and blending his poetic speakers with the "wavering women" they address and describe. In Crashaw's poetics of conversion, the poetic "I" is at once Protestant and Catholic, male and female, mature and infantile, English and European. By contrast, Dryden's poetics of conversion centers on experiments with intertextuality and allusion. Writing at the end of the seventeenth century, and at the end of his own career as a Protestant laureate, Dryden was keenly aware of religious change as a historical fact. Using complex echoes and repetitions, *The Hind and the Panther* deliberately invokes and inverts earlier English poems, Dryden's own earlier Protestant poetry, and indeed earlier moments in the poem itself, in order to represent the unstable history of English Christianity.

An interest in some form of conversion does not, in itself, set these poets apart; indeed, most early modern religious poets across the confessional spectrum shared a desire to express their respective understandings of *metanoia*, grace, or repentance in their respective devotional idioms. Critics have, for example, long noted the centrality of conversion to Protestant poetry, particularly that of George Herbert.[84] The recent resurgence of critical

---

[84] So Lewalski argues that the "introspective intensity and keen psychological awareness so characteristic of seventeenth-century religious lyrics" results from a specifically Protestant insistence on "a conversion experience, which is the great crisis or turning point of spiritual life." Lewalski, *Protestant*

interest in Robert Southwell has helped to demonstrate, as Louis Martz suggested more than half a century ago, that post-tridentine Catholicism also encouraged a poetically fruitful "conversion of the heart."[85] What makes the poetry of Alabaster, Donne, Crashaw, and Dryden distinct, I argue, is its consideration of conversion as an outward as well as an inward change, and its consequent willingness to address its institutional as well as spiritual dimensions. If such a tendency distinguishes this poetry from penitential verse within Catholic and Protestant traditions, it also distinguishes this poetry from the aggressively definitive poetic credos composed by other early modern converts between churches. In a ballad allegedly composed in Newgate prison, for instance, the early Protestant convert Anne Askew emphasizes her own steadfast belief:

> Lyke as the armed knight
> Appoynted to the fielde
> With thys world wyll I fight
> And fayth shall be my shielde.[86]

Askew's homely ballad stanzas elide their author's religious change. "I am not she that lyst / My anker to lete fall / For every dryslynge myst / My shyppe substantiall" (33–6), she announces – her declarations of firm piety drowning out any whisper of the uncertainties that preceded and produced them. Similar declarations can be found in the poetry of early modern Catholic converts. Henry Constable, for example, commemorated his turn to Rome with an English sonnet sequence arranged in the order of the Catholic *Confiteor*, or confession of faith.[87] These sonnets refer frequently

---

Poetics, 20–1, and *passim*. Cf. W. Halewood, *The Poetry of Grace: Reformation Themes and Structures in English Seventeenth-Century Poetry* (New Haven: Yale University Press, 1970). On Herbert in particular, see R. Strier, *Love Known: Theology and Experience in George Herbert's Poetry* (University of Chicago Press, 1983), and the darker vision of "letting go" in S. Fish, *Self-Consuming Artifacts: The Experience of Seventeenth-Century Literature* (Berkeley: University of California Press, 1972), 156–223.

[85] Martz's *Poetry of Meditation* centers on the Jesuit Spiritual Exercises as a technology of repentance. R. V. Young argues for a pervasive Catholic interest in election and conversion, citing the Council of Trent's *Decree on Justification*: "when it is said in Sacred Scripture, 'turn toward me and I shall turn toward you' (Zach. 1:3), we are reminded of our freedom; and when we respond, 'Convert us, Lord, to you and we shall be converted' (Lam. 5:21), we confess that we are anticipated by God's grace." Young, *Doctrine and Devotion in Seventeenth-Century Poetry* (Woodbridge: Brewer, 2000), 13. See S. Pilarz, *Robert Southwell and the Mission of Literature 1561–1595* (Aldershot: Ashgate, 2004); G. Kuchar, *Divine Subjection: The Rhetoric of Sacramental Devotion in Early Modern England* (Pittsburgh: Duquesne University Press, 2005), 37–91; and especially A. Sweeney, *Robert Southwell: Snow in Arcadia* (Manchester University Press, 2006). I will return to Southwell in Chapter 1 below.

[86] "The ballad which Anne Askew made and sang when she was in Newgate," in G. Braden (ed.), *Sixteenth-Century Poetry: An Annotated Anthology* (Oxford: Blackwell, 2005), 78–9; lines 1–4.

[87] Constable's "Spirituall Sonnettes" can be found in BL Harleian MS 7553 ff. 32–40, and in J. Grundy (ed.), *The Poems of Henry Constable* (Liverpool University Press, 1960), 183–92. Grundy surveys the evidence for their authorship in her introduction, 51–9. An anonymous manuscript in the

to Constable's earlier secular poetry, which he now regrets ("Why should I
any love, O Queene, but thee?" he exclaims, in the opening line of his
sonnet "To Our Blessed Lady"). Nowhere, however, do they acknowledge a
shift in denominational allegiance; Constable's poetic expressions of repentance offer no clue that he had not always been at least a nominal member of
the Roman church.[88]

But perhaps the most striking examples of this kind of poetic project – we
might call it a poetics *against* conversion – come from a more familiar early
modern convert and poet, Ben Jonson. Although details are sparse and
imprecise, we know that Jonson likely became a Catholic while imprisoned
in the 1590s, that in 1606 he and his wife were charged with recusancy, and
that by 1610 he had officially rejoined the established church.[89] Jonson's
devotional poetry, however, attempts to dispel the spectre of conversion as if
by aesthetic fiat, replacing doubt with declaration, change with certainty.
The poems he composed as a Catholic, like the epigram "On my First
Daughter," and "The Garlands of the Blessed Virgin," rehearse commonplaces of Catholic piety: in their evocations of innocence, virginity, and
martyrdom, they express what "Garlands" describes as a "firm ... flat" faith
in a correspondingly plain style.[90] The poems he composed as a recon-
firmed Protestant, in turn, present an equally stable system of beliefs in a
different theological key. "The Sinner's Sacrifice," for instance, describes an
act of supplication to the trinity in a neatly appropriate stanzaic form: each
quatrain invokes the three-personed God in a tercet of rhymed lines,
relegating man's entreaty to a fourth, shorter line:

> O Holy, blessed, glorious *Trinitie*
> Of persons, still one God, in *Unitie*
> The faithfull mans believed Mysterie,
>   Helpe, helpe to lift

Huntington Library contains some similarly hagiographic sonnets likely written by Constable's
contemporary and fellow Catholic convert, Toby Matthew. See A. Petti, "Unknown Sonnets by
Toby Matthew," *RH* 9 (1967), 123–58.

[88] Shell suggests that Constable "used ... the sonnet to express and encode the dubieties of Catholic
loyalism," (*Catholicism, Controversy*, 123), while Gary Kuchar stresses Constable's debt to medieval
mysticism in "Henry Constable and the Question of Catholic Poetics: Affective Piety and Erotic
Identification in the *Spiritual Sonnettes*," *PQ* 85.1 (2006), 69–89. Both accounts agree, however, that
the poems are clearly Catholic in their aesthetic and devotional stance.

[89] J. P. Crowley, "'He took his religion by trust': The Matter of Ben Jonson's Conversion," *Renaissance
and Reformation* 22 (1998), 53–70; Donaldson, *Jonson's Magic Houses*, 47–65; and T. A. Stroud, "Ben
Jonson and Father Thomas Wright," *ELH* 14 (December 1947), 274–82.

[90] Critics have long agreed with W. Trimpi that these poems "perfectly realize the virtues of the [plain]
style." Trimpi, *Ben Jonson's Poems* (Stanford University Press, 1962), 180–1. S. Booth demonstrates
how painstakingly Jonson works to create this illusion of plainness in *Precious Nonsense* (Berkeley:
University of California Press, 1998).

> My selfe up to thee, harrow'd, torne, and bruis'd
> By sinne, and Sathan, and my flesh misus'd
> As my heart lies in peeces, all confus'd
> O take my gift.   (1–8)

The truncated final line of each stanza neatly indicates the Reformed concept of prevenient grace, formally demonstrating the inadequacy of human efforts at devotion without divine "helpe."[91] For all its insistence on "confusion" and weakness, then, this poem nevertheless reflects an implicit confidence in the theological system that frames its pleas. Jonson's devotional lyrics convey a depth and range of religious feeling, with the accents of Rome replaced by those of Reformation. But in the content and form of the poems themselves, we find no hint of ambivalence.

The poetry of Askew and Jonson, like that of Constable and Matthew, conveys the zeal of the convert between churches, whether ultimately Protestant or Catholic. The poetry of Alabaster, Donne, Crashaw, and Dryden, by contrast, emphasizes something more surprising and more compelling: the *conversion* of the convert. While each of these four poets is distinctly aware of the idioms of contemporary prose polemic, none of these poets simply versifies its doctrinal or ecclesiological claims. None seeks to declare the permanence or stability of his current religious position, no matter how hard-won or heartfelt. Instead each of these poets acknowledges the linked experiences of inward and outward change as a subject, or perhaps *the* subject, of devotional poetry, each derives poetic energy from the experience of such change, and each associates such change with the particularly expressive dynamics of verse. In the chapters that follow, I will consider the contexts and pressures that set these four particular minds in motion. More importantly, however, I will trace some of their most striking poetic turns.

---

[91] As several critics have suggested, such self-effacement anticipates (or perhaps echoes) the chastised Protestant poetics of George Herbert. See S. L. Severance, "'To Shine in Union': Measure, Number and Harmony in Ben Jonson's 'Poems of Devotion,'" *Studies in Philology* 80.2 (Spring 1983), 183–99; and I. Bell, "Circular Strategies and Structures in Jonson and Herbert," in M. Maleski (ed.), *Fine Tuning: Studies of the Religious Poetry of Herbert and Milton* (Binghamton, NY: Medieval and Renaissance Texts and Studies, 1987), 157–70.

CHAPTER I

William Alabaster's lyric turn

In *Colin Clouts Come Home Againe*, Spenser's speaker catalogues those
men of letters at Elizabeth's court who deserve greater fame, among them
"*Alabaster* thoroughly taught / In all this skill, though knowen yet to few"
(400–1). William Alabaster's name is now known to fewer still, but his
mutable religious identity – and the inventive language he uses to describe
it – provides a useful beginning for a discussion of the early modern
poetics of conversion.[1] The story of this serial convert begins in 1567,
when Alabaster was born into a branch of the staunchly Protestant
Winthrop family of Hadleigh, Suffolk (a town that John Foxe proclaimed
a "Universitie of the Learned" for its early, fervent embrace of the
Reformation).[2] He was sent to study divinity at Cambridge, and became
a chaplain to the Earl of Essex on his 1596 mission to Cadiz. Shortly after
his return from Spain, however, Alabaster announced his turn to
Catholicism. He was imprisoned and interrogated in England, then
escaped to the continent, where he spent a period of exile among the
English Jesuits in Rome. Upon a brief return visit to England, he was again
imprisoned for recusancy; in 1603, after a pardon from James I, he began a
phase of anti-Jesuit Catholic loyalism in England and abroad. In 1610,
however, his book of cabalistic exegesis, *Apparatus in Revelationem Iesu
Christi* (Antwerp, 1607), caused him to be brought before the Inquisition,
charged with heresy, and briefly imprisoned by Catholic authorities.
Returning to England once more in 1611, Alabaster publicly announced

---

[1] The fullest account of Alabaster's career remains E. J. Coutts, "The Life and Works of William
Alabaster, 1568–1640" (unpublished Ph.D. dissertation, University of Wisconsin, 1956). See also
J. S. Alabaster, *A Closer Look at William Alabaster: Poet, Theologian and Spy?* (Oxford: The Alabaster
Society, 2003); A. Marotti, *Religious Ideology and Cultural Fantasy*, 98–109; and D. F. Sutton's
introduction to his edition, *Unpublished Works of William Alabaster*, Salzburg Studies in English
Literature, Elizabethan and Renaissance Studies 126 (University of Salzburg, 1997), xv–xxx.

[2] See S. Andrews and T. Springall, *Hadleigh and the Alabaster Family* (Ipswich: Sue Andrews, 2005). For
a revisionist reassessment of Hadleigh's reputation, see J. Craig, "Reformers, Conflict and
Revisionism: The Reformation in Sixteenth-Century Hadleigh," *HJ* 42 (1999), 1–23.

his reconversion to Protestantism, and by 1614 was Doctor of Divinity at Cambridge. His devotional affiliations would nevertheless remain persistently ambiguous; to Oliver Cromwell, one of Alabaster's Paul's Cross sermons contained enough "flat Popery" to inspire his first speech in the House of Commons, but to Robert Herrick "Dr. Alablaster" (*sic*) was "next the Gospell" in theological wisdom.[3] Alabaster's mutable devotional identity seems to have been a source of bewilderment for his contemporaries. One observer, John Dickenson, borrowed a phrase from Apuleius's *Metamorphosis* to describe him as the "vilest among bipeds" (*Alabastrium bipedum nequissimus*), John Chamberlain dismissed him as the "double or treble turncoat," while Ralph Winwood mocked him for the ease with which he prepared to "sing his recantation" (*palinodiam canere*).[4]

Borrowing Winwood's phrase, I want to present Alabaster not simply as a convert, but as a "singer of recantations" – a poet of conversion. My discussion will focus on the circumstances of his initial change from Protestantism to Catholicism, and, especially, on his self-conscious refractions of that change into text. Like his avowed spiritual forefather, St. Augustine, Alabaster describes his conversion as inspired by reading, and productive of writing. More specifically, he associates conversion with literary transformation; for Alabaster, a change of church involves a change of genre or style. His penchant for literary experiment began early; by 1592, he had gained repute in the world of university drama for his Senecan tragedy *Roxana*, closely modeled on Luigi Groto's Italian play *La Dalida*.[5] But Alabaster soon abandoned tragedy for epic, as Colin Clout notes praising "that heroick song, / Which he hath of that mighty Princesse made" and declaring that "when he finisht hath as it should be, / No braver Poeme can be under Sun" (404–5, 410–11). Spenser here refers to the first

---

[3] Cromwell, *Speech in the House of Commons, Feb. 11, 1628–9*, in W. C. Abbott (ed.), *The Writings and Speeches of Oliver Cromwell*, vol. 1 (Oxford: Clarendon, 1937, reissued 1988), 61 2; Herrick, "To Doctor Alablaster," in *Hesperides* (1648), line 20. Herrick's allusion to "the Trumpet which thou late hast found" (17) likely refers to Alabaster's late work of occult exegesis, *Spiraculum Tubarum* (n.d.–1633).

[4] For Chamberlain, see Alabaster, *Unpublished Works*, xvii, n. 1; for Dickenson and Winwood, see Coutts, "William Alabaster," 20 n. 12–13.

[5] J. C. Coldeway, "William Alabaster's *Roxana*: Some Textual Considerations," in R. J. Schoeck (ed.), *Acta Conventus Neo-Latini Bononiensis* (Binghamton, NY: State University of New York Press, 1985), 413–19. Samuel Johnson would describe Alabaster's dactylic hexameters a paragon of Renaissance *latinitas*, matched only by Milton's poetry. Johnson, *Lives of the Poets*, ed. A. Waugh, 2 vols. (London: Oxford University Press, 1955–6), vol. 1, 65. A more outrageous endorsement comes from Thomas Fuller, who notes that the tragedy was once "so admirably acted in [Trinity] College, and so pathetically; a gentle-woman present thereat (Reader, I had it from an Author whose credit it is Sin with me to suspect) at the hearing of the last words thereof, *sequar; sequar*, so hideously pronounced, fell distracted and never fully recovered her senses." Fuller, *History of the Worthies of England* (1662), 70.

completed book of the *Elisaeis*, a Latin epic meant to detail Elizabeth's defeat of Catholicism.[6] Alabaster never "finisht" this poem, but instead converted to the very faith whose destruction it heralded. This first conversion, in turn, led him to try his hand at two new literary genres: the spiritual autobiography and, most crucially, the English lyric. In this chapter, I will survey some of Alabaster's innovations in prose life-writing, but I will suggest that it is his turn to the lyric – and the sonnet in particular – that enables him to articulate his particularly dynamic understanding of conversion.

CATHOLIC LIFE-WRITING AT THE ENGLISH COLLEGE, ROME

The newly Catholic Alabaster arrived at the English College in Rome in 1598; in this year, he contributed to a set of autobiographical documents known as the *Responsa Scholarum*, or "scholars' answers," currently preserved in the College Archives.[7] These texts have gone almost entirely unnoticed by scholars of the early modern English spiritual autobiography, who still tend to define the "conversion narrative" as an exclusively Protestant genre.[8] Belying the implicit equation of the conversion narrative with a Reformed self-inventory about the workings of grace, however, these *responsa* follow a particular rubric: a questionnaire presented by the Jesuit superiors of the College to the men and boys who arrived there to study:[9]

---

[6] The single extant manuscript copy of this "heroick song" is held in Emmanuel College, Cambridge, and has been translated and edited by M. McConnell as *Studies in Philology* 76 (1979). McConnell suggests that the *Elisaeis* may have influenced Spenser's *Faerie Queene*, as well as Milton's Latin epyllion on the Gunpowder Plot, *In Quintum Novembris*.

[7] A. Kenny (ed.), *The Responsa Scholarum of the English College, Rome*, 2 vols. (London: Catholic Record Society, 1962–3). This edition reproduces the original Latin *responsa*, as well as English summaries of their contents. Further quotations from the *Responsa* will be my own translations unless otherwise noted, with volume and page number included in the text.

[8] The groundbreaking work of Nigel Smith, for instance, nevertheless frequently implies that the literary inventiveness of autobiographical texts is commensurate with the Protestant radicalism of their authors. See *Literature and Revolution* (New Haven: Yale University Press, 1994) and, especially, *Perfection Proclaimed* (Oxford: Clarendon, 1989). See also P. Caldwell, *The Puritan Conversion Narrative: The Origins of American Expression* (Cambridge University Press, 1993). For a discussion of the Catholic conversion narrative, see M. Murray, "'Now I ame a Catholique': William Alabaster and the Early Modern Catholic Conversion Narrative," in R. Corthell, F. Dolan, C. Highley, and A. Marotti (eds.), *Catholic Culture in Early Modern England* (University of Notre Dame Press, 2007), 189–215.

[9] This rubric is included before the first page of Volume 1 of the *Responsa*. For Catholic education in exile, see P. Guilday, *English Catholic Refugees*. For the English College in particular, see A. C. F. Beales, *Education Under Penalty: English Catholic Education from the Reformation to the Fall of James II* (London: Athlone, 1963), 49–72.

Capita, quibus ex Regularum praescriptis admittendi in hoc Collegium tenentur Respondere.

[Prescribed headings, to which those admitted into this College are made to respond.]

1. *Quodnam sit verum nomen suum et parentum? Quae aetas? Quis locus nativitatis et educationis? Ubi vixerit?*

   [What is [the student's] real name, and that of his parents? How old is he? Where was he born, educated, and raised?]

2. *Quae sit status et conditio sua et parentum praecipuorum amicorum? Si nobiles an plebii an mediae sortis? Divites an pauperes? Quosnam habeat fratres, sorores aut cognatos? Si haeretici an Catholici sint?*

   [What is his condition, and that of his parents and closest friends? Are they nobles, commoners, or of the middle sort? Rich or poor? Does he have brothers, sisters, or relatives? Are they Catholics or heretics?]

3. *Quibus studiis, et ubi, operam dederit, et quo progressu?*

   [What has he studied, and where, and with what progress?]

4. *Qua valetudine utatur? Secunda, an adversa? Si animae aegritudinem vel sentiat, vel aliquando senserit, quae vel a litterarum studiis, vel a regularum observatione aliquem retardare posset?*

   [How healthy is he? Does he now or has he ever felt any ailment of spirit that might inhibit his ability to study or to observe rules?]

5. *Si in haeresi aliquando aut schismate vixerit? Quando, quibus praesidiis, cuius industria, fidem Catholicam amplexus sit, si aliquando fuerit haereticus? Quando ex Anglia discesserit? Cur Romam venerit, quidve ipsum induxerit ad hoc seminarium petendum? Si quid perpessus sit aliquando ob fidem Catholicam? Quid demum illi contigerit circa vocationem ad fidem Catholicam?*

   [Has he ever lived in heresy or schism? If he was ever a heretic, how and under what circumstances did he embrace the Catholic faith? When did he leave England? Why did he come to Rome, and what led him to seek out this seminary? Has he ever suffered for the Catholic faith? What exactly happened around his vocation to the Catholic faith?]

6. *An propositum, et desiderium sentiat suscipiendi vitam ecclesiasticam? An decernat apud se constanter in virtute et literis operam ponere? An sentiat se paratum ad studendum iis rebus, et in ea classe, quam superiores assignabunt? An statuat submitterere se regulis, et disciplinae Collegii, et Superiorum directioni?*

   [Does he feel himself likely to embrace an ecclesiastic life? Will he undertake the work constantly and with virtue? Does he feel prepared to study those subjects assigned by the Superiors? Does he declare that he will submit to the rules and discipline of the College, and the direction of the Superiors?]

The particular circumstances in which these questions were presented and answered remain unclear. The *responsa* may have been composed in private or in consultation with a spiritual advisor, submitted in writing or delivered in front of a confessor or assembled body of seminarians. The questionnaire itself, however, reflects some of the practical goals of the Jesuit Mission.

First, and most obviously, missionaries wished to confirm the faith of those English recusants who endured penalties for continued Catholic practice. Second, they wished to encourage the greater commitment of "schismatics": those who maintained private Catholic beliefs, but who conformed outwardly to the established church. Finally, they worked actively to convert a new generation of born-and-bred English Protestant "heretics."[10] Given that entrants to the College could come from all three religious backgrounds, the Jesuit superiors wished from the start to ensure their institutional aptitude and to regulate potential dissent, as well as to determine which students had the physical stamina and social connections that would make them productive members of the Mission.[11]

By giving students an opportunity to compose accounts of their lives, however, the *responsa* produced a mode of Catholic life-writing not wholly determined by the exigencies of public propaganda. If dramatic martyrologies and memoirs of "hunted priests" like John Gerard or William Weston were meant to galvanize members of a persecuted church, these shorter and more intimate self-descriptions vary dramatically in both style and content. Most are simply terse replies to the list of questions, often in halting Latin (one student responds to Question 4 "*Aegrotus fui nunquam in mea vita nisi bis* and once of the measles & the small pockes" (1.25)). Occasionally, though, students volunteer fuller answers to questions they find particularly important or interesting. Question 2, for instance, led some to offer lengthy and pained admissions of "heresy" or "schism" in their immediate families, and encouraged others to proclaim their illustrious Catholic genealogies. In this latter vein, John Copley announces that "My parents come from a noble family: my father was called the Illustrious Baron of Hoo and Wells, and Lord Copley of Gatton; my mother came out of the Lutterell family ... my third sister called Margaret [Gage] with her husband was condemned to death after two years of imprisonment because a priest, later martyred, celebrated mass at her home ... Father fled England for religion, and died in

[10] See M. Questier, "'Like Locusts all over the World': Conversion, Indoctrination and the Society of Jesus in Late Elizabethan and Jacobean England," in McCoog (ed.), *The Reckoned Expense*, 265–84.
[11] Several years earlier, members of the College had disagreed violently over the issue of England's war with Spain; many objected to the pro-Spanish position of the church, arguing that their Catholic identity did not obviate loyalty to Elizabeth. See A. Pritchard, *Catholic Loyalism in Elizabethan England* (Chapel Hill: University of North Carolina Press, 1979), and M. Carrafiello, *Robert Persons and English Catholicism* (London: Associated University Presses, 1998), 90–102. A propagandistic account of earlier "dissention" at the College can be found in Anthony Munday, *English Roman Life* (1590), ed. P. Ayres (Oxford: Clarendon, 1980). See D. Hamilton, *Anthony Munday and the Catholics 1560–1633* (Aldershot: Ashgate, 2005).

Flanders in service of the King of Spain … Reverend Father Robert Southwell who was martyred is related by blood to my father's sister" (1.20). Copley may have been trying to impress the Jesuit superiors with this account, but his pride in his Catholic forebears seems nevertheless palpable and personal.

Questions 4 and 5 reveal a wide range of physical conditions among the seminarians. At one extreme, we find men like Thomas Hodgson who, in the words of the editors' summary, "describes, with a wealth of contemporary medical terms, how his stomach is weakened by an excess of cold and wet humours, how his head suffers from sympathetic pains, how his animal forces tend to sluggishness, how his distemper is offset and his superfluities voided by exercise or warm weather, how his loins are allergic to excessive heat and demand a doublet open at each side, how and why he has suffered twice from spermatorrhoea, thrice from fever, once from colic, and often from toothache and pains in the eyes" (1.94–5), while Hugh Anderton notes that "violent movement causes him to pant" (1.99). Thomas Pershall, by contrast, describes his daring flight from London hidden in the wares of a sympathetic English tailor (1.79–80), while Nicholas Hart, one of the few students who composed his answers entirely in English, recalls the various stratagems he used to conceal his Catholic conversion from friends and authorities at Oxford:

the night before I purposed to goe to confessione, I was very much tempted by one of my former companions to eat flesh it being a fastinge day at night, I endeavoringe by all meanes possible to shunne his companye & coud not but that I must needs supp with hime, I beinge loth to seeme unto hime to refuse to eate fleash, in this great perplexitie & vexatione of mynd … it pleased god that by this meanes I was delivered, for we walkinge home together to supper, it came in to his mind to goe into a Confectioners shopp wheare he did soe fill hime selfe with sweete meates, that he had noe stomack unto his supper, & I in lyke manner used the same excuse. (1.27)

Hart's feigned stomach ache, along with other tactics, managed to keep his secret safe until his departure for Rome.

The intellectual training among members of the College seems to have been equally varied. Edmund Smith, for instance, confesses that he spent his university years pursuing trifles and vain things (*nugis et vanitatibus*) (1.75), while John Smith, alias Carrington, recounts his early dilettantism at Oxford, where he made only the very slightest progress in his studies (*minutissimos progressus literis*) (1.97). Other seminarians, particularly the older Catholic converts, describe a more ruminative path to Rome. Henry

Chaderton offers a twenty-page account of his early religious opinions, devoting as much time to his progress in "study and devotion" as to his persecution and escape from England (1.30–52). Chaderton makes copious marginal references to the scriptural and controversial sources that bolstered his nascent Catholic beliefs, giving his *responsum* the appearance of a formal theological tract – but his emphasis on reading is, if extravagant, not unique. Of the twenty-seven former Protestants who entered the college before 1603, twelve ascribe their conversions to the influence of Catholic priests, and twelve to the persuasion of Catholic texts. Particular works mentioned include controversial tracts written against the Protestant bishop John Jewel, Robert Persons's *Spiritual Directory*, Edmund Campion's *Rationes Decem*, and Robert Bellarmine's work on Purgatory.

Given his credentials as a man who, by his own admission, had even before his conversion "eaten and drunk Grammar, Poetry, Rhetoric, Logic, philosophy, mathematics, history, criticism, philology, almost all the Greek and Latin fathers ... as well as the works of St. Thomas, Bellarmine, Suarez and Stapleton, and other Catholic books both great and small" (1.1), it should not surprise us that William Alabaster's *responsum* attributes his conversion to an encounter with a Catholic text. His description of that encounter, however, is idiosyncratic. When mentioning those polemical or theological writings that influenced their spiritual development, Chaderton and others take pains to mention the specific points of doctrine that those texts propounded. John Brown, for instance, recounts how he "was shown a book of St. Augustine which mentioned fire of hell and another fire besides this one; taking this as a confirmation of the doctrine of Purgatory, [I] became convinced of the truth of Catholicism" (1.102–3). By contrast, Alabaster omits any mention of doctrine, limiting his discussion of textual engagement to the act of reading itself. He explains that one day, while at court, he found himself "idly reading a certain book written by one Reginaldus, in favor of the Catholic cause. I had not yet finished reading the preface when suddenly I drank in so great a radiance of divine light, and perceived such a great scattering of unaccustomed joy in my soul, that at that very moment I leapt up gesturing, and my voice broke forth: 'Now I am a Catholic'" (1.2). Alabaster claims to have quit the court immediately after this cataclysmic moment. But his description of the moment itself raises at least as many questions as it answers. Who was this "Reginaldus"? How did Alabaster manage to find his book? Which Catholic tenets did it justify, and how did it manage to persuade Alabaster to abandon his promising career as a Protestant chaplain and poet?

ALABASTER'S CONVERSION AND *ALABASTER'S CONVERSION*

Alabaster provides some remarkable answers to – or, rather, revisions of – these questions in another text that has been unduly neglected by critics: a prose autobiography, over one hundred pages long, drafted during his first year at the English College.[12] The particular reasons behind this longer work have not been conclusively determined. The acting superior of the College, Robert Persons, began to translate the text into Latin shortly after the English version was completed, however, a project that suggests a plan for its eventual circulation in print or manuscript.[13] This translation project ceased in the early seventeenth century, after Alabaster's Catholic commitments had begun to waver. Before then, however, Persons might have wished to capitalize on this new convert's literary gifts and relative prominence among Elizabethan courtiers, preachers, and poets. It seems likely that Persons commissioned Alabaster's extended autobiography intending to use it to strengthen devotion and effect further conversions among both English and continental readers.

This narrative is more than a vehicle for Catholic propaganda, however. If Alabaster's lost *Seven Motives* was a work of self-justification offered in soberly theological terms, his conversion account is, by contrast, a work of artful self-representation.[14] The later sections of the text contain summaries of theological debate, carefully narrated as dramatic scenarios of encounter; the earlier sections, including the account of the conversion itself, eschew doctrine almost entirely. Alabaster elaborates on his brief *responsum*, in other words, not merely to clarify the theological grounds of his conversion, but also, and perhaps more importantly, to delineate the emotional, psychological, and literary aspects of the conversion experience. He begins by describing his early activities in "the heate of heresie ambition and vanitie,"

[12] This manuscript is held in the archives of the English College at Rome as *Liber* 1394. For a reproduction of the typescript made by a College archivist see Clara Fazzari (ed.), *Alabaster's Conversion (anno 1598)* (Florence: Università degli Studi di Firenze, 1983); I will quote from the version included in Sutton's edition of Alabaster's *Unpublished Works*, with page numbers noted in the text.
[13] The manuscript of this partial translation, entitled "De Conversione Gul.mi Alabastri ad fidem Catholicam opusc.m P. Rob. Personii ex Anglico in Latinum idioma translatum," is held in the English College as *Liber* 1395. See P. O. Kristeller, *Iter Italicum* (London: Warburg, 1963–97), 565.
[14] No copies of Alabaster's *Motives* are extant. The two printed refutations of it, however, Roger Fenton's *Answer to William Alablaster [sic] His Motives* (1599) and John Racster, *A Booke of the Seven Planets, Or, Seven Wandring Motives, of William Alablaster's Wit, Retrograded or Removed* (1598), both include extensive and identical quotations from Alabaster's text, allowing a reasonably confident reconstruction of its contents.

a time when he not only composed the *Roxana* and *Elisaeis*, but also participated in the avant-garde ecumenism of the Essex circle.[15] On the Cadiz expedition, Alabaster had close contact with Catholics and crypto-Catholics as well as extreme Protestants, and the heterodox opinions of this group would have accustomed him to theological debate.[16] Returning from Cadiz, Alabaster tells us, he was confident in his ability to counter any Catholic argument with Protestant "reasonableness," making frequent visits to London prisons to attempt the conversions of recusants.[17]

The text instrumental to Alabaster's conversion came into his hands from one of these recusants, the priest allegedly responsible for the Catholic conversion of Ben Jonson, Father Thomas Wright.[18] One night, Alabaster recalls, after a lengthy debate, Wright loaned him a book entitled *A Refutation of Sundry Reprehensions* (Paris, 1583), a defense of the Douai-Rheims New Testament written by William Rainolds (the "Reginaldus" of the *responsum*). Alabaster describes the consequences in a passage that expands on his earlier account:

I went to my lodging with this little booke of Mr William Reynaldes in my hand and sitting down after supper on my bedds side; to spend that ydle time, I begane to reede the preface therof, that treated very learnedly and lardgly out of the writinges of protestentes themselfes of their inconstant and deceatfull manner of proceedinges. I had not read for the space of a quarter of an howre (if I remember well) but as if those squames [i.e. scales] that fell from St Paules boddylye eyes ... so was I lightned

---

[15] In "Essex and Europe: Evidence from Confidential Instructions by the Earl of Essex 1595–6," *English Historical Review* III (1996), 380–1, Paul Hammer describes how Essex "deliberately cultivated an international reputation as a supporter of toleration for English Catholics." Although a staunch Protestant himself, Essex had a number of Catholics and crypto-Catholics among his friends and associates. For more evidence of Essex's reputation among Catholics as a proponent of toleration, see A. J. Loomie, S. J., "A Catholic Petition to the Earl of Essex," *RH* 7 (1963), 1–37.

[16] The theological variety of the participants in the Cadiz voyage, and of the Essex circle in general, has been discussed by R. Lacey, *Robert: Earl of Essex* (New York: Atheneum, 1971), 150–9, and by P. Hammer, *The Polarisation of Elizabethan Politics: The Political Career of Robert Devereux, 2nd Earl of Essex 1585–1597* (Cambridge University Press, 1999), 269–315. The commonplace book of Sir Edward Hoby (British Library Add. MS 38223) includes a list of regulations imposed upon the men, beginning with a frank acknowledgment of the company's heterodoxy: "VERY FIRST RULE: Imprimis: that you take especiall care to serve god by using of Comon prayer twise every daye unles urgent cause enforce the contrarie, and that no man, mariner, soldiers, or other so dispute of matters of religion except it be to be resolved of some doubtes, and in such case that he conferr with the Ministers fo the Armye, for it is not fitt that unlearned men should openly argue of such high misticall matters" (fo. 98). The fact that such "disputes" needed specific regulation indicates their predicted frequency.

[17] Alabaster, in other words, sought to counteract the vigorous Catholic proselytizing taking place in many of London's prisons. See P. Lake and M. Questier, "Prisons, Priests, and People," in N. Tyacke (ed.), *England's Long Reformation, 1500–1800* (London: University College Press, 1998), 195–233.

[18] See T. A. Stroud, "Ben Jonson and Father Thomas Wright," *ELH* 14 (1947), 277–9; and J. P. Crowley, "'He took his religion by trust': The Matter of Ben Jonson's Conversion," *Renaissance and Reformation* 22 (1998), 53–70.

uppon the suddene, feeling my selfe so wonderfully and sencybly chaunged both in iudgment and affection as I remaned astonished at my trewe state. I fownde my minde wholie and perfectly Catholique in an instante, and so to be persuaded of all and everie poynt of Catholic religion together, as I beleved them all most undoubtedly and every point and parcell therof, though I knew not the reasons of all, nor made perhaps sure the arguments of the contrary parte. Nor did I desyer any perticuler resolution in any other question of controversie, for I saw most evidently in my inward iudgment, that all were trewe and nothing could be false which the Catholic Roman Church dyd propose to be beleeved. And feeling this in my selfe uppon the suddene with such inward light of evidens as I cold not contradict and with such force of affection as I cold not resist, I lept up from the place where I satt, and saide to myself, now I ame a Catholique, and then fell down upon my knees, and thanked God most hartely humbly and affecteously for so rare a benefitt. (118)

Alabaster includes additional details that give this episode a striking verisimilitude: he opened the "little" octavo volume "after supper sitting on [his] bedds syde," he concentrated on the preface for about "a quarter of an howre," and had a violently physical reaction: he "lept up from the place where [he] satt ... and then fell down upon [his] knees." Conspicuously absent, however, is any more detailed account of the contents of Rainolds's preface. Alabaster does not mention the sacraments, Purgatory, papal infallibility, veneration of saints and martyrs, or the antiquity and visibility of the Catholic Church, topics which the preface treats at length.[19] Instead, he suggests that what Rainolds wrote in defense of Catholicism was less important, at least at this stage, than his way of expressing it. Rainolds, we learn, "treated very learnedly and lardgly out of the writinges of protestentes themselfes of their inconstant and deceatfull manner of proceedinges" – in other words, deftly converting Reformed arguments into support for a Catholic position. This manner of argumentation, rather than its matter, seems to have been of paramount importance to Alabaster, who goes on to announce his own consequent epiphany in terms as emphatic as they are vague: "Now I ame a Catholique." This statement, itself, seems also to rely on manner rather than matter for its effect; explanation is replaced by dramatic gesture, by an expression of fervor that we are to accept as true because of the way in which it is expressed. Alabaster, in fact, insists that his experience of conversion obviated any specific thoughts of doctrine: "I fownde my minde wholie and perfectly Catholique in an instante," he insists, requiring no "perticuler resolution" after that. Even as Alabaster refers to his "minde" and his "iudgment," then, he suggests that Rainolds's

---

[19] Rainolds defends the doctrine of papal infallibility explicitly from his first paragraph. *Refutation of Sundry Reprehensions*, sig. A2v.

book produced in him something more like sympathetic inspiration than intellectual persuasion.[20]

Over half of Alabaster's narration of his own conversion is, in fact, dedicated to the "lyff and happy death" of the author whose book converted him (115). A focus on exemplary character often marks Catholic hagiography and defenses of pastoral work. In his preface to the Douai-Rheims New Testament, for instance, Gregory Martin counsels his Catholic readers to seek out clergymen of character and learning who can better explain the contents of scripture to them.[21] Alabaster concurs in his *Seven Motives*: "when the question of truth in controversie of faith is turned too and fro, in the throng of so many particular quarrells ... *The question is at last removed from the text to the interpretor, from the scripture unto the men.* So that a mind studious of truth is now come to his last care, to determine of the worth, merit, and authority of those that are the expositours."[22] The Catholic Church, he continues, is led by "reverent and learned Fathers," in contrast to depravity of Luther, "an Apostata ... and an incestuous Monke" whose corrupt life inspires the "dregs of Hereticks."[23] In his prose conversion narrative, Alabaster presents Rainolds as a man of "worth, merit and authority," but further grounds that exemplarity precisely in his status as a Catholic *convert*. The inset biography of Rainolds is not merely hagiography, then, but a virtual *mise-en-abîme* within Alabaster's account of his own Catholic turn.[24] Like Alabaster, Rainolds had an early career as a fervent Protestant, even at times associating with "the familie of love and other new sects springing up" (115). Like Alabaster, Rainolds "departed from a most prosperous and flourishing worldly state" when he left the Church, exchanging this prosperity for "the state of Catholiques disgraced, empoverished and made odious to our Realme" (117). In fact, Rainolds's dramatic conversion to Catholicism was something of a popular legend in late sixteenth-century England, since it was widely believed to have resulted from the proselytizing of his Catholic brother – whom he simultaneously converted to Protantism. Alabaster himself wrote a Latin sonnet about this episode (translated by the recusant Hugh Holland):

> Between two Bretheren Civil warres and worse
> The nice poynt of Religion long did nurse.

[20] Marotti describes this moment in the text as "sudden and beyond the framework of rational discourse and argument," *Religious Ideology and Cultural Fantasy*, 99–100.
[21] *New Testament* (Douai, 1609–10), sig. A3r. See also G. Tavard, *Holy Writ or Holy Church* (London: Burns and Oates, 1959), 230.
[22] "Alabaster's First Motive," quoted by Racster, *Booke of the Seven Planets*, sig. B3r.
[23] "Alabaster's Fifth Motive," quoted by Racster, *Booke of the Seven Planets*, sig. D3v.
[24] Alabaster, *Unpublished Works*, 5.

> For Reformation of the Faith he plyes;
> That Faith should be reformed this denyes.
> Reasons on both sides being apart propounded,
> Both met alike, both fell confounded.
> As hart could wish, each brother other takes,
> As fates would have it, each his faith forsakes.
> Without captiver both are captive led,
> And to the victors camp the vanquished fled.
> What fight is this, where conquered both are glad,
> Yet either, to have conquered other, sad?[25]

Holland's translation conveys the neatly balanced clauses of Alabaster's Latin, emphasizing the mirror-image quality of these opposite turns: "Both met alike, both fell confounded," their conversions "fated" by forces beyond particular points of doctrine. In his narrative, Alabaster's description of Rainolds's turn also avoids theology, concentrating instead on another moment of transformative reading: "[Rainolds] dyd so much detest Mr Jewels falshod in his wrytynge and was so angry with it," Alabaster writes, "as for revenge he was wont to pull out the leafe where he founde it, and for that he could not passe over all the booke while he was in Ingland, he resolved to carrie it with hym ... and styll to teare out leafes as he found treacherie" (116). Once he found himself carrying a book without pages, Rainolds realized that he had become a Catholic. Again, conversion is textually triggered: if Alabaster's conversion occurs abruptly after he begins Rainolds's book, Rainolds's conversion happens after he tears out every page in Jewel's book. In both cases, religious transformations – and subsequent acts of writing – result from particularly intense experiential engagements with books. Rainolds is a "rare example indeede" for Alabaster, then, in his inextricable identities as convert, reader, and writer (114).

Rainolds is not Alabaster's only model, however. In fact, Alabaster's conversion narrative owes its most striking and surprising debt to another conversion narrative: St. Augustine's *Confessions*. While scholars have surveyed the influence of Augustine in early modern England, most emphasize the influence of the *Retractationes*, the epistles and tracts, and the pseudo-Augustinian *Meditations*.[26] The Catholic convert Sir Toby Matthew's 1620

---

[25] *Ibid.*, 12–13. Alabaster's original title, appended in English to the Latin poem, was "Upon a Conference in Religion between John Reynolds then a Papist, and his Brother William then a Protestant."

[26] Martz notes the importance of the 1577 *Certaine select Prayers, gathered out of S. Augustines Meditations* – a book which would inspire a sonnet by Alabaster himself – in *The Poetry of Meditation*. Milward discusses the controversial use of Augustine and other patristics during the 1559 "Challenge" debate. *Religious Controversies of the Elizabethan Period*, 1–8. In their article,

translation of the *Confessions* caused a certain amount of intra-Christian dispute, but in general this text does not seem to have been particularly central to the English religious imagination in the period.[27] Henry Chaderton's contribution to the English College *Responsa*, for instance, refers to "the works of St. Augustine, which [he] possessed complete except for the 6th volume," but mentions specifically only the sermons, the anti-Donatist tract *De Unitate Ecclesiae*, and the work on Purgatory. Although he was a convert himself, Chaderton seems not to have known, or at least not to have thought seriously about, Augustine's own conversion narrative (1.57). Surveying the evidence, Anne Ferry categorically declares that "Augustine's *Confessions* were not known to sixteenth-century autobiographical writers, whose presentations of their experiences took very different forms."[28] Only slightly more cautiously, Paul Delany claims that early modern spiritual autobiographers were "remarkably little influenced by the *Confessions*," a claim for which he offers a circular explanation: "Conservatives in religion, who would have known Augustine's works, tended to write restrained autobiographies in which Augustinian fervour and self-accusation were carefully avoided. The Baptists and other enthusiastic sects were closer to the spirit of the *Confessions*, but his works were probably too scholarly and expensive for them, since he is very rarely mentioned in their writings."[29]

Alabaster's narrative, however, reflects the unmistakable influence of Augustine's *Confessions* in both "spirit" and form. The narrative, like the *Confessions*, consists of thirteen books, and is written as an extended second-person address: Augustine composes his book as a lengthy apologia to his God, while Alabaster writes his text in the form of a letter to an unnamed childhood friend.[30] Both texts begin by describing early religious delusion, intellectual pride, social ambition, and sexual entanglement, all to be

---

"Strategies in Jacobean Polemic," Robert Dodaro and Michael Questier consider two early Jacobean polemicists, one Catholic and one Protestant, who both use Augustine to bolster their doctrinal positions.

[27] Matthew, himself a convert to Catholicism, produced a number of translations of other conversion narratives, including a version of St. Teresa of Avila's *Vida*, entitled *The Flaming Hart* (Antwerp, 1642), which would influence Richard Crashaw's poem of the same name. I discuss that translation in Chapter 3 below, and Matthew's friendship with Donne in Chapter 2.

[28] A. Ferry, *The "Inward" Language: Sonnets of Wyatt, Sidney, Shakespeare, Donne* (University of Chicago Press, 1983), 39.

[29] P. Delany, *British Autobiography in the Seventeenth Century* (London: Routledge, 1969), 31–2.

[30] Letters by converts to friends and family were not uncommon in the period. See, for instance, Robert Markham's letter from Rome to his brother Griffith, now held in the British Library (MS Lansd. 96 fos. 81–2). Sutton speculates that Alabaster had a particular addressee in mind when he wrote his manuscript, and tentatively identifies this addressee as Hugh Holland, whose own conversion happened around the time of Alabaster's own. Alabaster, *Unpublished Works*, xix.

eradicated in the life of the (literally) chastened "*novus homo.*"[31] Augustine's early career involved petty crime, a lengthy affair, and above all his adherence to the intellectually fraudulent Manichaean cult. Following this Augustinian paradigm, Alabaster elaborates on the simple acknowledgment of youthful heresy set down in his College *responsum.* He reminds his unnamed interlocutor of his matriculations at Westminster and Trinity, where he swore "an oathe [against the Catholic religion se]ven or [eight times, if I remember right, for which ble]st Jhesu forgeve [me]" (104). He describes his subsequent achievements in Protestant divinity, and his desire for great fame in both theological and literary arenas. He admits that he began "[to write a wor]ke in Latyn verses [about the Queen and her re]ign [ag]ainst the Catholic Religion, and I presented to her the [first book, and I would have] presented the second, had not God in his mercy prevented me" (104). Alabaster concludes this account of his heretical activities with the admission that he was "chaplaine for six yeares to the Right Honourable the Earl of Essex ... and preached also at the Court and laide the plott to aspire in tyme to the highest dignities and honors, and for the upshott and seale of a sure protestant I was so nigh to have a wyfe that ther wanted nothing but the dispatche of that buisenes for which I have attendence at the Courte" (104). While this may be a factual description of Alabaster's early life, it nevertheless also approximates Augustine's account of his career in Carthage and Rome, where he spent his time "being seduced and seducing, being deceived and deceiving ... pursu[ing] the empty glory of popularity" in verse competitions, and pursuing the empty philosophy exemplified by Faustus the Manichee (72–3).

Returning to Alabaster's central description of his text-centered conversion, we can now see this episode as an unmistakable retelling of the central moment in Book 8 of the *Confessions.* In both cases, a man becomes familiar with the texts and arguments of an opposing creed (Augustine reads Christian theology, Alabaster studies Catholic polemic). Both borrow a book from a proponent of that creed, and would-be mentor (Augustine borrows the letters of St. Paul from Ambrose, Alabaster borrows the Rainolds text from Wright). Both take this book into a place of retirement, where they undergo a nearly instantaneous epiphany. Augustine the Manichaean classicist reads the letters of the Christian convert St. Paul – and is immediately and miraculously convinced of that which he had formerly doubted: "I neither

---

[31] A. H. Hawkins notes these characteristic components of the Augustinian narrative pattern: *Archetypes of Conversion: The Autobiographies of Augustine, Bunyan and Merton* (Lewisburg, PA: Bucknell University Press, 1985), 17–19, 21.

wished nor needed to read further. At once, with the last words of the
sentence, it was as if a light of relief from all anxiety flooded into my heart.
All the shadows of doubt were dispelled" (153). A few lines of St. Paul are
enough to transform Augustine, just as fifteen minutes' perusal of the
preface to the "little book" would convince Alabaster of the entire truth of
Catholic doctrine. In both cases, dry and fruitless intellectual inquiry is
replaced by the inspired "judgment and affection" of newly sanctified men.

Alabaster explicitly likens his own conversion to a story that "St. Augustine
reconteth" elsewhere in the *Confessions*: how "the booke of St. *Antony* the
monke his lyf" converted "two that lighted upon it" (115). While this particular
comparison might seem to elide the more significant parallel between
Alabaster's conversion and Augustine's own, it also indicates one of the
most crucial formal similarities between their narratives. As we have seen,
Alabaster places his description of his own religious change alongside an
extended discussion of the similar change of another (William Rainolds).
So, too, Augustine weaves the story of his own conversion into a tissue of
other conversion stories, all of which involve similar experiences of reading.
His friend Simplicianus, for example, tells him the story of Victorinus, the
author of some of the controversial works Augustine has been skimming.
Augustine learns that Victorinus (like Rainolds) is not just a theologian, but
a convert, and one whose conversion also happened in a moment of textual
inspiration: "He read holy scripture, and all the Christian books with special
care. After examining them, he said to Simplicianus … 'did you know that
I am already a Christian'?" (136). Simplicianus's story of the convert reader
and writer Victorinus is followed by the story mentioned by Alabaster, told
by the convert Ponticianus: once, long ago, he and his colleagues were
wandering, and came upon a house where "they found a book in which was
written the Life of Antony. One of them began to read it. He was amazed
and set on fire, and during his reading began to think of taking up this life"
(144). Here, again, a skeptical man "chances" on a book, and is converted
almost immediately after beginning to read. The contagious accumulation
of such stories in Book 8 ultimately makes the author's own conversion
(after an encounter with the writing of the convert Paul) seem both
miraculous and formally inevitable. Finally, just as his conversion is inspired
by and modeled on other texts and other readers, Augustine the convert
fashions a text that can, itself, continue the exemplary work. Within the
narrative, Augustine describes his successful efforts to convert his friend
Alypius. More importantly, however, Augustine follows his conversion by
composing a text that will serve the same function for readers yet unknown –
readers who would ultimately include William Alabaster.

By invoking the exemplary life of Rainolds, and by imitating the exemplary text of Augustine, Alabaster proposes his narrative as part of a tradition of other stories and other texts beginning with that of "St. Augustine's Master," Paul (140). The imitative conversions described in Alabaster's autobiography – and exemplified by it – finally seek to catalyze a similar encounter between Alabaster's text and its ideal reader. Like Antony, Victorinus, Ponticianus, Augustine, Alypius, Rainolds, and Alabaster himself, this future reader will experience an epiphany intimately connected to the act of reading. Inspired both by Alabaster's conversion and by its textual expression, the converted reader will then go on to imitate the convert author (and his predecessors) both by embracing a new form of worship and, ultimately, by attempting a new form of writing in order to commemorate, and perhaps even to perpetuate, that change. Alabaster describes this process in his prose autobiography, but it is a process that finally led him back to the composition of verse, and more particularly to the English sonnet.

"DESIRE POSSESSION, POSSESSION DESIRE": HOLY SONNETS

Alabaster claims that his turn to Catholicism inspired him to compose "verses of love and affection" in the form of seventy-nine English sonnets.[32] Although his prior poetic output had been almost entirely in Latin, Alabaster's intimacy with Elizabethan literary and courtly circles would have familiarized him with the works of secular English sonneteers.[33] Nor would he have been alone among his contemporaries in using sonnet conventions "to style Christ's praise with heavenly muse's wing," as Thomas Roche and others have shown.[34] In 1560, Anne Locke composed the first sequence of devotional sonnets in English: twenty-six poems based on Psalm 51.[35] A few decades later, Anne's son Henry produced two "centuries"

---

[32] These poems were not printed in Alabaster's lifetime, but seem to have circulated in manuscript; Story and Gardner survey the extant manuscripts, and discuss the date and order of the sonnets, in Alabaster, *Sonnets*, xxxvi–xliii.

[33] Alabaster certainly knew at least two sonneteers, Spenser and Holland. For a discussion of the courtly milieux of other Elizabethan poets, see S. W. May, *The Elizabethan Courtier Poets: The Poems and Their Contexts* (Columbia: University of Missouri Press, 1991), and C. Warley, *Sonnet Sequences and Social Distinction in Renaissance England* (Cambridge University Press, 2005).

[34] No full-length study of the Renaissance devotional sonnet exists; see, however, T. Roche, *Petrarch and the English Sonnet Sequences* (New York: AMS Press, 1985), 154–92, and L. Campbell, *Divine Poetry and Drama* (New York: Gordian Press, 1972), 130–8.

[35] Anne Locke, *A Meditation of a Penitent Sinner: Written in the Maner of a Paraphrase upon the 51. Psalme of David* (1560).

of sonnets on a variety of religious subjects.[36] His contemporary and fellow Protestant Barnabe Barnes, only slightly less ambitiously, produced *A Divine Centurie of Spiritual Sonnettes* (1595), meant as atonement for his occasionally salacious secular collection *Parthenophil and Parthenope* (1593). Fulke Greville's *Caelica* sequence uses Petrarchan conventions, meanwhile, to depict a soul's progress from erotic to spiritual devotion, while Henry Constable marked his conversion to Catholicism with a sequence of hagiographic "spiritual sonnettes."[37]

Because Alabaster was also a convert to Catholicism, the few critics who have studied his sonnets have categorized them as "recusant poetry," part of the English Counter-Reformation literary tradition exemplified by poets like Constable and, especially, Robert Southwell.[38] Louis Martz, for instance, classifies Alabaster's sonnets as examples of the "poetry of meditation" based on the *Spiritual Exercises* of Ignatius of Loyola.[39] Alabaster does seem to have known the *Exercises* by the time he composed his sonnets; John Gerard claims to have guided Alabaster through them shortly after his conversion,[40] and Alabaster himself describes his poetic process in recognizably Ignatian terms: "I was wont often to walke into the feildes alone, and being then summer ther I would sett mee downe in certaine corne feildes where I could not be seene or heard of others, and here passe the time

[36] Henry Locke (or Lok)'s *Sundry Christian Passions, contained in two hundred Sonnets* (1597) has been discussed by Roche, *Petrarch and the English Sonnet Sequences*, 157–66, and Campbell, *Divine Poetry*, 130–2. See also I. Clark, *Christ Revealed: The History of the Neotypological Lyric in the English Renaissance*, University of Florida Monographs in the Humanities 51 (Gainesville: University of Florida Press, 1982), 35.

[37] For Fulke Greville, see Campbell, *Divine Poetry*, 136–8; Roche, *Petrarch and the English Sonnet Sequences*, 168–85, 295–317. For Constable, see J. Grundy (ed.), *The Poems*, as well as Roche, *Petrarch and the English Sonnet Sequences*, 188–90; Campbell, *Divine Poetry*, 134; and the Introduction, above. See also T. W. N. Parker, *Proportional Form in the Sonnets of the Sidney Circle* (Oxford: Clarendon, 1999), 146–67.

[38] His poems debuted in a Catholic periodical: J. J. H. Pollen, "William Alabaster: A Newly Discovered Catholic Poet of the Elizabethan Age," *The Month* 103 (1904), 427–30; and are given pride of place in I. Guiney, *Recusant Poetry* (London: Sheed and Ward, 1938), 335–49. A. Marotti discusses the sonnets in *Religious Ideology and Cultural Fantasy*, 102–3. See also A. D. Cousins, *The Catholic Religious Poets from Southwell to Crashaw: A Critical History* (London: Sheed and Ward, 1991), 85–101; L. K. Donaldson-Evans, "Two Baroque Devotional Poets: La Ceppède and Alabaster," *Comparative Literature Studies* 12 (1975), 21–31; Shell, *Catholicism, Controversy*, 88–92; and Ilona Bell, who considers Alabaster so unproblematically "Catholic" that she uses his poems as a contrast to Herbert's "Protestant" poetics. Bell, "'Setting Foot into Divinity': George Herbert and the English Reformation," *MLQ* 38 (1977), 219–41.

[39] Martz sets up this influential category in *The Poetry of Meditation*, 1–24. While he does not discuss Alabaster in this volume, he includes Alabaster in an anthology, *The Meditative Poem* (New York University Press, 1963), 53–62.

[40] Gerard claims to have "looked after [Alabaster] for two or three months" after his conversion and before his departure for Rome, during which time he gave him the *Exercises*. Gerard, *Autobiography of a Hunted Priest*, 169.

in conferences between almightie God and my soule, sometimes with inter-nall meditation uniting my will to God, sometimes forming and contryving the same meditations into verses" (122–3). Bearing out the notion that Alabaster's lyrics are "meditations" in a specifically Jesuit sense, many of them contain a textbook *compositio* describing Jesus's passion, cross, or tomb, while others invoke the trinity of Augustinian faculty psychology (memory, understanding, and will) used by St. Ignatius in the *Exercises*.[41]

Describing Alabaster's poems as strictly "meditative," however, risks overstating the privacy of their purpose. In his narrative, Alabaster states explicitly that he composed these sonnets "not only for my owne solace, and conforte, but to stir up others also that shold reed them to soew [*sic*] estimation of that which I felt in my self" (123), suggesting a plan for their circulation. Indeed, the first sonnet in the collection announces that its aim is "to give the onset" to other readers. Responding to this stated intention, Robert Caro both extends and qualifies Martz's reading by proposing the equal influence of the Catholic rhetorical theory of Father Thomas Wright, the Catholic priest and rhetorician from whom Alabaster borrowed the fateful Rainolds text that triggered his conversion.[42] In *The Passions of the Mind in General*, Wright proposes an idiosyncratic method by which principles of rhetoric – assisted by Jesuit meditative techniques – can be used in writing in order to stir the passions of the reader toward Christian virtue.[43] Caro argues that Alabaster's sonnets put Wright's theory of medi-tative rhetoric into practice, achieving in poetry what the "silent ministry" of Catholic controversial texts achieved in prose: a way both to convince readers of the truth of Catholic doctrine and to move them toward embracing it.

Caro's sensitive discussion of the simultaneously affective and rhetorical quality of Alabaster's poetry nevertheless presumes that these poems were written primarily as an expression of their author's firm Catholic beliefs. In fact, the collection contains hardly any clear doctrinal declarations or catechetical entreaties. Even as they address the Virgin Mary, martyrs, and saints, Alabaster's sonnets ultimately fail to sound forth the tenets of a theological system clearly or confidently. Instead, as in his conversion narrative, Alabaster foregrounds the subjective dynamism of belief: its

---

[41] For instance Sonnet 41, which explicitly associates these faculties with "palace," "parliament," and "lordship."

[42] R. Caro, "William Alabaster: Rhetor, Meditator, Devotional Poet," *RH* 19 (1988), 62–79, 155–70.

[43] For this text, see T. Sloan, "A Renaissance Controversialist on Rhetoric: Thomas Wright's *Passions of the Mind in Generall*," *Speech Monographs* 36 (1969), 38–54, and "The Crossing of Rhetoric and Poetry in the English Renaissance," in T. Sloan and R. Waddington (eds.), *The Rhetoric of Renaissance Poetry from Wyatt to Milton* (Berkeley: University of California Press, 1974), 212–42.

unfolding in time, its connection with personality and sympathy, and its demand for indirect, artful expression. To look for Catholic dogma in these poems, then, or even to diagnose a single devotional or rhetorical "method" of composition, obscures their avowed subject: "that which [Alabaster] felt in [him]self" during a period of transition, and that which he wanted to "stir up" others to feel with him. Alabaster's poems may invoke the signifiers of confessional identity, but they are not statements of achieved conviction; they are instead records, rehearsals, and models of change.

TEARS AND TURNS

This can be seen most strikingly in two poems that seem most superficially "Catholic" in orientation. In the first, Sonnet 10 in the Story and Gardner collection, Alabaster presents the voice of St. Peter. Peter's penitence after betraying Christ provided subject matter for many influential poems of the English Counter-Reformation, notably Robert Southwell's long poem, *St. Peter's Complaint*. In this poem, adapted from Luigi Tansillo's *Lagrime di San Pietro*, the titular saint offers a lengthy and extravagant statement of his contrition:

> Launch foorth my Soule into a maine of teares,
> Full fraught with griefe the trafficke of thy mind:
> Torne sayles will serve, thoughts rent with guilty feares:
> Give care the sterne: use sighes in lieu of wind:
> Remorse, thy Pilot, thy misdeede, thy Carde:
> Torment thy Haven: Shipwracke, thy best reward.   (1–6)

Brian Cummings points out that by moving the poem into the first person, where Tansillo had used the third, Southwell creates an expression rather than a description of penitence. The poem thus becomes "St. Peter's confession to Father Southwell, or in some sense Southwell's own confession to himself."[44] Speaking in the self-catechizing voice of the repentant saint, Southwell can simultaneously offer "an authentication of the [inward] self," and a reaffirmation of his own Catholic piety in the face of Protestant persecution.[45]

---

[44] Cummings, *Literary Culture*, 347; Sweeney suggests that Southwell's speaker is also the reader of the poem (see *Robert Southwell*, 79). P. Janelle discusses the tradition that follows Tansillo in *Robert Southwell, the Writer* (London: Sheed and Ward, 1935), 205–27.

[45] Cummings, *Literary Culture*, 348. For a discussion of Southwell's often violent clarity of poetic purpose, see G. Hill, "The Absolute Reasonableness of Robert Southwell," in *The Lords of Limit* (Oxford University Press, 1984), 19–37. Sweeney, however, points out the "flexible" and "dialogical" quality of the poems (*Robert Southwell*, 28–9).

Alabaster's sonnet also uses the first person, and while it shares with Southwell's poem a remarkable psychological complexity and intensity, it entirely alters Southwell's depiction of saintly penitence and abjection. Alabaster's Peter sonnet appears, first of all, immediately after a poem that indicts Luther for "forsaking" Christ's church and destroying its community of members.[46] It opens with a contrasting statement of loyalty:

> Though all forsake thee, lord, yet I will die,
> For I have chained so my will to thine
> That I have no will left my will to untwine,
> But will abide with thee most willingly.
> Though all forsake thee lord, yet cannot I,
> For love hath wrought in me thy form divine
> That thou art more my heart than heart is mine:
> How can I then from myself, thyself, fly?

The voice, here, initially appears to belong to Alabaster himself: a newly committed Catholic who, unlike the renegade Luther and his followers, will not "forsake" his savior. The repetition of "will" in the first quatrain, moreover, seems deliberately to invoke the Catholic theological emphasis on human volition in worship, lately reaffirmed by Trent. Unlike the solifidian apostate of the preceding poem, this speaker *will* will his *will* to obey as if he were transformed into Christ himself.[47] The ninth line, however, opens with a breathtaking turn: "Thus thought St. Peter and thus thinking fell." Using the sonnet's *volta*, Alabaster shifts our sense of the octave completely. What seemed a straightforward profession of faith by the newly Catholic poet has been suddenly revised into a quotation from St. Peter. This is not, moreover, Southwell's penitent Peter, a fallen disciple tormented by sorrowful self-recrimination. It is, by contrast, Peter before his dark act, bluffly denying the betrayal that we know he will eventually commit. Alabaster's sonnet begins as a confirmation of the speaker's firm devotional will, only to transform before our eyes into a dramatic depiction of devotional instability.

This instability is not Peter's alone. The sestet introduces the poem's "real" speaker (in contrast to the reported speech of the octave) who suffers

---

[46] According to Alabaster's editors, the two sonnets are in this order in all extant manuscripts, suggesting that Alabaster intended them to be read in sequence; the deliberate repetition of the word "forsake" from one poem to the next seems to confirm this. Alabaster, *Sonnets*, 46. George Klawitter addresses the issue of sequence in "Alabaster's 'Ensigns' Sonnets: Calm Before the Storm," in E. Cunnar and J. Johnson (eds.), *Discovering and (Re)Covering the Seventeenth-Century Religious Lyric* (Pittsburgh: Duquesne University Press, 2001) 62–79.

[47] For Alabaster's expressions of the *imitatio Christi*, as well as his use of Old Testament figures, see Clark, *Christ Revealed*, 51–9.

from the knowledge that he may, or may not, follow Peter's unfortunate
example:

> Thus thought St. Peter and thus thinking fell
> And by his fall did warn us not to swell,
> Yet still in love I say I would not fall,
> And say in hope I trust I never shall,
> But cannot say in faith what might I do
> To learn to say it, by hearing Christ say so!

Just as Christ's betrayer cannot foresee his imminent act of hypocrisy, the
poem's speaker cannot predict his own spiritual future with absolute confidence – and the difficult syntax involves the reader in this confusion. In
the critical introduction to their edition of Alabaster's poetry, Story and
Gardner assert that "this sonnet is spoiled by the weak sestet."[48] I would
argue that the "weakness" of the sestet, and the abruptness of the turn before
it, is an essential part of the poem's achievement: it demonstrates how a
profession of faith can become a confession of frailty. Blending his own
voice with that of St. Peter, Alabaster acknowledges that he too "cannot say
in faith what might I do." Having set us off-balance with these shifts in
poetic *personae*, he suggests that we might do well to question our most
seemingly certain beliefs – to remember that faith, especially faith in one's
own faith, can never be relied upon implicitly or for ever.

This emphasis on subjective mutability does not, however, inevitably
lead to despair. Alabaster uses similarly dramatic shifts in perspective to an
entirely different effect in his sonnet on Mary Magdalene. Here again,
Alabaster revisits and revises a common *topos* of Catholic devotional writing,
from Southwell's *Marie Magdalenes Funeral Tears* (1591) and *Mary Magdalen's
Complaint at Christ's Death* (1596) to Thomas Lodge's *Prosopopoeia,
Containing the Teares of the Holy Marie* (1596) and Nicholas Breton's *Mary
Magdalen's Love* (1595).[49] This sonnet, like those other works, presents a
grieving Magdalene whose ostentatious sorrow at Christ's death renders her
another model penitent:

> I weep two deaths with one tear to lament:
> Christ, my soul's life, out of my heart is fled,

---

[48] Alabaster, *Sonnets*, xxx.
[49] Other roughly contemporary poems include the anonymous *Magdalens Lamentations* (1601), and
Nicholas Breton's *The Ravish't Soul and the Blessed Weeper* (1601). Henry Constable's *Spiritual
Sonnettes* contain three Magdalene poems; as Gary Kuchar points out, these are atypical in that
they are apostrophes to the saint, rather than monologues by her. Kuchar, "Henry Constable," 72.

> My soul, my heart's life, from me vanished,
> With Christ my soul, and with my soul, life went.
> I weep, yet weeping brings mere discontent,
> For as Christ's presence my tears seasoned,
> When through my tears his love I clearer read,
> So now his loss through them doth more augment.

As in the St. Peter sonnet, Alabaster uses the first person to blend his own poetic voice with that of the Biblical speaker. In a number of other sonnets in the collection, Alabaster presents himself as a weeping sinner "seek[ing] Christ out." The tone of this sonnet is utterly consistent with those poems, and the title alone – "Upon Christ's saying to Mary, 'Why Weepest Thou?'" – informs us that this is, again, reported speech rather than the voice of Alabaster himself.[50] The identification of the poet with the penitent speaker is so seamless that, for example, Alison Shell persuasively reads the poem as Alabaster's own "apologia directed towards those whose devotional practices are different," its invocation of the Magdalene justifying a religiosity that is affective and emotional – that is, in other words, recognizably Catholic.[51]

The title, however, reveals a significant difference between this sonnet and more conventional Magdalene poems, one that further indicates Alabaster's own particular style of devotional self-presentation. Again, the title is "Upon Christ's Saying to Mary, 'Why Weepest Thou?'" and not, for example, "Mary Magdalen's Funeral Tears." Rather than a private expression of penitence, however exemplary, this sonnet presents part of a dramatic scene, based on a particular episode from the gospel of John. In this passage (John 12:14), the resurrected Christ encounters the grieving Mary and asks her the titular question before she recognizes him. It is precisely this epistemologically and ontologically pivotal moment, *between* Christ's resurrection and his ascension, and *between* Mary's mournful ignorance and her joyful recognition, that Alabaster chooses to depict. Our understanding of the sonnet's situation, then, transforms our understanding of the lament uttered by its speaker. When the speaker cries,

> Yet let my tears once after him fast run
> To seek Christ out, and when my tears are done

---

[50] According to Story and Gardner, the sonnet is prefaced with this title in the one surviving manuscript copy. It is possible that a later scribe might have added the title, but there is no reason to think that the title is not Alabaster's own, particularly since there is little in the sonnet itself that would have suggested a specific reference to Magdalene.

[51] Shell, *Catholicism, Controversy*, 89.

> Mine eyes and heart shall after him pursue,
> Until his grace into mine eyes return,

we perceive an acute dramatic irony, as Mary unwittingly speaks to the very man she mourns. Alabaster's Magdalene sonnet thus becomes a mirror image of his Peter sonnet. In that poem, the conflation of Alabaster's voice with Peter's fearfully acknowledges the fragility of faith: Peter temporarily abandons his savior, and Alabaster (undergoing a conversion betweeen churches) fears the same loss. In this sonnet, by contrast, the blurring of the poet's voice with that of Mary Magdalene adumbrates a joyful epiphany: Alabaster associates himself with a weeping disciple about to recognize her resurrected savior. Once the speech in Sonnet 10 breaks off, the adoring speaker (Peter) will abandon Christ; after the speech in this sonnet breaks off, the despairing speaker (Mary) will rediscover him. In both sonnets, Alabaster invokes and resists Catholic convention by refusing to depict the saints as mere penitents. Instead, he presents both Peter and Mary Magdalene at highly charged moments of incipient movement, moments just before a dramatic recognition – and moments that Alabaster associates with his own transformation.[52]

Alabaster composes a number of other poems of tearful lament in which he is the sole and unequivocal speaker. But these poems also center on radical perspectival shifts, further evoking the disorientation of both inward and outward change. Shell helpfully places these eight "penitential sonnets" in a tradition of Catholic lachrymal poetry that includes the poetry of Southwell and culminates in the poetry of Richard Crashaw, arguing that Alabaster uses tears to signify his own "repentance and conversion."[53] Taking this argument further, I want to suggest that these sonnets demonstrate Alabaster's particular and historically situated understanding of conversion in late Elizabethan England. As we have seen in his autobiography, Alabaster insists upon conversion as a function of regenerative reading. So, in these penitential sonnets, Alabaster transforms the conventions of Catholic lachrymal poetry to signify precisely this kind of transformative hermeneutics. Several of them, for instance, figure tears as miraculous lenses through which religious truths can be better seen or "read." In the Magdalene sonnet already discussed, Alabaster describes tears as means to "augment"

---

[52] For a discussion of Mary Magdalene as an exemplar of spiritual transformation in later seventeenth-century poetry, see W. Leiner, "Metamorphoses Magdaléennes," in *La Metamorphose dans la poésie baroque française et anglaise* (Paris: Éditions Jean-Michel Place, 1979), 45–56.

[53] Shell, *Catholicism, Controversy*, 88–92; cf. Martz, *The Poetry of Meditation*, 194–203. The so-called "penitential sonnets" are numbered 12–19 in Story and Gardner's collection.

both the weeper's initial joy at seeing Christ alive and her sorrow at seeing him dead. In Sonnet 71, tears create "The Difference 'twixt Compunction and Cold Devotion in Beholding the Passion of Our Saviour":

> When without tears I look on Christ, I see
> Only a story of some passion,
> Which any common eye may wonder on;
> But if I look through tears Christ smiles on me.

Here, Alabaster's tears transform a dead "story" into a live experience of Christ's mercy. This presentation of reading through the lenses of tears recalls a passage from the conversion narrative:

As in thinges that are seene in owr eye though the power of the eye be never so good, and the coulour be seene never so freshe … yett if the Medium that delivereth it be obscure or infected with yvell coulours it cannot be well and surely seen as by experience wee finde, when a man looketh thorow painted spectacles, all seemeth to be of that coulour with the spectacles that give the medium do give unto it. (144)

Alabaster elaborates upon the Catholic emphasis on mediation with an optical metaphor: the church is a lens to read God's word correctly. In the sonnet, tears function as a similarly transformative medium, effecting the Pauline conversion from carnal to spiritual reading. Typically, however, Alabaster complicates this idea by representing tears as a medium of self-consciousness as well as devotional intensification, a mirror as well as a lens:

> *Yea, there I see myself,* and from that tree
> He bendeth down to my devotion,
> And from his side the blood doth spin, whereon
> My heart, my mouth, mine eyes still sucking be;
> Like as in optick works, one thing appears
> In open gaze, in closer otherwise.

Images of spinning blood and sucking eyes gesture ahead toward the phantasmagoria of Richard Crashaw's poetry. More important for Alabaster, however, is the complex transformation of tears themselves; they are a device by which he can both read the phantasmagorics of the passion and read himself reading the passion. The phrase "if I look through tears Christ smiles on me" pivots on a crucial ambiguity, since the phrase "through tears" could modify either the "look" of the sorrowing poet or the smile of the suffering Christ. Ingeniously, Alabaster uses the very phrase "through tears" to effect a miraculous conflation of himself and his savior, the weeper and the watcher – and the reader as well. Looking through tears, the converted speaker sees both his savior and himself; reading the phrase "through tears," we are also enabled to see "otherwise."[54]

Alabaster's tears sonnets also reiterate his understanding of conversion as a spur to writing as well as a consequence of reading. Sonnet 24, "The Sponge," presents the speaker in verbal crisis, unable to articulate his emotional response to the Passion: "How shall I full express such loss, such gain?" Tears, once more, offer a practical solution. Rather than a pair of supernatural reading glasses, here they become part of a surreal transformation of the poet into a human source of stationery:

> My tongue shall be my pen, my eyes shall rain
> Tears for my ink, the place where I was cured
> Shall be my book, where, having all abjured
> And calling heavens to record in that plain
> Thus plainly will I write: no sin like mine.

While the earlier poem imagined tears as the means of interpreting the Passion, here tears are the means (the "ink") by which the poet's religious feeling can be legibly expressed on the "book" of his heart. The second "Morning Meditation" (Sonnet 70) again returns to the dual function of tears in the imaginative presence of Jesus: they can be both "glasses to behold him" (a means of interpretation), and as "words … upon my lips as pictures to unfold him" (a means of expression).

In Alabaster's sonnets, tears are not only mechanisms of transformation, but examples of transformation: miraculously shifting "pictures," described with a constantly changing array of metaphors. We have already seen the comparison of tears to ink, lenses, and prisms. In Sonnet 12, tears are likened to a group of supplicants, sent to Christ to plead for the speaker's soul. Echoing the Magdalene poem, in which her tears "run / To seek Christ out," the speaker in this sonnet implores his tears to "run … and strive you one the other to overtake" en route to the "heavenly throne" of judgment. There, tears will perform a Portia-like role: after the speaker's sins have made their "indictment" according to his "just deserts," tears can make a powerful "suit" for mercy according to "Christ's grace." Sonnet 17 abandons the forensic for the aesthetic, as tears become jewels to "spangle" Christ. Elsewhere, tears are not Christ's adornment, but simply his stored

---

[54] Discussing this poem as part of a larger Plotinian reading of Alabaster's tears-poetry, Gary Kuchar suggests that here, "the fully penitent subject catches a glimpse of quasi-divine perception through the perfecting of phenomenal modes of apprehension." Kuchar, *The Poetry of Religious Sorrow in Early Modern England* (Cambridge University Press, 2008), 112–14. I want, here, to stress the provisionality and ambiguity of this transformative "glimpse," and the dynamic imperfection of tears as a medium.

"treasure." More humbly, tears are likened in a number of poems to a variety of meteorological conditions: "rain" or "showers," "dew," "vapours," "springs." These tears poems, like Crashaw's later poem "The Weeper," energetically unfold the signifying possibilities inherent in a conventional trope; by multiplying the significance of tears, Alabaster makes his penitential poems into instances of dynamic figurative possibility.

Alabaster's sonnets on the incarnation continue this tendency to modify – and to multiply – figurative strategies. Sonnet 53 begins with an epic invocation: "I sing of Christ, O endless argument / Profaner thoughts and ears begone, begone." Having declared his intention to "spread the carpets of invention / Before the eyes of all the firmament" in this sonnet, however, the speaker becomes tentative and vexed in the next. Here, instead of confident "invention," we find paradox: Alabaster writes,

> Two, yet but one, which either other is,
> One, yet in two, which neither other be,
> I see it so, but how I do not see
> Nor could I reach the possibility
> Of being if it were not so in practice;
> For who can fathom God's omnipotence?　　(1–6)

The impossibility of describing "Th'unbounded sea of th'incarnation" leads Alabaster to statements of the *via negativa*: "Gaze no more my mind!" he cries, concluding that "God is best discernèd, not discerned" (14). Nevertheless, the sequence goes on to suggest various ways in which the incarnated Lord *could* be figured: a love-token for mankind (Sonnet 61), an embroidered textual margin (Sonnet 62), "the handle of the world's great ball" (Sonnet 64). As in many of the tears sonnets, Alabaster sometimes presents more than one metaphoric option in a single poem. In Sonnet 63, for instance, the incarnation is likened to a diamond encircled by two rings, which turns out to be also "that fair tablet / Wherein is drawn the angel's alphabet." Sonnet 66 presents the extreme version of this tactic, responding to a question about representation with a variety of answers that are also questions:

> By what glass of resemblance may we see
> How God and man, two natures, meet in one?
> Or is it like unto that union
> Whereby the soul and body do agree?
> Or like as when a graft of foreign tree
> Grows in some other by incision?
> Or like as when about one diamond
> Two rings are fasten'd which one jewel be?

> Or as when one same party is both man
> And is together a musician?
> Or like as iron is unbodied
> With interfused fire into one mould?

After listing metaphoric options in the first twelve lines, Alabaster concludes in the final couplet that "these resemblances are dead." And yet the sonnet, and indeed the sequence as a whole, undermines that conclusion; insisting, over and over again, that metaphors are inadequate to the mystery of his subject matter, Alabaster nevertheless produces a lively survey of figurative options. Christ's incarnation both resists and inspires constant paraphrase, so that in individual sonnets such as this one, as well as in the sequence as a whole, Alabaster makes his own process of poetic likening into an "endless argument," a serial conversion of metaphor.

This willingness to question and revise his own poetic choices within individual sonnets leads to another aspect of Alabaster's transformative poetics: the interrogation and qualification of elements between poems. In the group of sonnets "On the Ensigns of Christ's Crucifying," Alabaster repeats and revises phrases from one poem to the next. In Sonnet 1, for instance, Alabaster describes "the starless night of passion ... When Christ did sound the onset martial, / A sacred hymn," only to ask, in Sonnet 2, "What meaneth this, that Christ an hymn did sing?" After bidding his fellow believers to accompany him "Over the brook of Cedron" in Sonnet 3, Alabaster points out, in Sonnet 5, that "'Tis not enough over the brook to stride" if one's "spirits are not deified." Such linking devices have led Alabaster's editors to remark on the particular unity and coherence of this sequence.[55] Discussing one such device, the *concatenatio*, or the exact repetition of the last line of one sonnet in the first line of the next, Heather Dubrow suggests that Elizabethan poets could use it to "represent the complex relationship between movement and stasis" in a sonnet sequence.[56] The most famous example of such a concatenated sequence, Donne's *La Corona*, uses the device to weave individual sonnets into a seamless "crown of prayer and praise." In Alabaster's hands, by contrast, this variation on the *concatenatio* contributes to a sense of dramatic alteration in the speaker's position. Repeating himself, the speaker also interrogates himself, engaging in a contentious inner dialogue. The technique not only demonstrates

---

[55] Alabaster, *Sonnets*, xl–xli.

[56] H. Dubrow, *Echoes of Desire: English Petrarchism and its Counterdiscourses* (Ithaca, NY: Cornell University Press, 1995), 58. Dubrow notes the use of *concatenatio* in the Elizabethan sequences of William Percy, William Smith, Samuel Daniel, and George Gascoigne.

Alabaster's facility as a sonneteer, but also reaffirms his devotional temperament. It suggests his tendency to find static moments of self-figuration, like
static declarations of faith, intolerable.

Alabaster's eagerness to alter the significance of a single metaphor, or to
change metaphors within a poem or sequence, is complicated still further by
his frequent use of figures that depict instability and alteration in a basic and
literal sense. The incarnation, unsurprisingly, requires images of physical
change: a grafted tree "grows" after its incision, molten metal is "unbodied"
in the fire before being reshaped – vehicle and tenor are, here, ideally matched.
Returning to the penitential sonnets, we find equal transformative potential
in the vehicles themselves. When Alabaster likens his tears to jewels, for
instance, he refers specifically to jewels formed by processes that transmute
the worthless into the precious. They are pearls – precious stones formed by
an animal's endurance of pain – which are themselves compared to "drops
of amber" – precious stones formed by the solidification of plant matter over
the "scorned fly." In other poems, likening tears to weather allows Alabaster
further to imagine processes of liquefaction, vaporization, or solidification,
for instance in Sonnet 15:

> My soul a world is by contraction,
> The heavens therein is my internal sense,
> Moved by my will as an intelligence,
> My heart the element, my love the sun.
> And as the sun about the earth doth run,
> And with his beams doth draw thin vapours thence,
> Which after in the air do condense,
> And pour down rain upon the earth anon,
> So moves my love about the heavenly sphere,
> And draweth thence with an attractive fire
> The purest argument wit can desire,
> Whereby devotion after may arise.
> And these conceits, digest by thoughts' retire
> Are turned into april showers of tears.

Following Martz, Alabaster's editors praise the central conceit of this sonnet
as a splendid instance of meditative poetics.[57] But the poem is striking not
simply for its meditative intensity, but for its metaphoric dynamism. After
the opening quatrain, the operative metaphor is not simply a "world," but
an ecosystem filled with natural transformations; poetry ("wit") and tears
can be "turned into" each other as easily and inevitably as dew becomes rain.

[57] Alabaster, *Sonnets*, xxviii.

If Alabaster is preoccupied with the poetic vehicle, then, these images of mutability indicate that what interests him most is that vehicle in motion. Indeed, Alabaster's sonnets abound with images of physical movement. We have already seen, in a number of poems, how the speaker invites his tears to "run." In other poems, the speaker himself refuses to stand still. Sonnets 40 and 41 repeat the same crucial question: "Lo, here I am, Lord, whither will thou send me?" The question presupposes that the speaker must be sent somewhere; for Alabaster, sanctification requires movement in unforeseen, perhaps impossible directions. In Sonnet 22, he uses meditative techniques to try to imagine these marching orders: "Sink down, my soul, into the lowest cell," he commands, in remembrance of the Passion. Four lines later, memory of the resurrection changes his instructions: "Rise up my soul, as high as God doth dwell." The rhyme, here, underscores the paradoxical state of being both up and down, a paradox that the rest of the poem tightens into an analysis of the incarnation itself.

> Descend in patience with him to die
> Ascend in confidence with him to reign,
> And upwards, downwards by humility.
> Since man fell upwards, down by Satan's train,
> Look for no fairer way unto thy crown,
> Than that that Christ went up, by going down.   (9–14)

Christ, Alabaster implies, transcends directionality, moving in two directions – "upwards, downwards" – at once. Mortal men, by contrast, while they must try to escape the "dull languor" of religious apathy, will then be subject to the wild, confusing movements originating in "thoughts' unrest" (Sonnet 73, lines 4, 6). Exemplar of such bittersweet "unrest," Alabaster ends a number of his sonnets with dizzy cries of disorientation, as in the closing couplet of Sonnet 3: "Now we are up, now down, but cannot stand / We sink, we reel, Jesu stretch forth thy hand." In a poem entitled "Ego Sum Vitis," Alabaster's Ignatian imagining of himself as the vine "whose arms with wandering spire / Do climb upon the Cross" ends with a question: "*O where was I that was not where I am?*" (Sonnet 33, lines 4–5, 14). Such questions reflect the same spiritual displacement described in Alabaster's other writings on conversion, and in another sonnet, directed to another convert: "Where are we, Austin? Are the heavens come nigher, / Or is my earthly soul aspired higher?" (Sonnet 35, lines 13–14). Addressing his model in confessional change, Alabaster suggests that he and Augustine are, equally and literally, ecstatic – converts who stand for ever outside and beyond themselves, inviting their readers to follow.

"COUNTERCHANGE" AND CONVERSION

I have attempted to show how Alabaster's sonnets extend key aspects of his understanding of conversion, both formally and conceptually. Alabaster sees conversion as a profound, and even distressing transformation of the inner and the outer man; it unsettles the spirit, and revises the outward signifiers of social and confessional identity. His sonnets demonstrate a comparable mutability of tenor and vehicle; the poems describe subjects in flux, through a shifting set of metaphors. Such poetic dynamism reaches its apotheosis, fittingly, in the sonnets explicitly describing Alabaster's own turn to Catholicism. Here, the dramatic scenarios of the poems on the saints are blended with the dynamic figurations of the poems on tears and the incarnation, effectively registering the linked experiences of inward and outward change. Sonnet 46, for instance, entitled "Of his Conversion" in most manuscripts, begins with a statement of confidence which, typically, is interrupted by a dramatic self-qualification, followed by a turn to figurative motion. "Away, fear, with thy projects, no false fire / Which thou dost make can ought my courage quail," Alabaster begins (1–2). This stern self-admonition, however, almost immediately yields a surprise turn: instead of the expected association of fear with flight, Alabaster proclaims that he will resist the fear that would have him "strike [his] sail" (4). In the mind of the convert, we realize, to keep faith is to keep moving. The reader, moreover, must keep moving with the syntax, which characteristically offers more abrupt transitions: after providing a catalogue of the indignities which he would gladly suffer in order to continue on his voyage, Alabaster moves, in the sestet, to explain how he is able to be so brave. This is not, however, a counter-catalogue of Catholic blisses, but rather a series of "the fears which make [him] quake" at the thought of a return to heresy:

> The smouldering brimstone and the burning lake,
> Life feeding death, death ever life devouring,
> Torments not movèd, unheard, yet still roaring,
> God lost, hell found ...

Having banished fear from the beginning of his poem, his final argumentative recourse is once again to fear. This is hardly "the accent of the convert to Catholicism" described by Herbert Grierson, "the joy of the troubled soul who has found rest and a full expansion of heart in the rediscovery of a faith and ritual and order which give entire satisfaction to the imagination and affections ... [who] is set free from the painful diagnosis of his own emotions and spiritual conditions."[58] The converted Alabaster, as we have seen, uses quite a different "accent," one which suggests that "expansion of heart" offers little "rest." He is, in this poem, literally at sea; unable to "strike his sail" although his destination is far from achieved.

Alabaster begins Sonnet 48 with another image of ambivalent ecstasy: "Lord, I have left all and myself behind." By converting, Alabaster suggests, he has embarked on a hazardous journey to an unknown destination. This journey requires that he take leave of family and fortune, and even of himself. The ensuing catalogue of loss underscores how intertwined such outer and inner renunciations could be:

> My state, my hopes, my strengths, and present ease,
> My unprovoked studies sweet disease,
> And touch of nature and engrafted kind
> Whose cleaving twist doth distant tempers bind,
> And gentle sense of kindness that doth praise
> The earnest judgements, other wills to please:

This list seems to describe the socially dire consequences of Alabaster's Catholic turn, described in his narrative as "the overthrowe of my whole course of lyf hitherto ledd and designed: the leesing of my lyving, freends, honors, and other worldly comodities" (119).[59] In the sestet, however, Alabaster manages to imagine an unusual kind of compensation for such losses. Rather than envisioning a secure arrival in a safe harbor, or a Griersonian moment of relieved "rest," Alabaster instead comforts himself with an image of endless and painful transformation, imploring God to create in him a productive wound:

> O strike my heart with lightning from above,
> That from one wound both fire and blood may spring,
> Fire to transelement my soul to love,
> And blood as oil to keep the fire burning,
> That fire may draw forth blood, blood extend fire,
> Desire possession, possession desire.

As in the poem on the microcosmic soul, Alabaster imagines that conversion will create not a resting place for a restless spirit, but rather an engine of perpetual change, underscored by the last line's chiasmus. In *The Art of English Poesy* (1589) Puttenham terms this figure the "Counterchange," and

---

[58] H. Grierson, *Metaphysical Lyrics and Poems of the Seventeenth Century, Donne to Butler* (Oxford University Press, 1959), xlvi–xlvii.

[59] He makes particular mention of having "to breake of the mariage which I had so earnestly treated," and the consequent "discontentment ... both of [his fiancée's] frendes and my owne parents" (121).

associates it with the more general category of divided lines which "the Greeks call … *antistrophe*, the Latins *conversio*," but which he terms "the Counterturn, because he turns counter in the midst of every meter."[60] By ending his poem with such a bold "Counterchange," Alabaster wittily harnesses an aspect of poetic form to the central insight of the last line, and of the poem as a whole: that conversion does not provide stasis, but instead inaugurates an endless alternation.

In the sonnet "Captivity Great Liberty to the Servants of God," Alabaster reiterates this notion of conversion as perpetual motion rather than achieved certainty. This sonnet has only thirteen lines, leading its editors to describe its "defective octave" as "beyond … patching."[61] If the sonnet's length is unconventional, however, its seven-line "octave" and regular sestet are nevertheless coherent in terms of grammar and rhyme scheme. I quote the poem in full:

> Unbalanced irresolution
> Long time did hold my mind with even suspense,
> When first how best to show my conscience
> Burning with flame of true religion
> As he who in the rain of July's sun
> Oft dips his foot and oft withdraws it thence
> Till that the brunt of cold be overgone.
> So now my stay by this restraint is chanced,
> To live in open as in dream I dare,
> And hoot at that whereat before I glanced
> And speak my thoughts as big as they now are.
> Free men are bound: I never knew ere this,
> That so great liberty in prison is.

The circumstances of the sonnet's composition may have been those of actual imprisonment. Alabaster, having proclaimed his Catholicism, was jailed in order to be cross-examined by a series of English Protestant divines before departing for Rome.[62] Read autobiographically, the sonnet is Alabaster's statement of willingness to endure those punishments meted out to recusants under Elizabeth. The new Catholic declares that "free men" – those not imprisoned for recusancy – are nevertheless "bound," trapped in heresy. Story and Gardner thus gloss line 9 as "My firmness [in Catholicism] has come about through this imprisonment."[63]

---

[60] Puttenham, *The Art of English Poesy*, 283, 293.   [61] Alabaster, *Sonnets*, 58.
[62] *Ibid.*, 58; cf. Alabaster, *Unpublished Works*, 131–57.   [63] Alabaster, *Sonnets*, 58.

Yet Alabaster, again, explicitly refuses to propose the replacement of sinful flight by faithful "firmness." Instead, the sonnet suggests that true devotion requires movement and change. He regrets the "unbalanced irresolution" of his pre-conversion life not because it resulted in excessive wandering, but because it "did hold my mind in even suspense" – not in errancy, but in spiritual stasis. This "unbalanced irresolution" was, paradoxically, all too balanced, suggested by the precarious balance of the two words in the first pentameter line. In his autobiography, Alabaster recalls an early flirtation with "that opinion which be-gynneth now to be very generall amonge the learneder sorte of protestants to witt that a man may be saved by both religions, or by a mixture of them both" (112). In this sonnet, he likens this conciliatory attitude to the hesitant posture of a swimmer on an icy Atlantic beach, afraid to launch himself on the waves (the constricted seven-line "octave" might be a deliberate echo of this idea of sinful caution). True devotion is the antithesis of such cold circumspection, and it is the convert, more than the irenic liberal on the one hand or the closed-minded dogmatist on the other, who best exemplifies such devotion. Even though his Catholic conversion may have immediately produced literal, physical "restraint," then, Alabaster claims that it has also permitted him to live and to write "as open as in dream I dare." Conversion involves a two-fold courage: to be changed, and to announce that change to others. But the phrase "to speak my thoughts as big as they now are" also implies the simultaneous awareness of conviction and contingency; it indicates a desire to utter thoughts that are "big," and at the same time to acknowledge that they exist in a necessarily ephemeral "now." For Alabaster, this kind of "speaking" is the language of the convert, and it is also the language of the poet. His holy sonnets may have been written in the fervor of his first conversion, but in their turns and tropes he demonstrates a deep and paradoxical commitment to change, proclaiming both the fervor of those beliefs that "now are," and the exhilaration of their passing away.

CHAPTER 2

John Donne and the
language of de-nomination

Two young poets joined the Earl of Essex on his expedition to Cadiz in 1596. Shortly before this voyage, or shortly after it, both poets converted, but in opposite directions: one became a Catholic, the other a Protestant.[1] This is not the only difference between William Alabaster and John Donne. If Alabaster's sonnets celebrate the vertiginous rapture of spiritual motion, much of Donne's poetry registers his own changeability with regret or even disgust. In a verse letter to the Countess of Bedford ("On New-Yeare's Day"), Donne describes himself as "meteor-like, of stuffe and forme per-plext, / Whose *what* and *where* in disputation is" (2–3). Such mutability creates a crisis of self-representation, a predicament acknowledged in the poem's next line: "If I should call mee *any thing*, should misse" (4). This idea of inevitable mis-designation recurs throughout Donne's religious writings, in which the identities of the true believer and the true church – especially in a time of ongoing "disputation" – become equally hard to pinpoint. The Holy Sonnets, in particular, seem to reflect the superimposition of two kinds of perplexity, the personal and the ecclesiastical. In Sonnet 19, for instance, Donne's speaker acknowledges a "constant" tendency to "change in vowes and in devotion," even when he "would not" (3–4). Elsewhere, he implies that this confusion is produced, or at least enabled, by the prolifer-ation of devotional possibilities. Asking his "dear Christ" to "show me ... thy spouse, so bright and clear!" in the first line of Sonnet 18, he seems desperate not so much to receive an answer as to believe his own adjectives.

The obvious vexation of this speaking subject has produced centuries of equally vexed critical attempts to clarify, resolve, and understand Donne's religious "*what* and *where*." According to some, Donne's prayers for spiritual

---

[1] I discuss Alabaster's conversion from Protestantism in Chapter 1 above. For a relatively even-handed presentation of the facts known about Donne's early life and Catholic upbringing, see R. C. Bald, *John Donne: A Life* (Oxford University Press, 1970), Chapters 2 and 3. For Donne's participation in the Cadiz expedition, see Bald, *John Donne*, Chapter 5.

and devotional certainty were answered; poems like the Holy Sonnets thus become the poetic birthpangs of a particular kind of conversion, evidence of Donne's status as, in Izaak Walton's phrase, "a second St. Austine [Augustine]."[2] Walton's Augustinian allusion implies a move from self-division and sin to devotional security. In Donne's case, the "Jack" who praises sexual promiscuity as "the nursery / of musicke, joy, life, and eternity" ("Elegy III," 36) becomes "the Doctor" who travels a proto-liberal Protestant *via media*, arriving safely in the deanery of the church named after his fellow convert, St. Paul.[3] Donne's conversion, according to this reading, is an escape not only from the maelstrom of inner spiritual conflict, but also from the maelstrom of outer confessional "disputation." Donne's imaginative efforts may be anguished, but they are, finally, "efforts at unity" that achieved a qualified success, leading him away from both libertine looseness and Catholic rigor and toward a broadly Reformed church "open to most men" and most ideas.[4]

Those critics who object to this teleology generally claim that Donne's conversion – either from sinner to saved, or from Catholic to Protestant – was either insincere or incomplete.[5] Louis Martz identifies in Donne's poetry, particularly the Holy Sonnets and *Anniversaries*, the enduring influence of Jesuit meditative techniques.[6] Dennis Flynn reminds us of the strong connections Donne maintained with his recusant Heywood relatives, even in the years after his Protestant ordination.[7] Most notoriously,

---

[2] Izaak Walton, *The Lives of John Donne, Sir Henry Wotton, Richard Hooker, George Herbert and Robert Sanderson (1640)*, ed. G. Sainsbury (Oxford University Press, 1947), 37.

[3] Walton compares Donne's libertinism to Saul's pharisaical zeal, *ibid.*, 43. Nicholas Tyacke includes the converted Donne among proto-Laudian "Arminians" in *Anti-Calvinists: The Rise of English Arminianism c.1590–1640* (Oxford: Clarendon, 1987), 182, 261. This view has been challenged by, among others, Jeanne Shami, who sees Donne as a more stringent Calvinist. Shami, "Anti-Catholicism in the Sermons of John Donne," in L. A. Ferrell and P. McCullough (eds.), *The English Sermon Revised* (Manchester University Press, 2000), 136–66.

[4] The phrase "efforts at unity" comes from R.-J. Frontain, "'Make all this All': The Religious Operations of John Donne's Imagination," in R.-J. Frontain and F. Malpezzi (eds.), *John Donne's Religious Imagination: Essays in Honor of John T. Shawcross* (Conway: University of Central Arkansas Press, 1995), 8, 20. Frontain characterizes all the essays in the collection as efforts to show Donne's poetry resisting the "threat of dissolution" in various ways.

[5] These critical speculations have been ably surveyed by Gregory Kneidel, who notes the subtleties of religious affiliation at the time of Donne's conversion to Protestantism. "John Donne's *Via Pauli*," *Journal of English and Germanic Philology* (2001), 224–46. Kneidel goes on to suggest that Donne's sermons on the Feast of the Conversion of Saint Paul celebrate the flexible nature of Pauline rhetoric, and so the religious "prudence" essential to Donne's own conversion.

[6] Martz, *The Poetry of Meditation, passim*. See also the foreword to Donne, *The Divine Poems*, ed. Helen Gardner, 2nd edn. (Oxford: Clarendon, 1978).

[7] D. Flynn, "Donne's Catholicism," *RH* 13 (1975), 1–17, and *John Donne and the Ancient Catholic Nobility* (Bloomington: Indiana University Press, 1995).

John Carey speculates that Donne turned to Protestantism as much from "ambition" as from any genuine religious conviction – and that residual Catholic sympathies, and guilt over this pragmatic "apostasy," create a constant psychic strain in his life and writing.[8] In stark contrast to the readings of Donne as an inclusive Protestant "unifier," Carey's psycho-biographical reading makes him out to be the exemplar of a divided, proto-modern consciousness.[9] On this reading, the religious poems, and especially the Holy Sonnets, do not reflect the anguish of the pre-converted soul destined to be calmed by God's grace, but rather a subject locked in an ongoing and aesthetically productive struggle against itself.[10]

In this chapter, I will resist reading Donne's devotional poetry as clear statements of a broad, bland middle way. I will also resist the temptation either to unmask Donne as a crypto-Catholic or crypto-Calvinist, or, con-versely, to congratulate him for those poetic moments where he seems "undone," unable or unwilling to resolve his own spiritual difficulties.[11] Instead, I will begin by taking Donne at his word: that he was born into the Roman Catholicism of his family, and that he converted to the Protestantism of his nation. This conversion seems to have been sincere, and it was certainly final; mere months before his death, Donne's will reiterated his "constant and cheerfull resolution … to live and dye in the Religion nowe professed in the Churche of England."[12] But this resolution

---

[8] J. Carey, *John Donne: Life, Mind and Art* (New York: Oxford University Press, 1981).

[9] Far less charitable about these divisions is Stanley Fish, who can barely contain his disgust at Donne's "sick," and specifically "bulimic," attitude toward most of his poetic subjects. Fish, "Masculine Persuasive Force: Donne and Verbal Power," in E. Harvey and K. E. Maus (eds.), *Soliciting Interpretation: Literary Theory and Renaissance Poetry* (University of Chicago Press, 1990), 223–52. For an explanation of this self-division in terms of Calvinist theology, see J. Stachniewski, "John Donne and the Despair of the Holy Sonnets," *ELH* 48 (1981), 677–705.

[10] The various versions of this reading are summarized and helpfully complicated in R. Strier, "John Donne, Awry and Squint: The 'Holy Sonnets' 1608–1610," *Modern Philology* 86 (1989), 357–84. Strier argues, subtly and persuasively, that the sonnets show the "pain and confusion … of a person who would like to be a convinced Calvinist but who is both unable to be so and unable to admit that he is unable to be so" (361). While this chapter focuses neither on Donne's holy sonnets nor on Calvinism, it does in a broad sense share Strier's interest in the "actual, peculiar shapes" of Donne's devotional poems, particularly when they present aspects of confessional identity (384).

[11] This latter critical tactic has a long history; see, for instance, Helen White's admiring claim that "Donne had at the heart of his being a whirlwind of incompatibilities that would have made living with himself difficult at any time," and that he was thus "quite unlike anybody else." White, "John Donne and the Psychology of Spiritual Effort," in R. F. Jones (ed.), *The Seventeenth Century* (Stanford University Press, 1951), 355–6. A similar point is made, in dramatically different language, by the "symptomatic" post-structuralist reading of T. Docherty, *John Donne, Undone* (London: Methuen, 1986). Docherty, in fact, includes us in his diagnosis: "writers in this epoch were obscure to themselves: neither affirming nor denying substantive propositions directly, they simply could not know the full extent and implication of what they were writing, and nor can we" (7).

[12] The will is printed by Bald, *John Donne*, 563.

did not preclude an ongoing interest in confessional change as a subject of speculation, an object of representation and, as I will argue, a model for expression. We see this interest in his library, which was full of polemical texts about conversion.[13] We see it in his letters, in comments like "A Gent. that visited me yesterday told me that our Church hath lost Mr. *Hugh Broughton*, who is gone to the Roman side," or "*We hear (but without second as yet) that Sir* Rich[ard] *Philips brother* in France *hath taken the habit of a Capuchin.*"[14] And, I will argue, we see it most clearly in his religious poetry. Donne's ongoing sensitivity to conversions taking place around him need not, and I think should not, be mistaken as a sign of instability in his own devotional loyalties. Instead, I want to suggest that Donne remains imaginatively compelled by movement between Christian churches because, in considering and describing this movement, he finds an ideal way to combine devotional certainty with spiritual inscrutability, conviction with concealment.

I have suggested that the dynamism of Alabaster's sonnets calls the reader's attention to the process of change itself as the central characteristic of devotion. Donne, by contrast, continually asserts the necessary conclusions of this process, the particular and single results of change. Yet Donne also refuses to describe those conclusions in clear or specific terms, ingeniously using the very forms and formulae of contemporary polemical discourse to demonstrate the ineffability of its alleged subject. Rather than inventing a completely original account of conversion, in other words, Donne deliberately borrows from other contemporary treatments of the subject of religious change. Read alongside these texts, Donne's religious writing becomes more intelligible, but at the same time it becomes more resistant to single, conclusive interpretation. By using the commonplaces of other writings on conversion, Donne highlights their intended polemical consequences, stressing the ecclesiastical embodiment of grace, and the need to "fix" religious truth within a particular church through an act of deliberate adherence. To use one of his favorite words, Donne emphasizes the need to "choose."[15] But by emphasizing precisely those moments at which Catholic and Protestant polemics on religious choice share terms, or

---

[13] Izaak Walton announces that Donne left at his death "the resultance of 1400 Authors, most of them abridged and analysed with his own hand"; Geoffrey Keynes provides a list of those titles proven to be in Donne's library in *A Bibliography of Dr. John Donne* (Oxford: Clarendon, 1973), 263–79.

[14] Letter, Donne to Henry Goodyer (1609), in C. E. Merrill (ed.), *Letters to Severall Persons of Honour* (New York: Sturgis and Walton, 1910), 30; Letter, Donne to Goodyer (1615), in *ibid.*, 191.

[15] Forms of this word appear twenty-six times in Donne's poems, half of them in poems on religious subjects. C. Florén, ed., *John Donne: A Complete Concordance of the Poems* (New York: Olms-Weidman, 2004), 177–8.

are reduced to a shared silence, Donne also moves the consequences of choice beyond the reach of argument or debate. In their evocations of conversion, his religious poems thus manage to hide in plain sight; they remind us both of the need for all believers to declare themselves on earth, and of the essential mystery within any such self-declaration.[16]

PSEUDO-MARTYR AND DONNE'S MIXED MOTIVES

Any account of Donne's conversion must begin with his own failure to provide such an account himself. Unlike a great many of his contemporaries who abandoned their original churches, Donne would never compose an extended or explicit account of his own confessional change. Seeking a direct description of his conversion, we must make do with the few autobiographical passages in his prose, none perhaps more provocative than the remarks at the beginning of *Pseudo-Martyr* (1610). This work of polemic, written during Donne's association with the Protestant controversialist Thomas Morton, argues "that those which are of the Romane Religion ... may and ought to take the Oath of Allegeance" proposed by James I, and, moreover, that those who suffer for refusing it should be considered suicidal, not heroic.[17] As Camille Wells Slights has demonstrated, Donne's text is entangled with contemporary casuistical debates about the proper relationship between royal prerogative, papal authority, and private conscience.[18] In simplest terms, however, *Pseudo-Martyr* is an energetic denunciation of silence, particularly silence in matters of confessional allegiance. This work of controversial prose is in this sense a double defense of publicity in matters of religion: a "publicke act" of controversy that defends the necessity of "publicke acts" of religious self-declaration.

[16] Here, I both follow and depart from J. Herz's argument in "'An Excellent Exercise of Wit that Speaks so Well of Ill': Donne and the Poetics of Concealment," in C. Summers and T.-L. Pebworth (eds.), *The Eagle and the Dove: Reassessing John Donne* (Columbia: University of Missouri Press, 1986), 3–14. Herz suggests that throughout the poetry "what sounds like confession is in fact concealment" (3), suggesting the radical dislocation of both poetic *persona* and reader. In the following pages, I will argue that while Donne does indeed aim at concealment in his devotional poetry, this strategy exists in tandem with devotional certainty, rather than in tension with it. My reading comes much closer to Jeanne Shami's account of Donne's verbal "discretion," but unlike Shami I see this as a feature of the poetry even more than the prose. "Donne on Discretion," *ELH* 47 (1980), 48–66; see also Shami, *John Donne and Conformity in Crisis*, 20–2.

[17] Donne, *Pseudo-Martyr*, ed. A. Raspa (Buffalo: McGill-Queen's University Press, 1993). Further citations will be noted parenthetically in the text by page number.

[18] C. W. Slights, *The Casuistical Tradition in Shakespeare, Donne, Milton and Herbert* (Princeton University Press, 1981), 144–9.

Such a defense would seem to require of its author an equally "publicke" declaration of his own orthodoxy. But what Donne offers in *Pseudo-Martyr*, first in a prefatory "Advertisement to the Reader," and then in an address to "priests and Jesuits, and their disciples in this Kingdome," is not an explicit statement of his Protestant beliefs, but rather an admission of their relative novelty, and a declaration of his status as a Protestant convert. On the first page of the book, Donne announces that he is "derived from such a stock and race as, I beleeve, no family ... hath endured and suffred more in their persons and fortunes, for obeying the Teachers of Romane Doctrine, than it hath done." He declares, in other words, that he was born and raised a Catholic, and is therefore no mere "impious and profane under-valewer of Martyrdome" (8). Donne proceeds to describe his embrace of Reformed religion as the result of rigorous intellectual reconsideration:

I ... used no inordinate hast, nor precipitation in binding my conscience to any locall Religion. I had a longer worke to doe then many other men, for I was first to blot out, certaine impressions of the Romane religion, and to wrastle both against the examples, and against the reasons, by which some hold was taken, and some anticipations early layde upon my conscience, both by Persons who by nature had a power and superiority over my will, and others who by their learning and good life seemed to me justly to claime an interest for the guiding and rectifying of mine understanding in these matters. (13)

Donne declares that he postponed all doctrinal adherence, in fact, "till I had, to the measure of my poore wit and judgement, surveyed and digested the whole body of Divinity, controverted beween ours and the Romane Church." This was, he confesses, an extended process, making him subject to "many mis-interpretations ... misconceivings and imputations" by those "who think presently that he hath no Religion which dares not call his Religion by some newer name then Christian" (13–14). Donne counters that this process of bringing his religious attitudes to an "equall and indifferent" position was in fact necessary to settle his "understanding and judgement."

In contrast to the abrupt Augustinian epiphany offered in Alabaster's conversion narrative ("nowe I am a Catholique"), Donne's account of prolonged "wrestling" does not pivot on a moment of instantaneous trans-formation. This deliberately undramatic account of gradual intellectual realignment seems, in fact, to be anything but a story of cataclysmic conversion. An overlooked subcategory of polemical writing on conversion, however, provides a historical and generic context for Donne's self-description: first-person accounts of motive, in which early modern

Christian converts attempted to explain and justify their turns.[19] These texts, written by both Catholics and Protestants, describe similar experiences of religious doubt, search, and, finally, confident adherence to a new creed. For instance, in his *First Motive* (1609), the Catholic convert Theophilus Higgons offers an account of "such peculiar things, as prevayled with me in the beginning, and rowsing me out of my lethargy in schisme, and heresy, provoked me unto a diligent investigation of the truth."[20] In his account of this investigation, Higgons describes not only how he found the Catholic doctrines of Purgatory and prayers for the dead convincing, but also details his increasing disillusionment with the "egregious falsehood" of various Protestant controversialists, including Thomas Morton.[21] Offering a methodical account of his gradual acceptance of reasons for belief, he asks his reader to use the same technique that he himself used for settling his doubts: "peruse diligently, compare exactly, and give thy verdict uprightly, in the presence of the all-seeing Eye."[22] Higgons, in other words, describes his own process of seeking in order to provide a model of action, as well as a source of information, for wavering readers.

Donne owned a copy of Edward Hoby's refutation of Higgons's *First Motive*, as well as another such refutation, Roger Fenton's *Answer to William Alablaster [sic] His Motives* (1599).[23] We do not know for certain that Donne met Alabaster in Cadiz or in London, but he certainly would have been aware of Alabaster's highly publicized conversion to Catholicism, and we can assume that he was familiar with the text of Alabaster's *Motives*, which is reprinted in its entirety by Fenton.[24] Alabaster begins with a description of preliminary doubt: "the understanding unquiet by nature, passeth through all formes of opinions, untill he resolve his assent upon some principle that standeth only upon his owne ground."[25] His own conversion consisted in moving through these "formes," which he describes

[19] This genre has not received sufficient attention from scholars of early modern spiritual autobiography, perhaps because it foregrounds matters of doctrine rather than detailing the development of the "inner man." See D. Ebner, *Autobiography in Seventeenth-Century England: Theology and the Self* (Paris: Mouton, 1971).

[20] Theophilus Higgons, *The First Motive of T. H. … to suspect the integrity of his Religion, With an Appendix intituled, Try Before You Trust* (Douai, 1609), sig. 2v–3.

[21] Higgons mentions Morton by name in the full title of his text. Later the same year, Morton published *A Direct Answer unto the Scandalous Exceptions, which Theophilus Higgons hath lately obiected.* Donne owned a copy of this book, and would have been aware of the progress of this exchange as he prepared the text of *Pseudo-Martyr*. Bald, *John Donne*, 206–8; Keynes, *Bibliography*, 273.

[22] Higgons, *First Motive*, sig. 3r.   [23] Keynes, *Bibliography*, 268, 271.

[24] In 1614, Donne would mention Alabaster, newly reconverted to Protestantism, in a letter to Henry Goodyer: "Mr. Alabaster hath got of the King the Dean's best Living worth above l.300, which the Dean had good hope to have held a while," *Letters*, 146.

[25] Fenton, *Answer to William Alablaster [sic] his Motives* (1599), 1. See Chapter 1.

in detail, until he found that Catholicism could best "stay the assent of the scholar."[26] Alabaster here uses terms echoed by a slightly later Catholic convert, and friend of Donne, Sir Toby Matthew. Arrested for recusancy in 1607, Matthew received visitors in prison, Donne among them.[27] On that occasion, Matthew might have described his conversion in the language of a later autobiographical letter sent to Dame Mary Gage, O. S. B., sister of another Catholic convert, George Gage.[28] In this text, Matthew explains that during a trip to Italy he encountered the Jesuit Robert Persons, who "prayed me only that I would make the search of true religion my greatest business."[29] After a period of indecision, Matthew agreed:

I began to consider what I was, how I lived, what I believed … These considerations cast me often into so great perplexity, and anxiety of mind, as drew me, in short time, to be half asking that question – *Domine, quid me vis facere?* I knew that religion was the foundation of all Christian life; that without true faith it was impossible to please God. I considered that the world was so extremely divided in the judgment which it made of true and false religions in this age, every man pretending for his own, and censuring, excommunicating, and even damning such as differ from it. I knew that falsehood might be infinite, but that truth could be but One.[30]

Despite his fear of incurring the wrath of the English Protestant authorities and destroying his relationships with family and friends, Matthew, like Alabaster, adopts an initial attitude of open-mindedness toward religious affiliation. This disinterested investigation ends, however, at a point of certainty. Eventually identifying the "One" as the Catholic Church, Matthew dismisses his Protestant interlocutors as "mere libertines" who "thought me too saucy, for presuming to show them the right way."[31]

Donne's self-descriptive claims in *Pseudo-Martyr* mirror closely the motives of yet another prominent Jacobean Catholic convert, Benjamin Carier, who would publish his letter to James I explaining his reasons for refusing to take the Oath of Allegiance several years after Donne's defense of

---

[26] Fenton, *Answer,* 5.
[27] See R. Sorlien, "Apostasy Reversed: John Donne and Sir Toby Matthew," *John Donne Journal* 13 (1994), 105. See also J. P. Feil, "Sir Tobie Matthew and his Collection of Letters" (unpublished Ph.D. thesis, University of Chicago, 1962), 54. Feil offers the fullest biographical account of Matthew, and describes this period of imprisonment, 44–57.
[28] This work was likely circulated in manuscript during Matthew's lifetime, but was not printed until the twentieth century. See Toby Matthew, *A True Historical Relation of the Conversion of Sir Tobie Matthew to the Holy Catholic Faith,* ed. A. H. Mathew (London: Burns and Oates, 1904).
[29] *Ibid.,* 33–4.   [30] *Ibid.,* 36.
[31] *Ibid.,* 86. Matthew singles out Sandys, whose "resolution to reduce all religion to human reason, made me apt to fear him a little and to like him less" (87).

it.[32] Just as Donne begins his preface with an account of his recusant family, Carier begins with a description of his Puritanical father: "a learned and devoute man, who althoughe he were a Protestant and a preacher yet he did so season me with the principles of pietie and devotion, as I could not chuse but ever since be very zealous in matters of religion."[33] So zealous was Carier, in fact, that he felt compelled in his early adulthood "to enforme myselfe" about the question of the day: "whether the religion of England were in deed the verie same, which being prefigured and prophesied in the ould testament ... or whether it were a new one for privatt purposes of statesmen invented, and by humane laws established."[34] Just as Donne claims to have meticulously separated himself from childhood indoctrination in order better to see the true contours of religious debate, so Carier claims to have spent his college years

[trying] to looke as far into the matter as possibly I could, that I might find out the truth. And having the oportunitie of a verie good Librarie in that Colledge, I resolved with myself to studie hard ... and betooke my self wholie to the reading of the church history and the ancient fathers which had no interest in either side.[35]

Only after such a process of "disinterested" study was Carier persuaded to the truth of Catholicism, quite against his initial expections.

Contemporary Protestant converts, of course, composed similar texts of autobiographical motive.[36] John Harding recounts his rejection of Catholicism after painstakingly heeding "that worthy precept of St. John, when he saith, Trust not Every Spirit, but try the Spirits, whether they bee of God or no."[37] Accounts of such "trials" abound: "Godefridus Coruinus," for instance, "being diligent in reading the Scriptures the longer he read, the more he found, that Poperie might in no sort be made like thereunto, but that the Papists erronious doctrine for the most part was grounded upon no scripture at all."[38] Jean Le Vager, a Frenchman and "sometimes a Priest in

---

[32] Benjamin Carier, Letter to James I (1613), BL Additional MS 72415, fos. 52–71. This was printed as *A Treatise written by Mr. Doctor Carier* (Brussels, 1614), and reprinted as *A Missive to His Majesty of Great Britain King James* (Paris, 1649). For a discussion of Carier's career, see Questier, "Crypto-Catholicism, Anti-Calvinism and Conversion," 45–64.

[33] BL Additional MS 72415, fo. 52v. Cf. Toby Matthew's account of his father, the Archbishop of York in *Historical Relation*, 5.

[34] BL Additional MS 72415, fo. 52v.   [35] BL Additional MS 72415, fo. 53r.

[36] For a survey of the polemical importance of converts to Protestantism, see Michael Questier, "John Gee, Archbishop Abbot, and the Use of Converts from Rome in Jacobean Anti-Catholicism," *RH* 24 (1993), 347–60.

[37] John Harding, *A Recantation Sermon ... by J. H., late Priest and Dominican Fryer* (1620), 3.

[38] *The Confession and Publike Recantation of thirteene learned personages, lately converted in France, Germanie and the Lowe-Countreys, from Poperie to the Churches Reformed: wherein they have zealously*

the Church of Rome," asserts that "it behooveth us to travaile and study, in the search of this Church, to ioyne and incorporate our selves into the same." Le Vager describes how, afflicted with the "perplexitie, in the conflict of opinions, which we daily see about the matter of Religion," he withdrew to consult the scriptures until he was able to determine that Catholic teachings were but "fantasies" – or, in the more piquant words of another French convert, "the Onions, leekes, and garlike of Aegypt."[39] Like his many contemporaries who converted in the opposite direction, Le Vager provides a list of the "certainties" found in his new faith and the "errors" of his old. So, too, does Richard Sheldon, who converted to Protestantism in 1612. Sheldon explains how his initial state of being "unsatisfied in my understanding" led to much reading and conferring with "doctors and learned men," and finally to a conclusion that the teachings of Catholicism were "full of lies, contradictions, impertinencies."[40] Sheldon is so convinced of the infallibility of his new faith that he dares Catholic priests to "read over distinctly my Motives," and try to find places "wherein I have abused, or misapplied, either holy scripture or Fathers, or wherein I might have calumniated their doctrine or persons."[41] Like the Catholic Higgons, the Protestant Sheldon offers his text of motive not only as a testimony to his own conviction, but also as a means of converting the reader to it.

As this survey indicates, texts of motives for conversion had a number of recognizable generic characteristics; the occasional forgery of motives by controversialists on both sides (justified, in the words of one forger, by "Poeticall freedome") attests to their widespread familiarity.[42] Donne's brief account of his own change in the preface to *Pseudo-Martyr* seems obviously modeled on these texts: it announces the author's early commitment to religious error, explains the difficulty of separation from that error, and describes a period of prolonged, painstaking, and dispassionate "trial" in search of surer belief. This account of an extended intellectual investigation and reconsideration, in other words, does not make Donne's account

---

and learnedly set downe the reasons that moved them therunto (1602), sig. 2v. Donne's familiarity with French conversions to Protestantism can be surmised by his possession of Bertrand Avignon's *Declaration présenté en la Faculté de Théologie et Sorbonne, Par Laquelle il deduict les raisons qui l'ont meu de quitter la Religion Romaine, pour embrasser la verité de l'Évangile* (Paris, 1605). Keynes, *Bibliography*, 264.

[39] *The Voluntarie Recantation of foure great Learned Men, Professed Fryers in Sundry Monasteries in France, latelie converted from Poperie to the True Religion* (1611), 1, 4, 13.

[40] Richard Sheldon, *The Motives of Richard Sheldon, Pr., for his iust, voluntary, and free renouncing of Communion with the Bishop of Rome, Paul the 5th, and his Church* (1612), 7–9.

[41] Sheldon, *Motives*, 3.

[42] [Edward King], *The Bishop of London his Legacy, Or: Certain Motives of Dr. King, Late Bishop of London, for his Change of Religion* (1623), sig. 3v.

unusual. What is unusual, however, is his failure to describe in clear terms what he came to believe *after* this period of "irresolution" – his failure, in short, to write the end of his own story. In texts of motive, authors invariably detail not only their early miseducation and the process of provisional separation from childhood error, but also the details of their corrected opinions. Donne, indeed, seems to encourage his reader to expect such details, alluding to the "rectifying and reducing [of] mine understanding and judgement" (13). "Reduction," here, appears to carry the force of its Latin etymology, suggesting that Donne will explain how he was "led back" (*re-ducere*) from error, away from Catholic doctrinal innovations, and toward religious conviction more firmly grounded in truth.[43] Donne alters the expected contours of the story with a pun, however, and immediately announces that his treatise will now be "*reduced* to a narrow issue and contracted to a strict point" (14). He sets aside his own "motives" for leaving the Catholic Church, and turns to a more circumscribed and more obviously polemical subject: the "motives" that should move Catholics to swear allegiance to King James. Compared to Carier's insistence that "It is not in my power not to know that which I know,"[44] or Matthew's confident dismissal of Protestant "mazes and confusions," Donne's abbreviated account makes the work's title into another sly pun: it is a "pseudo-Martyr," literally a false witness, to its author's conversion.

Donne explains the abrupt end to his autobiographical account with an equally abrupt disclaimer: the text is, in fact, "not of Divinity, but meerely of temporall matters," specifically, the political legitimacy of the Oath (14). But even in his consideration of "temporall matters," Donne broaches the subject of conversion only to fall silent. Specifically, he omits the two final chapters promised in the table of contents. According to the table of contents, the last of these was to have dealt specifically with the matter of royal converts, arguing "[t]hat no pretence, eyther of Conversion at first, Assistance in the Conquest, or Acceptation of any Surrender from any of our Kings, can give the Pope any more right over the Kingdome of England, than over any other free State whatsoever" (7). From this brief heading, we can reconstruct the missing chapter's central claim: that, even in the

---

[43] This particular meaning of "reduce" was common in religious discourse; discussing the recent Catholic conversion of Toby Matthew, for instance, Dudley Carleton mentions various Protestant attempts at "*reducing* him by conference" (Carleton to Thomas Edmonds, July 11, 1607), BL Stowe MS 169, fo. 84 (my italics). Similarly, the anonymous author of *The Reclaimed Papist* (1655) declares that "people are now run into new ways of [religious] errour, and therefor new ways must be thought on to *reduce* them" (sig. 4r, my italics).

[44] BL Additional MS 72415, fo. 54v.

unlikely event that James I were to become a Catholic, he would thereby admit no papal power over his political realm – in other words, that royal conversions would have no necessary consequences. Even this, however, appears to have been too explicit a discussion of conversion for Donne's liking. Instead of making the claim himself, he refers his readers to the writings of "the reverend and learned Edward Coke" (9), pleading his own [...] final chapters, however, makes the [...] rally inconclusive, if not Jacobean [...] After [...] in [...] t to the Reader, that he [...] perly be called a Reader, [...] nne's failure to write the [...] f Jacobean polemic, Jesse [...] final two chapters before [...] nse to "ideological inter-[...] ep potentially inflamma-[...] vertheless leaves a "trace [...] ecomes an object of fan-[...] ight see this provocative [...] invite but ultimately to [...] text and as a conversion [...] rmal principle of preter-[...] sity of making particular theological and polemical claims, but then refuses to make them clearly or definitively. This is not to question Donne's own Protestant loyalties, or his text's status as a work of Protestant polemic. Donne uses the first-person plural when discussing the Jacobean church, and explicitly objects to the "unwholesome and putrifying Traditions and Postscripts" of Rome (21); his claim that "we are not sent into this world to suffer, but to Doe" (27) would seem implicitly to differentiate his own strenuous religious investigations from what he calls the "drowsie and stupid adoration of the Pope" (19). Nevertheless, Donne consistently avoids unequivocal statements of the truth or persuasiveness of Protestant doctrine, or of the tenets of his own belief. Instead, he offers statements of seemingly calculated inconclusiveness.

[Handwritten annotations across the page: "Do not question his protestant loyalties"; "Avoids unequivocal statement / Ambiguous devotional language"; "Taking oath not just a protestant idea"]

---

[45] Lander, *Inventing Polemic*, 155–8.

[46] "Preterition" can refer to the rhetorical technique of mentioning a subject while declaring its omission. I am here using another definition, one which Donne himself used, indicating the *actual* rhetorical omission of a significant point. Cf. Donne, *Sermons*, ed. G. R. Potter and E. M. Simpson, 10 vols. (Berkeley: University of California Press, 1953–62), vol. VI, 318: "As long as they are but preteritions, not contradictions, but omissions, not usurpations, they are not worthy of a reproofe."

When, for instance, he alleges that "more Catholique princes admit toleration of the Reformed religion than princes of our Profession" (22), it is
momentarily unclear which side he means to praise. Even the text's central
point, that English Catholics should subscribe to the Oath of Allegiance,
was far from an exclusively Protestant position in 1609.[47] Throughout
Pseudo-Martyr, as Alison Shell and Arnold Hunt argue, Donne "tries to
detach certain words from their generally accepted Catholic interpretation,
and reclaim them for Protestant use."[48] Faced with such evasions and
redefinitions, Anthony Raspa prefaces his edition of *Pseudo-Martyr* with
an acknowledgment that "no one can claim [the text] comfortably to his
side" (liv).

In this way, the confessional equivocations of *Pseudo-Martyr* echo the
ambiguous devotional language of Donne's *Litanie*, composed around
the same time. This poem has been described both as a poetic "vestige
of Catholic loyalty" and a statement of Protestant orthodoxy, and this
confusion seems to have been calculated on Donne's part.[49] Writing to
Goodyer, he offers this account of the poem:

I have made a meditation in verse, which I call a Litany; the word you know
imports no other than supplication, but all Churches have one form of supplication, by that name … That by which it will deserve best acceptation, is, That
neither the Roman Church need call it defective, because it abhors not the
particular mention of the blessed Triumphers in heaven; nor the Reformed can
discreetly accuse it, of attributing more then a rectified devotion ought to doe.[50]

Here, Donne seems to describe the *Litanie* as a deliberately ecumenical
poem, available to all "lesser Chappels, which are my friends," no matter
what their religious positions. We might see the truncated self-description
at the beginning of *Pseudo-Martyr* as a similarly inclusive gesture. Describing
his own conversion in a way that is equally indebted to Catholic and Protestant
writings, Donne stresses the shared elements of polemic language used by all
early modern Christian converts, interrupting his account precisely at the
moment where Catholic and Protestant authors would differentiate themselves from one another. And yet a crucial element of this inclusive vision of

[47] For accounts of Catholic arguments in favor of taking the Oath, see T. Clancy, *Papist Pamphleteers* (Chicago, IL: Loyola University Press, 1964), 89–93.
[48] A. Shell and A. Hunt, "Donne's Religious World," in A. Guibbory (ed.), *The Cambridge Companion to John Donne* (Cambridge University Press, 2006), 65–82, 74.
[49] Carey, *Life, Mind, and Art*, 51; Lewalski, *Protestant Poetics*, 259–60. For recent surveys of the criticism of the *Litanie*, and readings suggesting the strategic ecumenism of the poem, see the paired essays in *John Donne Journal* 21 (2002): A. Patterson, "A Man is to Himself a Dioclesian: Donne's Rectified Litany" (35–49); and D. Haskin, "Is There a Future for Donne's 'Litany'?" (51–88).
[50] Donne, *Letters*, 29–30.

Christianity is, paradoxically, an abiding insistence on singular choice. In *Pseudo-Martyr*'s dialectic between declaration and silence, Donne never suggests the irrelevance or unimportance of conversion to a particular church. Indeed, by imitating texts of motive and removing the final account of an achieved conversion, Donne finally draws the reader's attention more powerfully to that necessary, unspoken end.

But Donne also addresses conversion in another, less preteritive mode, a mode that we might see as an alternative to the poles of explicit speech and abrupt silence so radically juxtaposed in *Pseudo-Martyr*. He describes this alternative in a stanza of the *Litanie*:

> Thy eagle-sighted Prophets, too,
> Which were thy Churches Organs, and did sound
> That harmony, which made of two
> One law, and did unite, but not confound;
> > Those heavenly Poëts which did see
> > Thy will, and it expresse
> In rhythmique feet, in common pray for mee,
> That I by them excuse not my excesse,
> In seeking secrets or Poëtiqueness.   (64–72)

In these densely self-reflexive lines, Donne asks for the intercession of the prophets who have excelled him in the composition of devotional poetry. In contrast to the work of these sanctified prophets, who clearly and eloquently express God's will "in rhythmique feet," Donne describes his own devotional poetry as "excessive" and obscure. This "poëtique" refusal to speak plainly in his religious verse is, Donne insists, a sin for which he requires holy forgiveness. As usual, Donne is his own best reader as well as his own harshest critic; such obscurity is, in fact, the signal achievement of his devotional verse. Hardly a gratuitous "seeking [of] secrets," the language of poetry becomes for Donne the best means, or perhaps the only means, by which the convert can both proclaim and preserve those secrets that he has found.

"TRY BEFORE YOU TRUST": DOUBTFUL RESOLUTION IN *SATYRE III*

The earliest and in some ways the clearest example of Donne's "poëtique" approach to religious choice and change can be found in *Satyre III* ("Kinde pitty chokes my spleene"). This poem does not immediately seem to foreground the problem of denominational allegiance. In its first forty-two lines, in fact, the bravely scornful, kindly pitying speaker considers the

plight of "our Mistresse faire Religion," indicating that the subject of the
satire will be the "malady" of irreligion generally, rather than the inadequacy of particular creeds. But in line 43, the urgent injunction "Seeke
true religion" is followed immediately by an equally urgent, and more
particular, question: "O where?" (43). This question, which moves the
satire into the realm of "locall Religion," is one that Donne would have
had ample reason to ask at this particular moment.[51] By the late 1590s,
continued public loyalty to his Catholic upbringing would have presented
not only a hindrance to further court employment, but a positive danger:
the increased stringency of the Elizabethan penal laws had recently claimed
the life of his brother Henry, who died in prison after his arrest for
harboring a missionary priest.[52] Coming from the scion of a persecuted
recusant family, Donne's question could be taken as a statement of provisional independence, the very fact of posing it evidence that he had
"already parted from the Catholic position."[53] Although the motto of
his contemporary portrait brashly declared him to be "*antes muerto que
mudado*" (sooner dead than altered), Donne seems in these years to have
been actively altering his religious affiliation, volunteering for Essex's
military attack on Catholic Spain, and entering the service of Thomas
Egerton, a man who presided over the trials of several high-profile
Catholics, including Mary Queen of Scots.[54]

The recommendation to "seeke" has seemed, to some, an indication of
Donne's unusually restive temperament. Paul Oliver suggests that "the
poem is … ahead of its time in its stress on the need to find the truth
for oneself, a concept which would have been simply incomprehensible to
most of Donne's contemporaries, whatever their religious allegiance."[55]
Arguing for the poem's conceptual radicalism, Richard Strier asserts that
"for most Europeans in the period, religion was not something to be sought,
it was something given … it was not the object of an intellectual quest.
Donne's injunction requires a highly unusual detachment from existing

---

[51] The date of the satire has not been established beyond doubt, but has been persuasively set in the years
   around the Cadiz voyage. See Donne, *The Satires, Epigrams, and Verse Letters*, ed. W. Milgate
   (Oxford: Clarendon, 1967), 139–40; Bald, *John Donne*, 72; and Donne, *Complete Poetry*, ed. J. T.
   Shawcross (New York: Anchor, 1967), 412.
[52] For Henry's imprisonment, see Bald, *John Donne*, 58–9. The penal laws leveled against Catholics in
   the late Elizabethan period, and the strategies that Catholics used to confront them, are discussed by
   P. Holmes, *Resistance and Compromise: The Political Thought of the Elizabethan Catholics* (Cambridge
   University Press, 1982).
[53] G. Parry, *Seventeenth-Century Poetry: The Social Context* (London: Hutchinson, 1985), 49.
[54] For Donne's service to Thomas Egerton, and for Egerton's anti-Catholic activities, see Bald, *John
   Donne*, 80–1, 94.
[55] P. M. Oliver, *Donne's Religious Writing* (London: Longmans, 1997), 61.

commitments, a detachment like Donne's own in the 1590s."[56] But in fact, as we have seen, religion was very much "something sought" at this time, and not just by radical Erasmian humanists. Throughout the previous decade, Donne would have witnessed his two Heywood uncles participating in the Jesuit mission that worked to re-Catholicize England, convert by convert.[57] His future patron Sir Thomas Egerton, by contrast, had converted to Protestantism before becoming Lord Keeper – a fact that Donne might have known from Thomas Egerton Jr., his companion at Lincoln's Inn and on the Cadiz voyage. As we have seen, the Cadiz company itself contained a number of models of religious affiliation and re-affiliation. Here, Donne would have encountered not only Catholics, Protestants, and politic ecumenists such as Essex himself, but also Protestants reputed to have once been Catholics, such as John Reynolds, and Protestants about to become Catholics, such as Essex's chaplain, William Alabaster.

Satyre III reflects its author's acute sense of religion as emphatically *not* "something given." Donne instead describes a culture of confessional flux, a culture in which his contemporaries not only differed from each other in their definitions of "true religion," but were also themselves changeable, keen to "seeke" that truth in new places. He paints the scene by identifying the kinds of choice being made around him, his sharply ironic tone mocking each in turn. The figure of "Mirreus," for example, whose name completes the line in which the reader is asked to "[s]eeke true religion," is not simply a Catholic, but a Catholic *convert*. Like Toby Matthew, or Benjamin Carier, or William Alabaster, Mirreus was not born into the Roman faith. Instead, he is an Englishman "fled from us" who now "seekes [true religion] at Rome," for the evidently unsatisfactory reason "that shee was there a thousand yeares agoe" (44–5). While the exiled convert Mirreus pursues the "ragges" of Rome, Crants chooses another destination: Calvinist Geneva. While we cannot be sure where Crants's journey originated, we learn that he has handily rejected the temptation of Roman "inthrall[ment]" (49), preferring a religion that was "plaine, simple, sullen, young, / Contemptuous, yet unhansome" (51–2). Donne thus implies an ironic flaw in Crants's rationale for conversion: his is the religion of predestination, but he turns to that religion in an ostentatiously, willfully perverse exercise of "lecherous" choice.

Both of these converts appear, at first, in contrast to the English Protestant "Graius," who "stays still at home here," with "still" implying

[56] R. Strier, *Resistant Structures: Particularity and Radicalism in Renaissance Texts* (Berkeley: University of California Press, 1995), 134.
[57] See Flynn, *Donne and the Ancient Catholic Nobility*, 98–114.

both a judicious silence and a physical and historical permanence (55). The pun, however, is misleading: "staying still," Donne points out, will in fact require a turn according to "laws / Still new like fashions" (56–7). Remaining "home," and accepting the latest religion officially established in England, Graius is a convert despite himself. Extending the connection between religious and erotic choice, Donne tells us that Graius

> Imbraceth her, whom his Godfathers will
> Tender to him, being tender, as Wards still
> Take such wives as their Guardians offer, or
> Pay valewes.   (58–61)

Although Graius prides himself on avoiding the explicitly sexualized choices of his compatriots, he is in fact dependent, weak, and ultimately forced to "imbrace" something new and less than desirable. His outward "stillness," in fact, disguises a fretful capitulation to the leaders of England's church, depicted as thuggish pimps who will exact penalties for refusing their most recently proffered alternative. Donne's initial Christian triumvirate, then, is produced by three equally objectionable conversions. Mirreus's adoration of the "ragges" of Rome (47), Crants's ardor for the "contemptuous yet unhansome" lady of Geneva (52), and Graius's willingness to accept the offerings of "vile ambitious bauds" (55) are "all bad" scenarios that elicit erotic disgust (77).

After such a scathing, equal-opportunity critique, it is tempting to read the ensuing invitation to "doubt wisely" as an idealized alternative to local confessional conversion, a principled refusal to adopt any particular religious position.[58] Read this way, the speaker's recommendation to "doubt," and to "stand enquiring right," can thus be aligned with the "humanistic"

---

[58] For the Christian skepticism argument, see L. Bredvold, "The Religious Thought of Donne in Relation to Medieval and Later Traditions," in *Studies in Shakespeare, Milton, and Donne* (New York: Haskell House, 1964), 293–32. Richard Strier connects the satire's mode with the skepticism of Edward Herbert, and with the earlier "Erasmian" position of Sebastian Castellio, in *Resistant Structures*, 152–4. Thomas Hester has argued that "for Donne's satirist, the cure for which he searches is one with the mode of discovery itself," rendering the satire a performance of true religion. Hester, *Kinde Pitty and Brave Scorn: John Donne's Satyres* (Durham, NC: Duke University Press, 1982), 72 and ch. 3 *passim*. See also H. White, "John Donne and the Psychology of Spiritual Effort," in Jones (ed.), *The Seventeenth Century*, 355–67. John Lauritsen offers a more pessimistic version of this point: "the quest itself, rather than the end of the quest, has become, *in this fallen world*, the only attainable objective." Lauritsen, "Donne's *Satyres*: The Drama of Self-Discovery," *SEL* 16 (1976), 119, my italics. So Joshua Scodel suggests that in this satire "skeptical inquiry [is] the true religious mean." Scodel, "John Donne and the Religious Politics of the Mean," in Frontain and Malpezzi (eds.), *John Donne's Religious Imagination*, 45. Dominic Baker-Smith similarly identifies a dynamic *via media* in Donne's satire, which he associates with the Christian humanism of George Cassander and Paolo Sarpi. Baker-Smith, "John Donne's 'Critique of True Religion'," in A. J. Smith (ed.), *John Donne: Essays in Celebration* (London: Methuen, 1972), 404–32.

end of a *via media*, with an attitude of skeptical detachment or "proto-ecumenical Anglicanism."[59] This, however, would be a serious misreading. Recommendations of doubt, in fact, are just as frequently encountered in the kind of texts which critics have implicitly praised Donne for *not* writing in *Satyre III*: texts of controversy, particularly the genre of case divinity that I will term the text of resolution. Produced by Catholic and Protestant presses throughout the Elizabethan and early Jacobean periods, texts of resolution address those numerous men and women who found themselves in denominational crisis as they attempted to "seek true religion" among the rival churches.[60] The Jesuit Leonardus Lessius, in the preface to one such text, *Quae Religio Sit Capessenda? (What Religion Should be Embraced?)* diagnoses the problem:

> Great is the variety of Religion in this our age, and great is the contention about the truth thereof. Many in this point do continually waver, nor can they determine any certainty, passing from one Religion to another, as it were from house to house for trialls sake, thereby to find tranquillity of mind. Others, through an inconsiderate boldness, do imbrace any Religion which by chance they light upon, without either examining or understanding the same: who, when they are demanded why they preferre that Religion before others, they have no other answere, but that it seems better to them, or els (which comonly all do bragge of) because they follow the very pure word of God.[61]

Lessius and authors of similar texts of resolution wish their readers finally to stop "wavering." They insist on the importance of meaningful choice in a time of extreme "variety of Religion," discouraging a groundless obedience that needs to be rationalized after the fact. Though they ultimately aim to convert their readers definitively either to Catholicism or to Protestantism, these texts of resolution nevertheless acknowledge the process of struggle and search to which texts of motive offer testimony. Authors of these texts encourage individuals to compare a variety of competing theological and ecclesiological claims, and outline methods for the proper conduct of such a religious investigation.

[59] Frontain, "Make all this All," 20.
[60] Thus, the text of resolution addresses the particular problem of church adherence, rather than the general moral or spiritual topics treated in other works of casuistry or guides to devotional practice. Donne's writing has been read in light of these other traditions; see M. L. Brown, *Donne and the Politics of Conscience in Early Modern England* (Leiden: Brill, 1995), as well as Slights, *The Casuistical Tradition*, and Martz, *The Poetry of Meditation*.
[61] Leonardus Lessius, *A Consultation what Faith and Religion is Best to be Imbraced*, 2nd edn. (St. Omer, 1621), Preface, 1–2. The work was originally published in Latin in 1609. For an earlier description of such denominational "trouble," see Richard Bristow, *A Briefe Treatise of Divers Plaine and Sure Waies to Finde Out the Truthe in this Doubtfull and Dangerous Time of Heresie* ([Antwerp,] 1574, rpt. 1599).

A crucial characteristic of such texts of resolution, and one with particular relevance to *Satyre III*, is an insistence that their Christian readers cultivate an initial attitude of religious detachment in order to survey denominational options independently and objectively. We might perhaps expect to find such counsel in the work of Protestant writers: the polemical equation of priestcraft with confusion and duplicity, and Catholic worship with blind obedience, marks ecclesiastical satire from the *Friar's Tale* to *Lycidas*.[62] So George Carleton, writing in an effort to gain converts to Protestantism, implores his Catholic readers to "suffer not your selves to be blind-folded" by priestly subterfuge.[63] William Fulke suggests that by refusing to allow open debate about religious choice, Catholics "shew themselves thereby to be enemies of the trueth, that they flie the light and dare not abide the triall," a sentiment echoed some years later by the Protestant convert John Harding, who reminded his listeners of "that worthy precept of St. John, when he saith, Trust not every spirit, but try the Spirits, whether they bee of God or no."[64]

Such appeals to individual "triall" had equal prominence, however, in texts of resolution written by Catholics. The English Catholic priest Edward Weston promises his reader that, if "his watchefull Prudence be balasted beloe with humilitie and his humble obedience be reared up above to the height and light of discreete vigilancie," he will be able to "discrie the treacherous conceilement" of those who would prey on an unresolved conscience, settling it on the wrong object.[65] Weston's Protestant predators seem just as sinister as the blindfold-wielding papists described by Carleton or Fulke. The antidote Weston suggests is not simply "humilitie" or "obedience," but once again individual "Prudence" and "vigilancie." Similarly, the Jesuit Lessius asserts that strenuous investigation of doctrine is perfectly compatible with Catholic allegiance: "it is doubtlesse no disgrace, or signe of levity or inconstancy, by a diligent and iudicious examen, to try which of all these divers spirits is of God, and which is that Catholike Church so often commended to us in the Scriptures."[66] The Catholic convert Theophilus Higgons puts it in plainer terms in the text appended to his *First Motive*:

TRY BEFORE YOU TRUST: see both, compare both, examine both; Try all things and keep that which is good (Thess. 5.21). Try the cause and try the persons; try the faith

---

[62] Shell sensitively discusses this and other commonplaces of anti-Catholic slander in *Catholicism, Controversy*, 32–6.

[63] George Carleton, *Directions to Know the True Church*, 2nd edn. (1615), sig. A5r.

[64] William Fulke, *A Retentive to Stay Good Christians* (1580), sig. 4r.; John Harding, *A Recantation Sermon Preached in the Gatehouse at Westminster* (1620), 3.

[65] Edward Weston, *The Triall of Christian Truth … The Second Parte* (Douai, 1615), sig. A2r.

[66] Lessius, *Consultation*, Preface, sig. 5v.

and try the professours; try the sodality of the first, and try the fidelity of the second: follow that which is most credible, and believe them that best deserve your creditt.[67]

For Higgons, only a "diligent investigation of the truth" can counteract the human tendency toward "lethargy in schisme and heresy."[68]

In *Satyre III*, Donne depicts and decries such "lethargy" in the pair of figures who shirk responsibility for denominational choice entirely. "Graccus," for instance,

> loves all as one, and thinkes that so
> As women do in divers countries goe
> In divers habits, yet still are one kinde,
> So doth, so is Religion.   (65–8)

Donne's reaction, to disparage such a permissive attitude as a paradoxically enlightened "blindness," resembles Lessius's irritation with latitudinarianism: to believe that "all Christians [are] saved whether … a Papist, or a Lutheran, or a Calvinist, or an Anabaptist, or any other sect," Lessius points out, is "to make no account of any Religion."[69] Lessius argues that if a man ceases to care "what religion he hold, what he believeth or not believeth: he does not therefore seke after the truth."[70] Donne's satiric version of this point suggests, further, that the indifferent attitude toward doctrinal variety exemplified by Graccus exists symbiotically with the kind of spiritual torpor which Donne personifies in "careless Phrygius," who "doth abhorre / All, because all cannot be good, as one / Knowing some women whores, dare marry none" (62–4).

In contrast to the equivalent laziness of choosing "all" or "none," Donne insists that the search for true religion must end in a single, definitive result: "unmoved thou / Of force must one, and forc'd but one allow; / And the right" (69–71). With the dramatic caesura after "right," *Satyre III* re-emphasizes one of the crucial generic assumptions of the text of resolution: that a single and newly firm spiritual conviction will conclude the process of searching. Recording a debate between a Catholic and a Protestant, the Irish Jesuit Henry Fitzsimon makes explicit their shared assumption that a final, irrevocable, and particular choice will result from any temporary detour into religious "doubt": the interlocutors "agreed to abyde a lawfull resolution of

---

[67] Higgons, *Try Before You Trust*, appended to *The First Motive*, sig. 3v.   [68] *Ibid.*, sig. 4v.
[69] Lessius, *Consultation*, 228–9.
[70] *Ibid.*, 251. Cf. [John Radford], *A Directorie teaching the Way to the Truth, Whereunto is Added a Short Treatise Against Adiaphorists, Neuters, and Such as Say they May be saved in Any Sect or Religion, and Would Make of Many Divers Sects One Church* (1605).

the learned: which if it should justify M. Nugent's perswasion, then M. Rider would recant. Yf it could not; then M. Nugent would become a Protestant."[71] Both Catholics and Protestants see the process of religious search as finite, with one side destined to "convince" the waverer permanently. For this reason, both sides take great pains to accuse each other of identical failures of doctrinal coherence or conclusiveness, asserting their own contrasting certainty. The Protestant convert John Haren accuses Catholics of "a continuall mutabilitie and various exchanging of opinions ... for what was one day received and allowed by authoritie was the next day prohibited and utterly disannulled,"[72] while the Catholic convert Richard Broughton describes Protestantism as "a Religion tossed and tennised up and down, with so many bounds and reboundes, choppes and changes," based on the relativistic principle of *tot capita quot religiones* (as many religions as heads).[73] Broughton confidently declares that in his account of Catholicism "every point and proposition of religious duety will be prooved to be so certaine, that no infidell or false believer can make it doubtfull," while the Protestant Robert Crowley asserts that if his reader will agree to "examine both the English and the Romish Church by the same notes," he will realize that the latter is "neither Catholique, holy, one only, or Apostolique," and that the former indubitably is.[74] Both Catholic and Protestant texts of resolution advocate an initial period of wise doubt, but also insist that the process will end in the eradication of ambivalence, a process neatly summed up in the title of one Catholic contribution to the genre: *Instructions for your Search into Religion, with Reasons why the truth once founde, further conference is not to be admitted* (Douai, 1607).

Read against these contemporary texts, *Satyre III* anticipates the preteritive methods later used in *Pseudo-Martyr*. Donne rehearses the premises shared by both Protestant and Catholic writers on the subject of religious

[71] Henry Fitzsimon, *A Catholike Confutation of M. John Riders Clayme of Antiquitie* (Rouen, 1608), sig. J2r. Donne owned another of Fitzsimon's books, *Brittanomachia Ministrorum* (1614). Keynes, *Bibliography*, 269. Similar arguments are made by the Protestant convert Thomas Bell, who argues that a geunine "search" will inevitably lead one to "renounce" the Catholic Church (*Thomas Bels Motives* (1593), sig. 2v), and the Catholic convert Francis Walsingham, who claims that Protestant theology failed to offer a "sure ground ... on which to rest my salvation" (*A Search Made into Matters of Religion* (1609), 2).

[72] John Haren, *The Repentance of John Haren, Priest, and his Return to the Church of God* (1610), sig. E4r.

[73] Richard Broughton, *An Apologicall [sic] Epistle, Directed to the right honorable Lords and others of her Majesties Privie Counsell, serving as well as the Preface to a Booke entituled, A Resolution of Religion* (Antwerp, 1601), 24–5. For a flat denial of this charge, see Andrew Willet, *An Antilogie or Counterplea to an Apologicall (he should have said) Apologeticall epistle published by a favorite of the Romane Separation* (1603), 86.

[74] Broughton, *Apologicall Epistle*, 35 [mispag. 20]; Robert Crowley, *A Breefe Discourse Concerning the Foure Usuall Notes, whereby Christes Catholique Church is Knowen* (1581), sig. A4v.

choice, but avoids describing the object of that choice in terms more specific than "the right" or "the best." Even his positive suggestion that true religion "a little elder is" (73) seems a calculated equivocation, since the notion of antiquity appears in both Catholic and Protestant arguments: Catholics accuse Protestants of heretical innovation, while Protestants argue that the "Trent Councill" transformed the Roman Church into an institution which is "not Catholique but Schismaticall," and that the Reformation recovered an "elder" form of Christian worship.[75] Donne's reference to parental authority ("ask thy Father which is shee") recalls a subcategory of the "resolution" genre produced by both Catholics and Protestants: the letter of advice from the aggrieved parent of a convert, imploring the wayward child to return.[76] The conclusion of the poem, precisely the place where one would expect the speaker to lay his denominational cards on the table, only makes its message more difficult to discern. Donne here describes the "blest flowers" that "thrive and do well" at the head of "rough streames." Less fortunate are those which

> having left their roots, and themselves given
> To the streames tyrannous rage, alas are driven
> Through mills, and rockes, and woods, and at last, almost
> Consum'd in going, in the sea are lost.   (105–8)

With this bizarre image of suicidal flowers drowning themselves in a winding stream, Donne seems to repudiate the poem's earlier praise of "seeking." To leave one's "roots," he seems to suggest, might result in literal perdition, being for ever "lost"; conversion, here, is fatal errancy. Immediately, however, he qualifies the caution: "So perish Soules, which more chuse mens unjust / Power from God claym'd, then God himselfe to trust" (109–10). Religious choice is necessary, but choosing on the basis of human "power," or "mens laws," leads to spiritual death. This position, like the others I have just outlined, could be assimilated into both Catholic and Protestant arguments. Protestants associated post-Tridentine Catholicism with "popery," or the idolatrous veneration of a mortal man who claimed "power from God." Catholics, on the other hand, objected to the Elizabethan church settlement as an "unjust" attempt to legislate orthodoxy, taking "power from God" and investing it in the civil magistrate.

---

[75] Crowley, *Breefe Discourse*, sig. A6r.

[76] See, for instance, the reply to Theophilus Higgons by his Protestant father in Edward Hoby's *Letter to Mr. T.H. late Minister now Fugitive* (1609), or, by contrast, Francis Savage's *Conference betwixt a Mother a Devout Recusant and her Sonne, a Zealous Protestant* (1600). I will discuss this genre more fully in the following chapter.

Such evasions and equivocations ultimately suggest that while the message of *Satyre III* is certainly ambiguous, this ambiguity lies in a different place than is usually assumed. It is not, as Thomas Moore has argued, that Donne is simply "brave enough to face the fact that there is no certain way to Truth," finally concluding that "any way ... might be wrong."[77] By self-consciously imitating the shared features of Catholic and Protestant texts of resolution, Donne suggests that the "way to Truth" is absolutely clear, agreed upon by all sides in their advice to potential converts: the discovery of "true religion" in its earthly incarnation requires intelligent doubting, energetic searching, liberal inquiring. What remains essentially uncertain for that very reason, however, is the nature of that "right" religion which is the promised end to both search and satire. By placing "Truth" on a "huge hill," Donne does not create a shining exemplar, but a goal permanently hidden from view.[78] The seeker, and the satire itself, must circle around this goal, which can be reached only by circumnavigation and expressed only by circumlocution: it is "what the hilles suddennes resists" (82). By clarifying the way but obscuring the end, Donne makes *Satyre III* into a formally recognizable text of resolution that nevertheless avoids any final denomination.

But, unlike *Pseudo-Martyr*, *Satyre III* ultimately manages to say more than this. It does so precisely because of its status as a *poetic* contribution to early modern religious controversy, as an instance of a kind of poetry distinct from the privacy of devotional or meditational verse. By choosing poetry as the medium through which he will engage in contemporary religious debate, Donne makes his central point implicit from the very beginning: that neither the difficult, tortuous progress of conversion, nor the mysterious goal toward which it tends, can be adequately addressed in denotative statement. To express conversion fully and faithfully requires, in other words, *other words* – or perhaps a different kind of language entirely. Critics have long agreed that the poem is a stylistic tour de force, breathtakingly rough in its abrupt reversals, and in the urgency of its unanswered questions. Such formal characteristics are familiar as marks of classical satire, but Donne uses them to make an implicit claim about the subject matter addressed in the poem itself: that religious choices are, finally, best or only

---

[77] T. V. Moore, "Donne's Use of Uncertainty as a Vital Force in *Satyre III*," *MP* 67 (1969), 41–9. I agree with Moore's emphasis on the satire's ultimate praise of the inconclusive, although I disagree about the nature and purpose of that uncertainty.

[78] Compare, for instance, the contemporary account of conversion in BL Lansdowne MS 776, fo. 43, where the newly Catholic author celebrates his own arrival at "this heavenly citty builded upon an hill, this mountain prepared on the top of the mountains, this tabernacle placed in the sunne," where he finds "the edge of my curiosity fully rebated."

articulated obliquely. The poetry is, indeed, "trying" – both in the sense of "attempting" to convey the movement of spiritual quest (famously in the enjambed phrase "about must / And about must go"), but also "trying" in the sense of irritating the reader, creating an unsatisfied longing for stasis, for the promised "end" of the search, for a calm that will conclude the agitation of decision. Thomas Hester argues that "satire *is* religion in *Satyre III*," but by this he means that the poem's hectic style indicates Donne's *own* religious skepticism and uncertainty.[79] I would agree about the essential importance of poetic form and style for Donne's message, but not about what that message is. Rather than seeing the poem as a sign of his own irresolution, we might instead see it as Donne's ostentatious withholding of security for his wavering or converting readers. Read against the reassuring narratives offered by contemporary texts of resolution, the satire's own insistent roughness seems all the more striking. *Satyre III*'s final innovation is its simultaneous emphasis on, and periphrastic obscuring of, the goal toward which it aims. In its peculiar combination of stridency and reticence, the poem is, itself, a version of the religious truth it defines: "like the Sunne, dazling, yet plaine to all eyes" (88).

"VERSE HATH A MIDDLE NATURE": DONNE'S CHANGING STYLE

In the *Second Anniversary*, Donne interrupts his meditation on the death of Elizabeth Drury with a moment of curious self-caution, one that seems to rescind the emphasis on choice so central to *Satyre III*. Addressing his own "insatiate soul," Donne instructs it to have patience "till Gods great *Venite* change the song" (44). At the last judgment, God will replace partial and inadequate human hymns with the clarity and completeness of his own divine language. Until that time, Donne tells his soul,

> Forget this rotten world; And unto thee
> Let thine own times as an old storie be.
> Be not concern'd: studie not why, nor whan;
> Doe not so much, as not beleeve a man.
> For though to erre, be worst, to try truths forth
> Is far more busines, then this world is worth.   (49–54)

These lines appear to present a despairing retraction of Donne's earlier, investigative optimism about devotion and belief. As we have seen, *Satyre III* represents a process of strenuous search and energetic choice as essential

---

[79] Hester, *Kinde Pitty*, 72.

to spiritual life. This gesture of renunciation, by contrast, seemingly rejects the vigorous processes in which all earthly conversion originates. Rather than inquiry, Donne here seems to encourage quiescence ("forget"). Rather than a diligent alertness to options, Donne here seems to advise apathy ("be not concern'd"). Read more carefully, however, these lines do not recommend an end to the individual search for truth. "To try truths forth," here, does not mean "to experiment in pursuit of truth" – a counsel that Donne never retracts. Instead, the phrase means simply to display truths, to declare and defend one's allegiances, in the arena of theological controversy. Here, Donne suggests that to "try" truth in this sense, to attempt to make belief explicit or intelligible, is to invite the endless, unproductive "busines" of public dispute. In the "rotten world" of human disagreement, one must – in the words of *Satyre III* – "keep the truth which thou hast found" (89). One must, that is, find ways to keep one's truth secret.

Donne offers similar advice in an undated letter to Henry Goodyer. Donne's correspondence with Goodyer often turned to religion, and the letters between the two men contain a number of Donne's most suggestive comments on his own religious position – from his account of the *Litanie* to his more striking statement that "I never fettered nor imprisoned the word Religion … immuring it in a *Rome*, or a *Wittemberg*, or a *Geneva*; they are all virtuall beams of one sun … connatural pieces of one circle."[80] In this particular letter to his friend, Donne offers a more pessimistic version of this latter notion of Christian community: "I will not, nor need to you, compare the Religio[n]s," he writes. "The channels of Gods mercies run through both fields; and they are sister teats of his graces; yet both diseased and infected, though not both alike."[81] The main burden of this letter, however, is a discussion of Goodyer's religious beliefs, which had apparently been reported as "irresolved or various."[82] Referring to "that sound true opinion, that in all Christian professions there is way to salvation (which I think you think)," Donne warns Goodyer against "incommodiously or intempestively" announcing this belief to others.[83] To "try truths forth," in this case, would have consequences that Donne describes with evident distaste: "When you descend to satisfie all men in your own religion, or to excuse others to all, you prostitute your self and your understanding, though not a prey, yet a mark, and a hope, and a subject, for every sophister in Religion to work on."[84] By "descending" to open self-description, in other words, Goodyer would present himself as a target for proselytizing. Donne's caution, while it certainly has much to do with the practical risks of

---

[80] Donne, *Letters*, 25.   [81] *Ibid.*, 88.   [82] *Ibid.*, 87.   [83] *Ibid.*, 87.   [84] *Ibid.*, 89.

heterodoxy in Jacobean England, is more than mere prudence. In *Essays in Divinity*, Donne quotes St. Augustine to assert that "*within me there is a truth not Hebrew, nor Greek, nor barbarous; which without organs, without noyse of Syllables, tels me true, and would enable me to say confidently to Moses, Thou sayest true.*"[85] For Donne, the deepest religious "truth" inevitably speaks, but it does so only "without noyse of Syllables." By exposing his particular convictions to the realm of "business," Goodyer would betray that truth; he would "prostitute" not only his own faith, but faith in general.

Here again, Donne expresses a commitment to the privacy of belief, and to the necessity of secrecy in the matter of religious affiliation. Nevertheless, he returns again and again to conversion as its own autonomous subject, re-emphasizing its necessity to any progress toward the "the right" or "the best" faith. In a late sermon, for instance, Donne returns to the topic of true and false conversion:

> to depart from that Church, in which I have received my baptism … deserves a mature consideration; for I may mistake the reasons upon which I goe, and I may finde after, that there are more true errours in the Church I goe to, then there were imaginary in that that I left.[86]

His advice seems, by now, familiar: men and women should doubt wisely for fear of "running wrong," and the first-person phrasing reminds us that Donne himself had reckoned with that possibility en route to the pulpit he now occupies. The paradoxical phrase "true errours," however, seems to predict something less straightforward than mere condemnation of Catholic apostasy. Sure enough, Donne proceeds "in strange way," admitting that

> I have been sorry to see some persons converted from the Roman Church, to ours; because I have known, that onely *temporall respects* have moved them, and they have lived after rather in a *nullity*, or *indifferency to either* religion, then in a true, and established zeale.

One might expect the Dean of St. Paul's to rejoice in any conversion from Rome. Instead, Donne explicitly objects to all conversions based on bad premises ("temporall respects" or "indifferency"). His point, here, seems to be that any sense of "the right" or "the best" church can be vitiated by a corrupt method of adherence.

---

[85] E. M. Simpson (ed.), *Essays in Divinity* (Oxford: Clarendon, 1952), 15–16. The quoted passage comes from *Confessions*, 11.3; Toby Matthew's 1620 version uses many of the same phrases (including "noyse of Syllables"), suggesting the intriguing possibility that Donne assisted his friend on this first English translation of the *Confessions*.

[86] Donne, *Sermons*, vol. x, 161.

Donne's correspondence with the Catholic convert Toby Matthew emphasizes their shared manner of conversion, and in doing so carefully avoids any specification of the different creeds to which their searches led them. "That we differ in our wayes, I hope we pardon one another," Donne writes.

> Men go to China, both by the Straights, and by the Cape. I never mis-interpreted your way; nor suffered it to be so, wheresoever I found it in discourse. For I was sure you took not up your Religion upon trust, but payed ready money for it and at a high Rate.[87]

Donne does not deny the difference between Matthew's convictions and his own, but his account here makes their achieved "Religion" identically ineffable; both men are headed for the mysterious "China" of God's grace. What *can* be discussed, and what Donne wishes here to point out, is their shared aversion to the blind "trust" that all texts on conversion, both Catholic and Protestant, inveigh against with equal vehemence. In a sense, even as Donne claims that he and Matthew "differ in [their] ways," the point of his letter is that they in fact share a "way," perhaps even a "strange way," of navigating their respective journeys – this way, Donne maintains, should be respected, and not "mis-interpreted" in the arena of "discourse." Donne's objection to the common "mis-interpretation" of Matthew's "Religion," however, should not be confused with a desire for its greater clarification. Instead, Donne continues to challenge the very notion that conviction can, or should, be described precisely. This challenge, and the assumptions underlying it, finally returns us to the resolute, deliberate obscurity of his poetry, and especially his devotional poetry. Camille Wells Slights suggests that in comparison to the satires and prose, Donne's devotional lyrics "are not casuistical in any precise, specific way," by which she means that these poems do not treat moral dilemmas in their worldly contexts as clearly as, say, the poems of Herbert.[88] This very lack of precision and specificity, however, makes Donne's devotional lyrics a powerful expression of one of his most deeply held beliefs: that it is a Christian's obligation first to seek out the "truth," and then to keep that truth from view. It is precisely in a poem – rather than a sermon, letter, or

---

[87] "Dr Dunne, with a kind of labour'd Complement, to a Friend of his," in J. Donne, Jr. (ed.), *A Collection of Letters Made by Sir Tobie Matthews, KT. With a Character of the Most Excellent Lady, Lucy Countesse of Carleile. To which are Added many Letters of his own, to severall Persons of Honour, who were contemporary with him* (1660), 68–9. For evidence that this "Friend" is in fact Matthew, see Bald, *John Donne*, 143, and Feil, "Sir Toby Matthew," 141.

[88] Slights, *The Casuistical Tradition*, 145.

Privacy

satire – that Donne most effectively demonstrates how even the clearest declarations of religious commitment can be refashioned into evidence of an essential, irreducible mystery.

Such a deliberate, strategic use of paradox marks one of Donne's most superficially orthodox Protestant poems, "To Mr. Tilman after he had Taken Orders." In this modified verse epistle, Donne reimagines priestly ordination – seemingly the clearest possible expression of a Christian's denominational position – as a process of radical concealment.[89] As a newly ordained Protestant minister, Donne's addressee has, it seems, definitively declared himself, has "tr[ied] truths forth." Addressing Tilman, however, Donne offers a series of complicated questions about the relationship of identity to faith. These questions are unanswered, perhaps unanswerable, and occasionally not even immediately recognizable as questions, for instance:

> as a Ship after much paine and care,
> For Iron and Cloth brings home rich Indian ware,
> Hast thou traffiqu'd, but with farre more gaine
> Of noble goods, and with less time and paine?   (9–12)

The importance of this question seems not to be in Tilman's potential response (indeed, what kind of response could he offer?) but in the exotic mercantile metaphors that Donne uses to pose the question. Again, as in his reference to "China" in his letter to Matthew, Donne here represents progress toward religious conviction as an arduous voyage (taken "with paine and care") to a strange and unknown realm. If such "traffique" is a source of certainty for Tilman himself, it is a source of uncertainty for all others who regard him. Donne imagines the newly ordained Tilman as subject to mysterious and unknowable "new thoughts and stirrings … new motions" (7–8). He is "new stamp[ed]" (18) and "new feather'd" (22), likened to a "new-found Starre" (46) and a "blest Hermaphrodite" (54). As an ordained minister, Tilman's "gainings doe surmount expression" (25) and his "joyes passe speech" (27). Self-declaration conveys, in the end, a profound secrecy, a secrecy that Donne describes with a literally pregnant image:

> *Maries* prerogative was to beare Christ, so
> Tis preachers to convey him, for they doe
> As Angels out of Cloudes, from Pulpits speake.   (41–3)

---

[89] For information on Tilman, see A. Pritchard, "Donne's Mr. Tilman," *Review of English Studies* 24.93 (Feb. 1973), 38–42; and Bald, *John Donne*, 302–4. Bald suggests that in this poem "Donne reveals a good deal about his own feelings" regarding his own recent ordination (302), a suggestion echoed by Oliver, *Donne's Religious Writing*, 198.

It is worth pausing to trace out the arrangement of vehicles and tenors here. "Preachers," like Tilman and Donne himself, are likened to Mary, in that both "beare" or "convey" Christ (like the "ship," the poetic vehicle is, literally, a vehicle). In the next line, preachers are likened to "angels," their pulpits to "cloudes" from which the divine presence emerges. Preachers here both receive annunciation (like Mary) and deliver it (like angels). But in both cases, their truths must be conveyed within some kind of protective container, be it made of vapor or flesh – or poetic language itself.

We have seen Donne describing the goal of religious conversion, firm adherence to a particular church, with a complex of exoticized, feminized metaphors that shroud that conviction in darkness. Religion – as embodied in a church – is China, the Indies, "our mistress," an obscure object of desire that must be "wooed" or "won." Holy Sonnet 18, one of Donne's most direct and well-known poetic treatments of the subject of confessional choice, centers on this kind of metaphor. Having asked his "dear Christ" to reveal his "spouse," Donne's speaker surveys the options in a bridal catalogue reminiscent of *Satyre III*, beginning with the "richly painted" Roman church and the lamenting, persecuted Protestant, "rob'd and tore." From this, he proceeds to survey the ways in which his fellow Christians attempt to define and designate their churches as the true Bride of Christ:

> Sleepes shee a thousand, then peeps up one yeare?
> Is she selfe truth and errs? now new, now outwore?
> Doth she, and did she, and shall she evermore
> On one, on seaven, or on no hill appeare?
> Dwells she with us, or like adventuring knights
> First travaile we to seeke and then make Love? (5–10)

These six lines neatly sum up several commonplaces of contemporary polemic, referring to the true church's alleged infallibility, immutability, visibility, and antiquity. In this way, Donne's sonnet explicitly demonstrates his familiarity with the accusations and defenses used by controversialists across the denominational spectrum. Donne returns to the original bridal metaphor, however, with a notoriously bold final quatrain:

> Betray kind husband thy spouse to our sights,
> And let myne amorous soul court thy mild Dove
> Who is most trew, and pleasing to thee, then
> When she'is embrac'd and open to most men. (11–14)

Donne's profane paradox revolves around a pun on the word "true," suggesting that Christ's "spouse" is most "true" in terms of theology when least "true" in terms of sexual fidelity; the best church is at once "embrac'd" by each and "open" to all. This striking image of promiscuity might seem to indicate Donne's latitudinarianism, his advocacy of a broad-based church that could comprehend "most" Christians. But if we stay within the terms of the sexual metaphor itself, we must also acknowledge that the particular thing that is "open" here is a negative space, a vaginal darkness. By linking the endpoint of conversion to feminine sexuality, Donne yet again defines the goal of conversion with radical explicitness and radical obscurity. Yet again, he gives us the impression of having been told both too much and too little, as he designates a "trew" church while at the same time managing to avoid any precise description of it. From the commonplace that the church is the bride of Christ, Donne suggests more specifically, and more scandalously, that if the spouse herself is visibly "bright and clear," conversion is a journey to the mysterious "centrique part" of her, the part which must be loved best, but also which cannot be viewed, and must not be named.[90]

In a sensitive discussion of this and other Holy Sonnets, Brian Cummings has argued that Donne's central concern in these poems – and the source of their striking lack of confessional clarity – is the inscrutable, inexpressible grace of God. "The grammar of these poems," he writes, "projects a bewildering confusion of theological accents, which refuse to conform to a rigid doctrinal pattern. Like the road to Damascus, this way is obscured by the 'noyse' of grace, demanding interpretation but not delivering it. The 'noyse' of the Holy Sonnets insists itself upon the reader's attention, but fails to provide a coherent 'voyce.'"[91] Cummings's account acknowledges Donne's preteritive mode, but I think moves too quickly from noting the poetry's theological "confusion" to assigning to it a more abstract (and implicitly Reformed) notion of ineffable grace. The shadowy theology of Donne's religious poetry may, as Cummings suggests, reflect his sense of the ultimate unintelligibility of "God's grammar." But it is also part of Donne's deliberate engagement with, and commentary on, the all-too-explicit human grammar of religious controversy. In the Holy Sonnets, as elsewhere in his writing, Donne alludes to contemporary polemical discourses of confessional change while at the same time insisting on their most equivocal, or equivalent, terms. Subjecting this language to various poetic tropings, Donne suggests, is one way that devotional

---

[90] Elegie XVIII ("Love's Progress"), 36. Shell and Hunt point out this sonnet's interest in "the dark side of religion" ("Donne's Religious World," 80), but this is meant as a moral darkness, as the metaphor's dangerous sexual "coarseness" finally taints the notion of religious inclusiveness. I'm suggesting, instead, that Donne's metaphor does not impugn the choice itself; the denominational "darkness" he proposes is politic, not profane.

[91] Cummings, *Literary Culture*, 397.

identity – his own, and that of his countrymen – can be at once expressed and obscured.

If Holy Sonnet 18 associates true religion with the shadows of erotic experience, the latest, murkiest, and most moving of Donne's poetic evocations of devotional mutability, "The Hymne to Christ on the Author's Last Going into Germany," invokes a different kind of darkness, the darkness of death. This poem has rarely been read as a reflection of Donne's attitudes toward heterodoxy and conversion, but these interrelated subjects would have been much on his mind at the time of its composition. Donne wrote the poem shortly before traveling with the Earl of Doncaster's embassy to Bohemia in 1619, a diplomatic mission intended to mediate between Catholic and Protestant factions on the brink of the Thirty Years' War.[92] This would be a journey into the heart of confessional conflict; in a valedictory sermon preached at Lincoln's Inn shortly before his departure, Donne described Bohemia as a place "where ambition on one side, and a necessary defence from unjust persecution on the other side hath drawn many swords."[93] In the same sermon, Donne suggests that his imminent departure has brought him explicitly to consider ideas of separation and reunion, both physical and ideological. He takes as his text Ecclesiastes 12:1: "Remember now thy creator in the dayes of thy youth." The sermon in general is a powerful evocation of "memory," which he defines as a faculty that links all religions: "howsoever the understanding be beclouded, or the will perverted, yet both Jew and Christian, Papist and Protestant, Puritan and Protestant, are affected … this issue of that faculty of their memory is alike in them all." In an earlier version of this sermon, however, Donne goes on to describe memory not simply as a shared mode of piety, but as a shared means of conversion: "this remembring which we intend, is an inchoation, yea it is a great step into our conversion and regeneration, whereby we are new creatures."[94] This "conversion and regeneration" is both a progress in grace, and a choice of earthly churches; it requires "a consideration, a

---

[92] For an account of the Doncaster embassy, see Bald, *John Donne*, 340–65, and especially P. Sellin, *So Doth, So Is Religion: John Donne and Diplomatic Contexts in the Reformed Netherlands, 1619–1620* (Columbia: University of Missouri Press, 1988). Writing to the members of Lincoln's Inn, Doncaster apologizes for "an act so prejudiciall to your service, as to frustrate you of [Donne] for so long a time," citing "his Maj: commandement." BL Egerton MS 2593, fo. 21.

[93] Donne, *Sermons*, vol. II, 235–49, 236.   [94] *Ibid.*, vol. II, 379.

deliberation, a debatement that a religion, a forme of professing the gospell, be not taken and accepted blindly, or implicitely ... that the true religion be really professed, and corrupt religion be utterly abolished."[95]

Despite his statement that there is a single "true" religion, to be distinguished from the "corrupt," Donne ends his sermon on a note of reconciliation. He and his congregation in Lincoln's Inn will be reunited after his journey, just as all men, despite their local differences in judgment, will be united at the Last Judgment:

Christ Jesus remember us all in his Kingdome, to which, though we must sail through a sea, it is the sea of his blood, where no soul suffers shipwrack; though we must be blown with strange winds, with sighs and groans for our sins, yet it is the Spirit of God that blows all this wind, and shall blow away all contrary winds of diffidence or distrust in Gods mercy; where we shall be all Souldiers of one Army, the Lord of Hostes, and Children of one Quire, the God of Harmony and consent ... where there shall be no difference in affection, nor in mind, but we shall agree as fully and perfectly in our Allelujah and gloria in excelsis, as God the Father, Son, and Holy Ghost agreed in the *faciamus hominem* at first; where we shall end, and yet begin but then; where we shall have continuall rest, and yet never grow lazie; where we shall be stronger to resist, and yet have no enemy; where we shall live and never die, where we shall meet and never part.[96]

As Donne traveled to Germany, however, his old friend Sir Toby Matthew would put this inclusive vision of Christian community to the test. Donne and Doncaster met with the Catholic convert Matthew as their embassy passed through the Spanish Netherlands. Shortly afterward, Matthew sought a place in Doncaster's service, raising the question of Donne's attitude toward Catholics, and toward converts, in a particularly awkward context. Writing to Donne, Matthew entreated him to "cast me ... at the feete of that excellent Noble man my Lord Embassadour [Doncaster]."[97]

Lest this importunity fail, Matthew also wrote directly to Doncaster, protesting his loyalty, and begging "leave to putt my selfe upon the ingenuity and prudence of Doctour Dunne, whether ... I deserve to be any otherwise obnoxious, then for the exercise of my relligion."[98] We do not know exactly what intercession, if any, Donne made on Matthew's behalf. In a slightly belated letter to Matthew, however, Donne asserted that he had "never forsaken [Matthew's] honour and reputation," adding that

we are fallen into so slack and negligent times, that I have been sometime glad to hear, that some of my friends have differed from me in Religion. It is some degree of

---

[95] *Ibid.*, vol. II, 380.   [96] *Ibid.*, vol. II, 249.   [97] Feil, "Sir Tobie Matthew," 142.
[98] Letter, Matthew to Doncaster from Naumurs, July 27, 1619, BL Egerton MS 2592, fo. 237.

an union to be united in a serious meditation of God, and to make any Religion the rule of our actions.[99]

Once again, and in striking contrast to many of Matthew's other Protestant friends, Donne minimizes confessional differences and emphasizes similarities of spiritual attitude.[100] Although they stand on opposite sides of the Reformed divide, both men have refused to "take up" their religion without making sure of its truth, and both now take their faith equally seriously. Again, Donne interprets religious sincerity not according to the particular form of religious practice, but according to how deliberately and carefully a particular Christian has come to choose – again, to "take up" – that particular form. Once more, Donne implies that the best kind of Christian is not a Catholic or a Protestant, but a convert.

The particular phrasing of Donne's reassurance to Matthew, however, bears some emphasis. He is, he insists, always "readie to shadow and defend [Matthew] from others malice" in the matter of religion.[101] Donne uses a now-obsolete meaning of "shadow": to "screen, protect from attack … blame, or punishment, or from wrong."[102] But the word also, inevitably, carries the force of a different kind of shadowing, the shadowing of concealment. To be "shadowed" in this sense is to be protected not merely from harm, but more particularly from the prying beams of "too much light." Individual religious beliefs, Donne once more implies, must be "shadowed" in both senses. This kind of shadowing haunts the "Hymne," a poem that moves inexorably toward "an everlasting night." Because of this last line, recalling the *nox perpetua* of classical elegy, the poem is almost always taken as desperately pessimistic, a sick man's contemplation of imminent death and oblivion.[103] The poem's opening lines, however, recalling the language of his valedictory sermon, suggest another sphere of interest:

[99] "A Letter of much kindnesse from Doctor Donne, to Sir Toby Mathew, from Colleyn," in Donne (ed.), *Collection of Letters*, 337.
[100] Dudley Carleton's letters to Thomas Edmonds provide a typical reaction to Matthew's conversion. Carleton notes that Matthew "is now so peremptorily and superstitiously Popish that I give him for gon without recovery. And his labor is not little to carrie others with him." BL Stowe MS 169 fo. 158. About Matthew's imprisonment for recusancy, Carleton is unsympathetic: "I wished him better entertainment, but I can not say he deserved better, considering his manifestation of his falling away from owr church to all cumers, and therby bringing himself into a needeles truble." BL Stowe MS 169, fo. 84. Matthew's close friend Francis Bacon declared him "miserably abused," and implored him to "receive yourself back from these courses of perdition." Francis Bacon, Letter to Matthew (1607–8), in Bacon, *Works*, ed. J. Spedding, R. Ellis, and D. Heath, 14 vols. (London: Longmans, 1862–74), vol. XI, 11.
[101] Donne, *Letters*, 336.   [102] *OED*, "shadow (v.)" 3.a, b.
[103] Ramie Targoff points out the allusion to the classical notion of *nox perpetua* in his "Facing Death," in Guibbory (ed.), *Cambridge Companion*, 217–32, 220–1. For a survey of readings of the poem that

> In what torne ship soever I embarke,
> That ship shall be my embleme of thy Arke;
> What sea soever swallow mee, that flood
> Shall be to mee an embleme of thy bloode.   (1–4)

On a literal level, these lines refer to the perils Donne anticipates for his physical crossing into Europe. On an allegorical level, they indicate difficulties in spiritual life, moments when God disguises his face with "clouds of anger" (5). Read against the metaphors of voyaging Donne often uses to describe religious choice, however, they also suggest his sense of the similar potential significance of various methods of religious exploration. "What soever" the means of voyage, and "what soever" the sea traversed, the progress can be equally sanctifying to a spirit engaged in what Donne calls in his letter to Matthew "a serious meditation of God."

In the next stanza, Donne methodically describes the preparation for his voyage, and the voyage itself, with the language of renunciation.

> I sacrifice this Iland unto thee
> And all whom I lov'd there, and who lov'd mee;
> When I have put our seas twixt them and mee,
> Put thou thy sea betwixt my sinnes and thee.   (9–12)

The goal of the voyage seems here to be the unmitigated and unimpeded love of God. In the third and fourth stanzas, Donne urges Christ to "free / My soul" from other, lesser objects of affection (21–2). Addressing Christ in terms reminiscent of Holy Sonnet 2 ("As due by many titles"), Donne longs for an assertion of holy jealousy. He wishes Christ to limit his loves, imploring him to "seale then this bill of my Divorce to all / On whom those fainter beames of love did fall" (8–9, 22–3). He asks, here, for Christ's help in accomplishing a particular kind of conversion, with the love of God replacing a life of what he elsewhere dismisses as "dancing, Mistressing and compliment" ("To Mr. Tilman," 30). Walton describes this conversion in his *Life*, describing Donne's post-ordination efforts to remove himself "from the sight of his dearest friends … and all those vanities, those imaginary pleasures, that are dayly acted on that restless stage."[104] In its evocation of a dangerous and solitary pilgrimage away

---

stress a "death-obsession," see J. Johnson, *The Theology of John Donne* (Cambridge: D. S. Brewer, 1999), 107–8. Johnson reads the poem alongside a contemporary sermon to suggest that Donne in fact longs only for the "sacramental death" of repentance.

[104] Walton, *Life*, 41.

from friends and family, however, this "sacrifice" also recalls the literal voyages of converts like Alabaster, Matthew, Carier, and others, men who renounced their "Iland" and their closest connections in order to seek and then to practice "true religion."[105] In the poem's penultimate stanza, Donne describes the "the amorousness of an harmonious Soule" (18) as a force requiring limitation and re-direction. God is not indifferent, nor does he condone indifference: "O, if thou car'st not whom I love / Alas, thou lov'st not mee" (23–4). These lines refer to the limitation of love from worldly "Fame, Wit, Hopes" to God alone, but they also suggest the need for a singular choice among God's churches on earth.

The results of such a choice, however, must once again remain just outside the descriptive reach of the poem itself. If Donne's hymn describes the process of leave-taking with some precision, the goal of the voyage remains deliberately dark:

> Churches are best for Prayer, that have least light:
> To see God only, I goe out of sight:
> And to scape stormy dayes, I chuse an everlasting night.   (26–8)

This expressed desire to remain in "everlasting night" might suggest the speaker's longing for literal or sacramental annihilation. But it also reaffirms Donne's ongoing commitment to maintaining the obscurity of denominational choices. Sea and night, here, stand as ideal obstructions, protecting the converted speaker from public view. The hymn records not so much a wish for death as a wish for invisibility. To put the sea between himself and the "Iland" of England is to preclude the kind of intrusive regard which, in "the Calme," Donne called "the queasie paine / Of being belov'd, and loving" (40–1). It is to escape the kinds of unwanted solicitude that religious change could occasion among friends – Donne's own experiences with Matthew and Goodyer would have been ample evidence of this kind of difficulty. And it is to escape the "stormy dayes" of outright religious conflict. The image of the Christian as *homo viator* here becomes, more particularly, the image of a Christian resolutely sailing beyond the influence, observation, and judgment of others. At the end of this stanza, Donne compares this renunciation to "trees sap ...

---

[105] In his autobiography, Toby Matthew recalls his fear of "the temporal afflictions and vexations which I was likely to incur" upon his Catholic conversion, including "the most certain deprivation of whatsoever I might expect in future times; the blasting of my poor reputation ... the loss of my friends, of my liberty, and peradventure also of my country; yea, and perhaps (as the times were then set) an odious and ignominious death, when I should return to England." Matthew, *True Historical Relation*, 44–5.

seek[ing] the root below" in winter (13). In both cases, survival and growth requires a search, and this search requires at least a temporary disappearance. Discovering the truth, Donne suggests, means retreating from sight; seeking demands hiding.

The story of conversion, in its most familiar form, is a story of darkness and uncertainty yielding to what Augustine calls the *lux securitatis*, or the light of assurance. "I was blind," says the convert, "but now I see." Donne's various accounts of conversion insistently struggle to reverse this teleology in the realm of representation. Christian conversion, he suggests, follows channels which are open and visible, known by all, acceptable to Catholics and Protestants alike, and equally illuminated by God's grace. That visible, legible process, however, will lead men to a variety of convictions that they must describe obliquely, if at all. Preparing to depart for Germany, Donne sent a manuscript copy of *Biathanatos* to his friend Robert Ker, with the caution that the work concerned a "misinterpretable subject." He advises Ker to "publish it not, but yet burn it not; and between those, do what you will with it."[106] The scandalous topic of Donne's manuscript was, of course, the legitimacy of suicide. But the notion of a "misinterpretable subject," to be held in a region somewhere between speech and silence, also provides a way to think about Donne's understanding of conversion, and of its expression. Like so many contemporary writers, Catholic and Protestant, Donne insists on conversion as the source of individual spiritual authenticity, as "true religion" truly defined. But by enfolding that truth in the "middle nature" of verse, in the twilight of trope, Donne also reasserts his belief that the truth, once found, must remain hidden for each of us, and from all of us. In one of his last sermons, on the feast of his church's patron, St. Paul, Donne suggests that "there are words in the text that will reach to all the Story of S. *Pauls* Conversion, embrace all, involve and inwrap all."[107] "Embrace," "involve," "inwrap"; in their simultaneous evocations of inclusion, protection, and concealment, these words also describe Donne's poetry of conversion, poetry that finally shadows any Christian belief – not merely his own – from those who would "possesse or denominate" it.[108]

---

[106] Donne, *Letters*, 18–19.
[107] Donne, *Sermons*, II.205 (Sermon Preached at St. Paul's, the Sunday after the Conversion of S. Paul, 1624/5).
[108] Donne, *Pseudo-Martyr*, 12.

CHAPTER 3

Richard Crashaw and
the gender of conversion

In contrast to the studied obliquities of John Donne's poetry, Richard Crashaw's devotional hymns have generally been considered among the least reticent poems in the English language. Crashaw's combination of a highly emotional tone, a tendency to overflow the metaphoric measure, and a preoccupation with the experiences of female saints and martyrs has led centuries of critics to repeat two linked condemnations: that Crashaw has "bad taste" in both religion and aesthetics, and that his imagination is essentially "feminine." This latter adjective has lately, and happily, begun to shed some of its pejorative critical connotations in Crashaw criticism.[1] What persists, however, is a scholarly tendency to explain Crashaw's distinctly feminine preoccupations with reference to a particular devotional milieu. Maureen Sabine and Anthony Low, among others, see in his work a straightforward expression of Catholic devotional traditions, borrowing equally from medieval mysticism and from the *humanisme dévot* popular at the court of Charles I's Catholic queen, Henrietta Maria.[2] More recently, Thomas Healy and Paul Parrish have attributed Crashaw's interest in

---

[1] J. Mueller, "Women among the Metaphysicals: A Case, Mostly, of Being Donne For," *MP* 87 (1989), 142–58, 144. For a survey of the misogynist critical disparagement of Crashaw, see J. M. and L. Roberts, "Crashavian Criticism. A Brief Interpretive History," in J. R. Roberts (ed.), *New Perspectives on the Life and Art of Richard Crashaw* (Columbia: University of Missouri Press, 1990), 1–29; A. Warren, "The Reputation of Crashaw in the Seventeenth and Eighteenth Centuries," *Studies in Philology* 31 (1934), 385–407; and Shell, *Catholicism, Controversy*, 93–104. Crashaw's feminine sensibility becomes a source of value in M. Sabine, *Feminine Engendered Faith: The Poetry of John Donne and Richard Crashaw* (Basingstoke: Macmillan, 1992). See also P. Parrish, "The Feminizing of Power: Crashaw's Life and Art," in C. Summers and T.-L. Pebworth (eds.), *The Muse's Common Weale: Poetry and Politics in the Seventeenth Century* (Columbia: University of Missouri Press, 1988), 148–62, and Parrish, "O Sweet Contest: Gender and Value in 'The Weeper,'" in Roberts (ed.), *Life and Art of Richard Crashaw*, 127–39.

[2] Sabine argues that Catholic mariolatry provided Crashaw with a sense of psychological wholeness akin to the child's "undifferentiated oneness" with the mother (*Feminine Engendered Faith*, 113), while Anthony Low argues that Crashaw found in Catholicism a feminized spirituality that "conquers through weakness, suffering, passivity and submission." Low, *The Reinvention of Love: Poetry, Politics, and Culture from Sidney to Milton* (Cambridge University Press, 1993), 125.

women's religious experience to his early familiarity with the high-church Protestantism of Mary Collet's "Arminian nunnery" at Little Gidding.[3] Such contextualizing accounts, however, can obscure an important function of feminine spiritual experience for Crashaw's poetry: such experience, as he represents it, can explicitly challenge or disrupt confessional boundaries. Indeed, Crashaw's "feminine" poetics invokes a specific discourse of conversion that, by the time of his poetry's composition in the 1630s, had become increasingly centered on Christian women. Like many of his contemporaries, both Catholic and Protestant, Crashaw represents female religiosity as affective and mutable, and particularly likely to shift from one confessional affiliation to another on the basis of emotional appeals. Rejecting the strenuous efforts made by other religious writers to contain or to manage that mutability, however, Crashaw both expands upon its most troubling implications and reappropriates it for his own linked *personae* as poet and as convert.

FEMININE CONVERSION AND MASCULINE ANXIETY IN EARLY STUART ENGLAND

In 1652/3, an anonymous Protestant controversialist published a reply to John Austin's *Christian Moderator*, a Catholic proselytizing text that ended by listing recent English converts to the Church of Rome.[4] This satiric reply, entitled *Legenda Lignea*, consists of a corresponding series of short anti-hagiographies, maligning the character of such new Catholics.[5] Among these is a description of Richard Crashaw:

[3] T. Healy suggests that "there is little in the poetry to demonstrate that it was not written by one who lived and died a high Anglican." Healy, *Richard Crashaw* (Leiden: Brill, 1986), 4. Parrish describes the femininity of Crashaw's Anglican milieu in "Richard Crashaw, Mary Collet, and the 'Arminian Nunnery' of Little Gidding," in C. Summers and T.-L. Pebworth (eds.), *Representing Women in Renaissance England* (Columbia: University of Missouri Press, 1997), 187–200. See also A. Maycock, *Chronicles of Little Gidding* (London: SPCK, 1954), and the documents included in E. C. Sharland (ed.), *The Story Books of Little Gidding* (1899), and B. Blackstone (ed.), *The Ferrar Papers* (Cambridge University Press, 1938), 231–312. Even Sabine, who mainly focuses on Counter-Reformation influences, mentions several Anglican writings centering on feminine worship, such as John Cosin's *Private Devotions* (1627) and Anthony Stafford's *Femall Glory* (1635). Sabine, *Feminine Engendered Faith*, 129. See also A. Warren, *Richard Crashaw: A Study in Baroque Sensibility* (Baton Rouge: University of Louisiana Press, 1939), 9–10.

[4] Austin's text, published in several parts under the pseudonym "William Birchley," consists mainly of a defense of Catholic doctrine; the list of recent converts concludes the revised edition of the second part, *The Christian Moderator: The Second Part, or Persecution for Religion Condemned ... whereto there are New Additions since the Octavo was Printed* (1652–3).

[5] The book's full title is *Legenda Lignea: with an Answer to Mr. Birchley's Moderator, Pleading for a Toleration of Popery. And a Character of some Hopefull Saints Revolted to the Church of Rome* (1653[2]). The title, literally "The Wooden Legend," satirically revises that of Jacob de Voragine's thirteenth-

This peevish sillie Seeker glided away from his Principles in a Poetical vein of fancy and impertinent curiosity, and finding that Verses ... much pleas'd some female wits, Crawshaw crept by degrees into favour and acquaintance with some Court-Ladies ... he got first the estimation of an innocent, harmless Convert, and, a purse being made by some deluded vain-glorious Ladies and their friends, the Poet was dispatch'd in a Pilgrimage to Rome.[6]

The author of this account denigrates both Crashaw's Catholic turn and his "verses" by associating them with the "female wits" and "vain-glorious ladies" at Henrietta Maria's court. His linking of Crashaw with women, delusion, and conversion, however, is more than mere misogyny, or an early version of the critical claim that Crashaw's Catholicism somehow unmanned him. The author's account of Crashaw's consorting with noble-women in fact makes a particular, anxious allusion to a particular early modern phenomenon: the increasing number of English women convert- ing from Protestantism to Catholicism in and around the early Stuart courts.

This trend, which reached its height during the reign of Charles I and Henrietta Maria, had begun even before the accession of James I. In 1600, while still in Scotland, James's wife Anna of Denmark converted from Lutheranism to Catholicism with the help of a Scottish Jesuit.[7] Anna's semi-secret religious turn, and the favor she showed to Catholic priests, courtiers, and noblewomen, contributed to a small wave of Catholic con-versions among the queen's coterie in Edinburgh and London. This trend only increased in intensity with the accession of Anna's son Charles I, who had been at least partially educated by Catholics according to the wishes of his mother, and who had nearly married a Spanish Catholic princess before marrying the French Catholic Henrietta Maria.[8] In contrast to her mother-in-law, who had dissembled her Catholic practices when politically neces-sary or expedient, Queen Henrietta Maria established London chapels where Capuchin priests openly celebrated elaborate Catholic masses before English recusants and continental visitors.[9] Her court not only offered a haven for native and foreign Catholics, but also served as the nexus for

century hagiography, the *Legenda Aurea* (*The Golden Legend*). The anti-Catholic parody extends to the physical presentation of the text: each convert's name appears in red-letter type, as in Catholic books of saints' lives.

[6] *Legenda Lignea*, 169–70.

[7] See T. McCoog and P. Davidson, "Father Robert's Convert," *TLS* (Nov. 24, 2000), 16–17; Barroll's biography of Anna reserves judgment about her religious identity, but acknowledges that rumors of her conversion circulated widely in the early years of the Stuart monarchy in England. *Anna of Denmark*, 166. See also M. Murray, "Performing Devotion in *The Masque of Blacknesse*," *SEL* 47.2 (Spring 2007), 427–49.

[8] Albion, *Charles I and the Court of Rome*, 195–215.   [9] Hibbard, *Charles I and the Popish Plot*, 51–5.

Catholic missionary efforts in England.[10] Under the direction of Catholic missionary directors George Con and Gregorio Panzani, the conversions of English noblewomen to the Roman church increased in frequency and in publicity, reaching an apotheosis in the late 1630s, particularly the "annus mirabilis" of 1638 when a midnight mass in the queen's chapel functioned as a kind of debutante ball for recent lady converts such as the Countess of Newport.[11]

This ever-increasing number of converting ladies posed a complex, sexualized threat to the Protestant establishment in England by the mid-seventeenth century. Not only did such conversions indicate a separate sphere of feminine religious power, but also, perhaps more alarmingly, they seemed to presage the eventual conversions of male associates and relatives, particularly those already worshiping along high-church lines. In his book of *Worthies*, Thomas Fuller recounts a story of a female convert who was a close friend of Archbishop Laud. The lady "was asked by Laud, in a rather pained tone, 'Why?' The lady retorted, 'My lord, it was because I ever hated a crowd.' As Laud looked puzzled, she explained, 'I perceived that your Lordship and many others are making for Rome as fast as you can, and therefore to prevent a press, I went before you.'"[12] If this story is apocryphal, it nevertheless suggests a pervasive worry about the implications of female conversions by the eve of civil war. In the early decades of the seventeenth century, Queen Anna's uncertain religious affiliation emphasized the inscrutability of Jacobean ecclesiastical policy. In the uxorious, ceremonial culture of Caroline England, the fear was more acute and more straightforward: the queen and her ladies were seen as spearheading a kind of feminized Catholic mission, one which would lead the court steadily and inexorably toward Rome.[13]

---

[10] See E. Dubois, "Conversions à la cour de la reine Henriette-Marie," in *La Conversion au xxiième Siècle: Actes du XXe Colloque de Marseille* (Marseille: CMR, 1983), 201–8. For other accounts of conversion at the Caroline court more generally, see M. Questier (ed.), *Newsletters from the Caroline Court 1631–8: Catholicism and the Politics of the Personal Rule* (Cambridge University Press, 2005).

[11] This mass was held five days after Laud's proclamation condemning attendance at Catholic services. Albion, *Charles I and the Court of Rome*, 226; Hibbard, *Charles I and the Popish Plot*, 57, 227. Hibbard discusses the work of Con and Panzani in *Charles I and the Popish Plot*, 71–5 and *passim*. The complementary English missionary work of the Benedictine Leander Jones has been detailed by Guilday, *The English Catholic Refugees*, 245–8. For some representative, if hagiographical, accounts of English converting ladies in the early Stuart period, see A. Hamilton (ed.), *The Chronicle of the English Augustinian Canonesses Regular of the Lateran, at St. Monica's in Louvain*, vol. I *(1548–1625)* and, especially, vol. II *(1625–1644)* (London: Sands, 1904–6).

[12] Fuller, *Worthies of England* (1662), vol. XI, 217.

[13] The publication of letters between Charles and his queen as *The King's Cabinet Opened* (1645) provided anti-monarchists and anti-Romanists with seemingly incontrovertible evidence of

English Catholic women did in fact exercise significant spiritual influence over their domestic spheres. Frances Dolan, John Bossy, and John Aveling have detailed numerous instances of recently converted Catholic Englishwomen actively and sometimes successfully encouraging their husbands, sons, fathers, and brothers to take up their newfound faith.[14] In letters to the Pope and his secretaries, both Anna and Henrietta claimed to be working to return the crown of England to the Roman Catholic Church.[15] Under the direction of agents such as Con and Panzani, English noblewomen such as Olivia Porter succeeded in converting both female and male relatives to the Catholic faith.[16] Fears that the court favorite the Duke of Buckingham might convert abounded after his sister and mother did so – since, as the author of *Legenda Lignea* notes, "there are little hopes of any quiet, if a deaf ear be turn'd to the female importunate motions."[17] When this same author links Crashaw the convert with the world of "Court-Ladies," then, he is reminding his readers of that insidious and powerful feminine "affection" which had reputedly drawn others such as Toby Matthew and Endymion Porter away from the established religion of England. Henrietta's court in exile, Austin Warren reminds us, included her "chief favorites … such as Walter Montague, Thomas Vane, Hugh

---

Henrietta Maria's power over her husband, in both political and religious spheres. Hibbard discusses these and other allegations of the queen's "Jezebelesque" influence on Charles. *Charles I and the Popish Plot*, 108–9, 221–5. For fears of Caroline and Laudian crypto-Catholicism in the 1630s, see also M. Smuts, *Court Culture and the Origins of a Royalist Tradition in England* (Philadelphia: University of Pennsylvania Press, 1988), 218–30.

[14] P. Crawford describes the autonomy of feminine devotion, particularly the persistence of Catholicism among women, in *Women and Religion in England 1500–1720* (London: Routledge, 1993), 53–73. See also A. Marotti, "Alienating Catholics in Early Modern England: Recusant Women, Jesuits, and Ideological Fantasies," in Marotti (ed.), *Catholicism and Anti-Catholicism*, 2–17. In a chapter suggestively entitled "Searching the Bed," Dolan offers evidence of the pervasive early modern fear that Catholic women would convert their husbands to Catholicism in the privacy of the domestic sphere. *Whores of Babylon*, 45–72. The book as a whole surveys the relationship of female sexuality and religious dissidence in the English Renaissance.

[15] So, for instance, Henrietta Maria assured Pope Urban VII that "I will not choose any but Catholics to nurse or educate [my] children," M. Green (ed.), *Letters of Queen Henrietta Maria* (1857), 8.

[16] Albion, *Charles I and the Court of Rome*, 208–14. See William Prynne, *Rome's Master Peece* (1644), 29: "Mr. Porter, of the King's Bedchamber, most addicted to the Popish Religion, is a bitter enemy of the king. He reveals all his greatest secrets to the Pope's legate: although he rarely meets with him, yet his wife meets him so much the oftener, who, being informed by her husband, conveys secrets to the legate." H. Trevor-Roper, *Archbishop Laud* (London: Macmillan, 1940), 332–3. An example of Olivia Porter's workings among her female friends can be found in a letter written by Con in October 1637: "The Marchioness of Hamilton, who, being brought up in Puritanism, has shown great violence against the Catholic Religion until some months ago … Mrs. Porter informs herself daily of what should be said to her, furnishing her with books and discourses, Catholic manuscripts, but her father, who is a Puritan Ass, being afraid, makes the pseudo-Bishop of Carlisle come to her." BL Additional MS 15390, qtd. in D. Townshend, *The Life and Letters of Endymion Porter* (1897), 165.

[17] *Legenda Lignea*, 233.

Cressy, Thomas Carre, and Stephen Goffe – all, save one, Catholic converts."[18]

In Protestant accounts of female conversions in this period, then, the commonplace references to the "seduction" of women by rapacious Jesuits can be read as efforts to deny a more frightening possibility: that Catholic women were succeeding in their efforts to lead men away from Protestant orthodoxy. Rather than acknowledge this possibility, Protestant authors insisted instead on the passivity of the lady convert, figuring conversion as a consequence of feminine vulnerability, a vulnerability which was typically sexualized. Reporting the Catholic turn of Lady Katherine Howard, for instance, one newspaper account asserts that "'tis love that hath bin the principall agent in her conversion, for, unknown to her father, the Earl of Suffolk, she is, or wil be, maryed to the Lord D'Aubigny … in France where he hath bin bred a Papist."[19] Instead of representing Lady Howard's conversion as an act of denominational choice, the author of this account explains it as a consequence of romance. Attributing her conversion to "love," the author reassures us that a man – even if Catholic – nevertheless continues to dictate the theological terms. Dudley Carleton had made a similar point earlier and more salaciously in a letter to Thomas Edmonds. Referring to the Catholic claim to maintain a more "visible church," Carleton jokes, "What, betwixt the visible church and the *sensible steeple*, our women even to the highest fall that way very fast" – his double entendre insinuating that women were being persuaded to Catholicism by sex rather than theology.[20]

Reimagining the Catholic conversions of women as the result of a sexualized "fall" enabled Protestant men to maintain the fantasy of a simple countermeasure: protecting women from eroticized Catholic temptation. After the Earl of Newport's wife converted to Catholicism in 1637, he did not target the likely proselytizers, the Duchess of Buckingham and Olivia Porter (Lady Newport's younger sister).[21] Instead, Newport accused Toby Matthew and Walter Montague of "having conspired with [Con] to seduce his wife," persuading Laud to urge the Privy Council to banish the triumvirate of Catholic "seducers."[22] Placed on trial by Parliament in 1644,

[18] Warren, *Richard Crashaw*, 52.
[19] Quoted in J. H. Aveling, *The Handle and the Axe: The Catholic Recusants in England from Reformation to Emancipation* (London: Blond and Briggs, 1976), 128.
[20] BL Stowe MS 169, fo. 158. Carleton to Edmonds, October 14, 1607.
[21] "One evening, after a play, [Lady Newport] got into a coach with the Duchess of Buckingham and Mrs. Porter, and drove off in secret to the house of a priest, and was there received into the Church of Rome." Townshend, *Life and Letters*, 166.
[22] Trevor-Roper, *Laud*, 333.

Archbishop Laud continually defends his orthodoxy in the language of chivalry, describing his gallant rescue of ladies from the clutches of wrong religion.[23] "Two daughters of Sir Rich. Lechford in Surrey," he recalls, "were sent to sea to be carried to a Nunnery. I heard of it, and caused them to be brought back, before they were got out of the Thames. I settled their consciences, and both of them sent me great thanks."[24] We might consider the too-much-protesting quality of this account; Laud was, in fact, defending his own Protestant identity against those who had accused him of crypto-popery.[25] But the rhetoric, here, is telling: Laud reasserts his own firm allegiance to the Church of England by exploiting the familiar idea of feminine devotional helplessness. In this account, the Lechford daughters become damsels in doctrinal distress, and Laud plays the valiant knight who thwarts their capture and "settles" their errant minds.

Laud was not the only Protestant man to make such public gestures of denominational heroics, however. An increasingly common genre of theological writing addressed other wavering women – often specified as relatives or patronesses of the male author – explicitly claiming to "protect" them from the seductive allure of Catholicism. This genre of controversial writing, while properly a sub-genre of the texts of resolution discussed above in relation to Donne, differs from these general guides in the foregrounding of their addressees' feminine frailty, and the particular kinds of anti-intellectual enticements to which they were supposedly susceptible. In *The Advise of a Sonne, now professing the Religion established in the present Church of England, to his deare Mother, yet a Roman Catholike* (1616), for instance, the Protestant convert Sir Anthony Hungerford warns his mother against those priests who would have her "beleeve in grosse, as doth their Church, without being able to render a reason of any article of the religion hee professeth."[26] "I malice not their persons," he continues, but

I cannot but condemne their craft, and pittie such as are inchaunted by them. The truth is they are cruell Iaylours, and mure up your understanding in these things as

---

[23] For Laud's trial, see Trevor-Roper, *Laud*, 422–4.   [24] Laud, *Autobiography*, 349.

[25] See, for instance, the anonymous *Letter Written by a Learned and Reverent Divine to William Laud, now Lord Bishop of Canterbury: Concerning his Inclination to Popery, perswading him not to halt betweene two opinions, but to be stedfast to the Protestant Religion* (London, 1643).

[26] [Anthony Hungerford], *Advise of a Sonne, now professing the religion established in the present Church of England, to his deare mother, yet a Roman Catholike* (Oxford, 1616), 10. A second edition of Hungerford's text, printed in 1639, also included *A memorial of a Father to his deare children, containing an acknowledgment of God his great mercy, in bringing him to the profession of the true religion, at this present established in the Church of England*. In both, Protestantism is associated explicitly with the masculine domain of father and son.

their close prisoner, well knowing, that if once they give you but libertie to heare freely what might be said against them, they are sure to loose you [*sic*].[27]

Hungerford presents Catholic priests as agents of obfuscation and "inchauntment," keeping his mother's "understanding" in darkness; the Protestant position, by contrast, encourages rational choice. His numerous quotations from scripture and patristic writers underscore his claim that Protestantism is not only a more plausible doctrine, but also encourages sober theological investigation as the basis for conversion.

Around the same time, the Protestant courtier and diplomat Sir Balthasar Gerbier composed a letter to his three daughters, Elizabeth, Suzanne, and Marie, who had recently left England for a Parisian convent.[28] The letter reads like that of a father whose daughters have eloped against his will; one thinks of Shakespeare's Brabantio or Father Capulet when Gerbier accuses his wayward daughters of disobedience, reminding them that "I have used my best Indeavours to instruckt you, and to keep you (as much as I could) frome being seduced by those whoe profess the Roman faith."[29] Here again, an author distinguishes the honorable Protestant "instruction" of women from sinister Catholic "seduction." Designating his own text as an example of the former, Gerbier appeals again and again to reason, asking for an opportunity to use it to convince his daughters:

My children, lett the Eares of your Souls incline to this my Sommons: Put yourself in a neuter place for a Conference ... [with] those whom I beleeve to be in the right way, so that you may have just cause to argue that you have don your duty toward God, your Parents, and yourself.[30]

Such a conference, Gerbier imagines, would inevitably convince his daughters of the truth of Protestantism, which he – like Hungerford – associates with sober mental effort. Gerbier's didactic pose extends into his dedicatory epistle to "the most Excellent and Serious Lady the Countess of Claire." Here, Gerbier declares that he will "never suffer those of your sexe to travell with ears fit for Charmers (Charme they never so wisely), without providing

---

[27] [Hungerford], *Advise of a Sonne*, 37.

[28] BL Harleian MS 3384: "Sir Balthasar Gerbier Knight His last Admonitions to his Daughters, His answears to theire letters, Theire refusall of a Conference, after they had accepted the Same, His more particullar declaration, and Sommons, Theire answeare on the said Sommons, His reply thereon, and the copie of his prayer to God for his said Daughters Elizabeth-Debora and Susanne retired in the English Nunnery at Paris," December 24, 1646. A much-shortened version of this text (not including the daughters' replies) was published as *A Letter from Sir Balthazar Gerbier, Knight, to his Three Daughters Inclosed in a Nunnery at Paris* (Paris, 1646). For Gerbier's career at court, see H. R. Williamson, *Four Stuart Portraits* (London: Evans Brothers, 1949).

[29] BL Harleian MS 3384, fos. 9v–10.   [30] *Ibid.*, fos. 5r–v.

a meanes to stop them."[31] He proposes himself as a champion of enlightened choice, eager to "provide a means" to protect his addressees from the subtle "charms" of predatory Catholics.

The emotional fervor and sensual vividness of much Catholic devotional literature directed specifically to women would seem to bolster the claims of such Protestant detractors. The *humanisme dévot* favored by Henrietta Maria emphasized the role of the affections in the development of holiness.[32] St. Francis de Sales's influential *Introduction to a Devout Life* is written as an address to the female figure of "Philothea," described as "a soul loving, or in love with God."[33] In his *Theologie Naturelle*, the French Capuchin Yves de Paris insists on "the way of love as the most direct means to attain to the goal of life. Not by the reasonings of the brain, but by the reasons known only to the heart, do we get any intimate knowledge of God and the spiritual life."[34] A number of prayerbooks explicitly described feminine spirituality as a matter of sensibility rather than intellect, aesthetic delight rather than rational deliberation. In the preface to his *Partheneia Sacra*, for example, Henry Hawkins admits to his female readers that he wrote his garden of flowery verses "Considering ... how much thou art taken and delighted ... with change and variety in all things."[35] Laud reports in his diary that "The Duchess of Buckingham ... shewed me a form of devotions, which another woman, unknown to me, had put into her hands. I read it. All was mean in it; nothing extraordinary; *unless that it was more like poetry.*"[36]

In contrast to the emotive rhetoric of such devotional handbooks, however, contemporary Catholic treatments of women's conversions, be they hagiographical or polemical, generally avoid the kinds of emotional appeal

---

[31] *Ibid.*, fo. 2v.

[32] For the highly affective Catholicism of the queen's court, see E. Veevers, *Images of Love and Religion: Queen Henrietta Maria and Court Entertainments* (Cambridge University Press, 1989). For a survey of major figures in the seventeenth-century "Ecole Française" influential in court circles, see H. Graef, *Mary: A History of Doctrine and Devotion*, 2 vols. (New York: Sheed and Ward, 1965), vol. II, 31–43.

[33] This work was originally published in France as a collection of de Sales's letters to Frenchwomen. It proved popular among English recusants, particularly in the circles around Henrietta Maria, and eventually was banned by the Parliamentarians, with the consent of Laud, in 1637. See Laud, *Autobiography*, 219–20. For an overview of Salesian spirituality, see introduction to Francis de Sales and Jane de Chantal, *Letters of Spiritual Direction*, ed. H. Nouwen, trans. P. M. Thibert (New York: Paulist Press, 1988), 18–33.

[34] Quoted in C. Cuthbert, *The Capuchins* (London: Sheed and Ward, 1928), 414–16.

[35] Hawkins, *Partheneia Sacra* (1633), A2v.

[36] Laud, *Autobiography*, 19–20. Compare Gertrude More's praise of the "plain, simple, easy and sweet" spiritual instructions of Augustine Baker: *The Holy Practises of a Devine Lover, or the Sainctly Ideot's Devotions* (Paris, 1657), reprinted in B. Weld-Blundell (ed.), *The Inner Life and Writings of Dame Gertrude More* (London: Washbourne, 1910–11).

that Protestants could discredit as affective or seductive. In his biography of the Catholic convert Queen Christina of Sweden, for instance, Galeazzo Gualdo Priorato assures the reader that Christina's religious doubts led her to apply her precocious mind to a careful survey of scripture, exegesis, and church history. "With these speculations, and the guide of the holy Fathers, exactly perpended by her; she saw a great light before her eyes … so among these new lights she walking in the best, and readiest paths, began to examine particularly the substance and foundations of the truest religion."[37] Offering guidance to a woman in the throes of denominational decision-making, Sir Kenelm Digby – a Catholic convert himself – proposes a similar technique.[38] His 1638 *Conference with a Lady about Choice of Religion*, contrary to allegations that "Sir Kenelm Digby is busy in seducing the King's subjects … from the Church of England," focuses on the head rather than the heart.[39] Digby addresses this treatise explicitly to his feminine reader's "great understanding … strong reasoning soul … [and] prudentiall judgement."[40] We approach God, he writes, "not by corporeall steppes and progressions, but by intellectuall actions: the highest of which, are mentall prayer and contemplation, in which exercises a man shall advance the more, by how much he is the more sequestered from the thought and care of any worldly affayres, and hath his passions quieted within him, and is abstracted from communication with materiall objects, and is untied from humane interests."[41] The superiority of Catholic doctrine, Digby informs his female reader, lies precisely in its capacity to suppress human emotional mutability and encourage the transcendence of worldly sensual pleasure. In sharp contrast to Hawkins's praise of "delightful" devotional variety, Digby notes that the soul successfully converted to Catholicism is "no longer

---

[37] Gualdo Priorato, Galeazzo, *The History of the Sacred and Royal Majesty of Christina Alessandra, Queen of Swedland. With the Reasons of her late Conversion to the Roman Catholique Religion* (1658), 23–4. This English translation was dedicated to Mary (Villiers) Stuart, Duchess of Richmond and Lennox, the sister of the first Duke of Buckingham.

[38] For Digby's conversion, see Hibbard, *Charles I and the Popish Plot*, 52–4. More detailed discussion of the grounds of Sir Kenelm's religious beliefs can be found in the correspondence he maintained with his brother, published as *Letters Between the Ld George Digby, and Sr Kenelm Digby Kt Concerning Religion* (1651). In a speech to Parliament, Digby confesses his recusancy, asserting that he was nonetheless "never offensive to the lawes of the kingdome, nor troblesom to any private person." BL Additional MS 41846.

[39] The allegation was made in the mid-1630s by the English ambassador at Paris, quoted by Hibbard, *Charles I and the Popish Plot*, 53. E. W. Bligh has plausibly identified the recipient of Digby's "very dull little book" as Frances Howard, Lady Purbeck, former sister-in-law of the Duke of Buckingham and eventual convert to Catholicism. *Sir Kenelm Digby and his Venetia* (London: Sampson Low, 1932), 198–9.

[40] Kenelm Digby, *A Conference with a Lady about Choice of Religion* (1638), 4–5.   [41] *Ibid.*, 89.

subject to any new impression, mutation, or change whatsoever."[42] Like many Protestant texts of counsel, then, Digby's encouragement of Catholic conversion elevates intellect over emotion as the appropriate basis for women's religious choice.

Whether written from a Catholic or Protestant perspective, early modern treatments of female conversion collectively demonstrate a number of linked dichotomies. First, and most basically, they presume a fundamental distinction between the Catholic and Reformed churches, creating a pair of options from which the wavering woman must ultimately and conclusively choose. Second, they posit a clear opposition between intellect and affect as a basis for that choice, praising the former and disparaging the latter. In "right" decision-making, the male guide encourages the woman to higher intellectual inquiry, while in "wrong" decision-making, the male seducer charms the woman with emotional appeals, blinding her reason. Conversion, then, maps onto a gendered understanding of devotional agency, in which women are naturally passive and men are active; women can be either the recipients of instruction or the objects of seduction, while men must initiate and direct both processes. Read with these presuppositions in mind, Crashaw's poems "To Mrs M. R., Councel Concerning her Choise" and "Epistle to the Countess of Denbigh" can be understood as unmistakable contributions to this contemporary genre of advice for converting ladies. And yet, as we will see, Crashaw invokes the genre's most fundamental premises, its dichotomies and distinctions, precisely in order to confound them.

SEDUCTION AND SEXUAL DIFFERENCE IN CRASHAW'S POEMS OF COUNSEL

The verse epistle entitled "To [Mrs. M. R.], Councel Concerning her Choise" first appeared in the second edition of Crashaw's *Steps to the Temple*.[43] The identity of his particular addressee remains unknown, but the titular word "choise" immediately identifies the poem as part of the literature of counsel for wavering ladies. Evidently, Mrs. M. R. faced a religious decision, and Crashaw adopts the pose, familiar from contemporary theological discourse, of the sage advisor who will guide her in making it. Although the poem does not immediately reveal the confessional

---

[42] *Ibid.*, 23.
[43] The poem was originally entitled, "To the Same Party Counsel Concerning her Choise," and followed the poem entitled "Ode on a Prayer-book sent to Mrs. M. R."

allegiance of its speaker, the opening lines suggest that he will employ an argumentative strategy familiar from both Catholic and Protestant texts.[44] Urging Mrs. M. R. to ignore those "suters that beseige your Maiden brest," Crashaw suggests that she has "seen all ready, in this lower sphear / Of froth and bubbles, what to look for here" (8–9). In fact, the "lower sphear," and the unscrupulous seducers in it, can offer the searching soul nothing

> But painted shapes,
> Peacocks and Apes,
> Illustrious flyes,
> Guilded dunghills, glorious LYES,
> Goodly surmises
> And deep disguises,
> Oathes of water, words of wind[.]   (11–17)

This denunciation of insincere devotional seduction thus seems entirely in line with the recommendations of sober choice made by Gerbier, Digby, and others. Warning Mrs. M. R. against such spurious charms, Crashaw's speaker seems to be preparing to echo the monitory messages of the texts discussed above, urging his addressee to seek "truth" and ignore the superficial glamour of those who would attempt to woo her to the wrong side. Conversion to right religion, the poem suggests, is properly aversion from the baser influences of human affection (8). Both Catholic and Protestant controversialists, we can imagine, would commend the anti-emotional rigor of such a claim.

A problem with this reading, however, is immediately obvious: after disparaging those pseudo-amorous "peacocks" who seek the lady's attention in the sublunary world, the poem does not offer any alternative to seduction itself. This poem's speaker in fact eschews the dispassionate tone *de rigueur* in most contemporary texts of counsel, and instead identifies himself from the beginning as "Amongst the rest / Of suters" who wish to gain the lady's love (2–3). The poem, in fact, goes beyond explicitly endorsing the rhetoric of seduction, and extends it into a kind of sexual procuring: the speaker confesses his desire to seduce the lady "not for myself alas, but for my dearer LORD" (7). With this gambit, Crashaw effectively makes the choice confronting Mrs. M. R. a choice *among* seductions. The lady ought to reject the inferior loves proffered by her other suitors, Crashaw argues, not on the basis of an abstracted Digbian "prudential judgment," but rather because

---

[44] Since the poem did not appear in the 1646 edition, it is likely that it was among those poems added by Crashaw after his conversion to Catholicism. See Crashaw, *Complete Poetry*, xxi. Nevertheless, the poem does not contain any unequivocal references to Catholic doctrine.

there is "a braver love, / Which from above / Calls [her] up higher" (20–2). His poem thus expressly reasserts that very erotic, seductive aspect of conversion which other contemporary controversialists – Catholic and Protestant alike – were virtually unanimous in disclaiming. Indeed, Crashaw represents even divine love as a matter of "stratagem." Apparently, "[t]he Mighty lover / Of soules" is not above some rather underhanded tactics. For instance,

> It was his heavnly art
> Kindly to crosse you
> In your mistaken love,
> That, at the next remove
> Thence he might tosse you
> And strike your troubled heart
> Home to himself; to hide it in his brest,
> The bright ambrosiall nest,
> Of love, of life, and everlasting rest. (45–53)

Crashaw removes the stigma of eroticized conversion by making the seduction of ladies the prerogative of God himself, who busily "crosses" and "tosses" them toward an eventual rest in the right religion.

The fact that Crashaw associates heavenly and erotic love, of course, does not make him particularly unusual among English devotional poets; Herbert frequently envisions his lord as an idealized "Spouse," while, more outrageously, the speaker of Donne's Holy Sonnet 14 had urged his God to "ravish" him into faith. Sexualized representations of devotion occur throughout Catholic and Protestant mystical writings, evident even in Crashaw's own "Ode on a Prayer-book" where he suggests that the same Mrs. M. R. consent "To have her GOD become her LOVER."[45] This poem of counsel differs from conventional invocations of the spiritual marriage *topos*, however, in two key ways. First, God is here not just a spouse, or even a "lover," but specifically an expert seducer. Second, the woman's affective response is not a passive, mystical submission, but rather a precondition for her active choice. Even as it praises God's seductive prowess above that of human "suters," Crashaw's poem preserves a space for the woman's erotic deliberations; her "wary love" will ultimately determine her *choice* of a religious position (34). This choice, moreover, is not merely a turn to holy love as opposed to worldly love. While God may be the ultimate seducer,

---

[45] A. F. Allison has discussed this poem as evidence of Crashaw's debt to de Sales, whose *Traité de l'Amour de Dieu* (1616) was translated in 1630 by Crashaw's friend and editor Thomas Car. "Crashaw and St. François de Sales," *Review of English Studies* 96 (1948), 295–302, 295. See also Cousins, *Catholic Religious Poets*, 140–2.

the lady no longer has the option of choosing Him as "lover," but instead must select her "roome / Among his fair sonnes of fire" (24–5). Even as Crashaw continues to avoid specifying the denominational direction of the lady's "choice," the overtones of filial marriage-planning in these lines reinforce the implication that Mrs. M. R. must, in fact, choose among God's sanctified representatives, among "sonnes of fire" rather than the Father himself. She must, in short, make a choice among churches.

By presenting this selection of spouses/churches as both God's doing and the lady's, by presenting both divine and human as agents in the eroticized process of confessional choice, the "Letter to Mrs. M. R." shows Crashaw beginning to express his particular understanding of the experience of conversion. Like being seduced, changing churches is here a paradoxically simultaneous act of effort and acquiescence, of willing and yielding. Proposing this as both erotically and spiritually desirable, the Epistle to Mrs. M. R. thus operates on two levels. First, it rehearses – and rehabilitates – the representation of feminine religious change as seduction encountered so often in texts of counsel. Second, it elaborates upon that cliché in order to suggest that seduction – if understood with the proper degree of erotic complexity – might, in fact, be the ideal metaphor for the inevitable, exhilarated blurring of agency in the experience of conversion. A. D. Cousins speaks for a great deal of Crashaw criticism when he observes that "Crashaw's religious verse is dominated by study of the love descending from God to man, of that reaching from man to God, and of those loves' intermingling."[46] But in this poem, Crashaw links Christian spirituality to a strikingly different form of love: not a transcendent and sublime *amour de Dieu*, but rather the kind of earthly enticement usually described with horrified suspicion in contemporary texts of religious controversy.

Unlike the Epistle to Mrs. M. R., Crashaw's other poem of counsel to a wavering lady seems from its very title to be a specific and a straightforward contribution to confessional polemic: "To the Noblest and best of Ladyes, the Countesse of Denbigh, Perswading her to Resolution in Religion, and to render her selfe without further delay into the Communion of the Catholic Church." The poem was first published in the posthumous volume *Carmen Deo Nostro* (1652) as the work of a publicly confessed English Catholic convert, and was addressed to a well-known court figure: Susan Villiers, lady-in-waiting to Henrietta Maria and the sister of the

---

[46] Cousins, *Catholic Religious Poets*, 127. A. Low, "Richard Crashaw: Sensible Affection," in *Love's Architecture: Devotional Modes in Seventeenth-Century English Poetry* (New York University Press, 1978), 116–59.

Stuart court favorite George Villiers, Duke of Buckingham. The Countess notoriously hovered between the Protestantism of her birth and the Catholicism of her queen for a number of years in the late 1640s, encouraging something of a bidding war over her confessional allegiance before she joined her newly converted mother in the Catholic faith in 1651.[47] As long as Susan Villiers remained undecided, papal emissaries rejoiced at the prospect of her Catholic turn, while members of the Protestant establishment, fearing her influence over her brother, attempted to reconfirm her loyalty to the Church of England. By composing a poem to this particular woman at this particular moment, Crashaw would have been intervening in a well-publicized debate, and announcing his own Catholicism in unequivocal terms.[48]

In his revisions to the poem, however, Crashaw alters aspects of his counsel precisely in order to mitigate this apparent confessional stridency.[49] Continuing his challenge to the elevation of theological reasoning as an adequate basis for conversion, he returns his focus to the affective, emotional foundations for choice, and particularly to the complicated erotic valences of conversion. Austin Warren has argued that "one can search in vain through the [poem] … without finding any hint, much less explicit statement, of Roman claims, or any answer to Anglican objections."[50] Indeed, the second version of the poem is entitled, simply, "A Letter from Mr. CRASHAW to the Countess of DENBIGH, Against Irresolution and Delay in matters of RELIGION." I do not follow Warren, however, in concluding from this revision that Crashaw wished to minimize the differences between Rome and the high-church Protestantism of Peterhouse. Instead, I would argue that this reluctance to spell out the particular coordinates of the countess's conversion, a reticence especially marked in the second version of the poem, recalls the preteritive technique that we have seen in Donne's poetry, as well as the kinetic preoccupations of

---

[47] Hibbard, *Charles I and the Popish Plot*, 55. The first edition of *Carmen Deo Nostro* contained this dedication to the Countess: "Must humbly presented To My Lady the Countesse of Denbigh by her Most Devoted Servant, R. C., In hearty acknowlegement of his immortall obligation to her Goodnes and Charity." Since Crashaw died before the book's first publication, and before the countess's conversion, this dedication was possibly added by Car.

[48] So, in *Feminine Engendered Faith*, Sabine calls this "a poem where the poet burned his bridges" (21). Cf. A. Raspa, *The Emotive Image: Jesuit Poetics in the English Renaissance* (Fort Worth: Texas Christian University Press, 1983), 159–61.

[49] After its first printing in *Carmen Deo Nostro*, a second revised version appeared in an independent pamphlet in 1653. Both versions are reproduced by Williams, who suggests that Crashaw left the initial version with his editor at Paris in 1646, producing the second version in Italy sometime between 1646 and his death in 1649. Crashaw, *Complete Poetry*, 146–7.

[50] Warren, *Richard Crashaw*, 50.

Alabaster. By eliminating the particular markers of confessional identity, Crashaw refocuses our attention on the feminine soul's transformation as it turns from one church to another.

Crashaw gestures toward this idea of conversion as metamorphosis even in the earlier version of the poem. The following passage, for instance, describes the pent and static quality of an unconverted soul with a natural metaphor:

> So when the year takes cold, we see
> Poor waters their owne prisoners be.
> Fetter'd, and lockt up fast they ly
> In a sad selfe-captivity.   (21–4)

The countess is here urged to cease her "sad selfe-captivity," and to unlock the "prison" of her own spiritual inaction. In the poem's first version, Crashaw follows this dynamic description of conversion with a somewhat incongruous plea for fixity: "Allmighty Love! end this long warr, / And of a meteor make a starr" (29–30). Several lines earlier, Crashaw had implored God to "thaw [the] cold" of the countess's indecision (27); by asking him now to "fix this fair INDEFINITE" (31), he seems to envision conversion as a paradoxical process of liquefaction and solidification.

In the second version of the poem, Crashaw resolves this paradox by removing all references to the stability and stasis of post-conversion belief. The revised poem preserves those images of thaw and release, but refuses to predict an "ending" or "fixing" for its addressee; omitting the earlier version's statement of hope that the countess "may write RESOLV'D AT LENGTH" (40–2), Crashaw here describes her religious change not as a source of resolution, but as the engine of an ongoing process of spiritual development. Crashaw offers the countess many more explicit examples of such dynamism from the "World's wide face" (29). So,

> The aiery nation of neat Doves,
> That draw the Chariot of chast Loves,
> Chide your delay: yea those dull things,
> Whose wayes have least to doe with wings,
> Make wings at least of their own Weight,
> And by their Love controll their Fate.   (45–50)

Earlier, Crashaw had likened conversion to meteors arrested in mid-heaven. Now, instead, he associates it with objects that move through the air without "delay," either actively (flying doves) or passively (falling objects). These lines themselves model this ideal, dynamic abandon; their only pause comes with the caesura at "delay" in line 47, after which the poem gathers weight with two monosyllabic spondees ("yea those dull things"), then resumes its tumble down the page in a series of rapid enjambments until it reaches its "Fate."

Crashaw's evocation of "falling" as an action that the countess should *emulate*, moreover, wittily returns to the erotic vision of feminine conversion presented in the poem to Mrs. M. R. As we have seen, Gerbier, Digby, Laud, Carleton, and others frequently use the word "fall" to liken the conversions of women to sexual error. In these lines, by contrast, Crashaw proposes the exemplarity of falling, adducing the gravity which makes heavy things "winged" as evidence of "love," and not sin (52).[51] This conceit recuperates the erotic "fallenness" often ascribed to lady converts by contemporary writers. Within the representation of conversion as an ideal dynamism antithetical to fixedness of place, then, Crashaw implicitly extends and complicates the erotic premises of his earlier poem. But he does something new with the erotics of conversion as well. Further challenging the dichotomies of emotion and intellect, activity and passivity implicit in most contemporary accounts of women's conversion, Crashaw here also begins to dismantle the underlying dichotomy of gender presumed by these accounts, depicting conversion instead as a vital and active hermaphrodism.

Returning to the opening lines of the poem, for instance, we can discern an erotic scene familiar from both classical love poetry and medieval courtly literature.

> What Heav'n-besieged Heart is this
> Stands Trembling at the Gate of Blisse:
> Holds fast the Door, yet dares not venture
> Fairly to open and to enter? (1–4)

The conceit, here, recalls the paradigmatic plot of courtly romances such as the *Roman de la Rose*, in which a love-lorn wanderer seeks entrance to his lady's well-guarded castle. It also draws upon the classical elegiac form known as the *paraclausithyron*, literally "gate-poem," in which an excluded lover (the *amator exclusus*) laments before the locked door, sometimes addressing the lady inside, sometimes lamenting his own plight, sometimes entreating the porter or the door itself to permit him access. As a well-trained classicist and translator, Crashaw would have known examples such as Ovid's *Amores* 1.6 (*"ianitor – indignum!"*) in which a lover addresses the

---

[51] In an editorial note to the poem, Williams notes "the scholastic thesis that stones, steel and other dull and lumpish objects demonstrated their love of God by falling." Crashaw, *Complete Poetry*, 151.

"shameful gatekeeper" who hinders him from entering the home of his beloved.[52]

The image of the lover at the threshold, with erotic overtones inherited from classical and medieval literary models, here becomes a metaphor for spiritual awakening, and its expression in choice of churches. Hesitation in religious commitment resembles an obstinate holding back from orgasm; entering the "Gate of Blisse," by contrast, the heart will attain both spiritual and sexual fulfillment. But the initial adjective, examined more closely, renders the threshold analogy paradoxical.[53] If the lady's heart is "besieged," then it is on the *inside* of an enclosure, fearfully "hold[ing] fast the door." Yet the ensuing lines make clear that her heart is also in the position of the male lover who must dare "to open and to enter" the protected space. The lady's heart is thus chided both for excessive resistance to penetration and for excessive timidity in penetrating. The prospective convert is both "besieged," unable to get out, and "trembling at the gate," unwilling to go in. In this state of incipience, the lady occupies both positions in the conventional erotic *mise-en-scène*; she is at once the overly guarded love object who must eventually open herself to sexual experience, and the overly tentative suitor who must eventually overcome his hesitations and enter the fortress of his heart's desire.[54]

The ambiguous rendering of the poem's opening threshold image is confirmed by the paradoxical description of the lady's heart in the next lines: "Whose definition is, A Doubt / 'Twixt Life and Death, 'twixt In and Out" (5–6). The liminal state of being "'twixt in and out" is not the same thing as simply being on the outside preparing to go in. Rather, the syntactic ambiguity of the phrase conveys the miraculously hybrid status of the addressee, who is presented as being both inside and outside the threshold at once, on the verge of a mysterious, as-yet-unspecified, and potentially impossible movement urged by the speaker of the poem:

> Ah! linger not, lov'd Soul: A slow
> And late Consent was a long No.   (7–8)

---

[52] Ovid, of course, also stood in the Renaissance as the quintessential poet of gendered transformations, as detailed in two complementary essays in P. Hardie (ed.), *The Cambridge Companion to Ovid* (Cambridge University Press, 2002), A. Sharrock, "Gender and Sexuality," 95–107, and C. Burrow, "Re-embodying Ovid: Renaissance Afterlives," 301–19, esp. 304–12.

[53] The initial version of the poem has "entreated" rather than "besieged." Crashaw's revised diction intensifies the allusion to *amour courtois* and heightens the urgency of the imagined scene.

[54] We might compare this state of incipience in Crashaw's poem with that which we saw in Alabaster's poems on St. Peter and Mary Magdalene; like Alabaster, Crashaw wishes to show the moment before a dramatic *peripeteia*, but goes further to make that *peripeteia* itself paradoxical.

The speaker again asks the addressee not to "linger," suggesting, as before, that the soul must enter the gates from the outside and so adopt the conventionally male role in a story of erotic achievement. But the obstacle in consummation is not simply the lady's lack of seductive energy, but her continued sexual withholding: "a slow / And late Consent" tantamount to outright refusal, "a long No." The word "Consent" restores the addressee to the conventionally feminine position on the *inside* of the gate, unwilling to permit entrance. Things are not much clarified by the ensuing two lines:

> Who grants at last, a great while try'de
> And did his best to have Deny'de.   (9–10)

The confused antecedents make it possible to understand the converting lady's soul both as the one who will finally "grant" her suitor access after long "Deny[ing]," and the one whose suit will finally be gratified after having long "try'de." In terms of medieval courtly literature, the addressee possesses the *froideur* of the *belle dame sans merci*; in terms of classical elegy, she is urged to demonstrate the persistence of the *amator exclusus*.

Crashaw continues to represent conversion as seduction, then, but at such moments he also suggests that the seduction he imagines is in a sense an *autoerotic* event, one in which the converting lady must occupy both conventionally defined gender roles. The ambiguous grammar creates a kind of poetic anamorphosis, showing the lady as two *personae* on the verge of two complementary but antithetical movements, and encouraged toward an eroticized conversion in which she would be both seducer and seduced. Crashaw's revisions to the poem only exaggerate these autoerotic qualities. In the earlier version, he makes an extended plea that the countess "yield" to God's love. Addressing that divine "love" directly, Crashaw asks it to "choose out that sure decisive dart / Which has the Key of this close heart" (33–4). By penetrating "the self-shutt cabinett of [the lady's] unsearcht soul" (36), this masculine dart would finally "kill this rebell-word, IRRESOLUTE" (40). Once successfully penetrated by Love, in other words, the lady would be "RESOLV'D AT LENGTH." In the poem's second version, Crashaw removes not only the wish that the lady be conclusively "resolved," but also the conventionally erotic account of ravishment by the "healing shaft" of divine love. He instead adds a passage describing "love" as a quality of the woman herself, the quality which will inspire the "move-ment" of her conversion – since even "lumpish Steel, untaught to move / Learned first his Lightnesse by his love" (51–3). This reimagining of "love" lends a new force to the final lines, urging the lady to "Yield, that Love may win / The Fort at last and let Life in" (85–6). In the first version, since love was part of God, the lady's yielding the "fort" to love meant acquiescing to an outside, masculine force. In the second version, since love is now an intrinsic quality of the lady herself, the countess's conversion becomes a miraculous moment of self-transformation.

Crashaw does not present this autoerotic vision as an onanistic dead-end. On the contrary, he imagines self-seduction as sexually fruitful. By taking on both active and passive sexual roles, the lady will create – and ultimately occupy – still another role: the converted soul, here likened to a newborn child. Crashaw represents this process in another second-person address:

> Say, lingring Fair, why comes the Birth
> Of your brave Soul so slowly forth?
> Plead your Pretences (O you strong
> In weaknesse) why you chuse so long
> In Labour of yourself to ly,
> Not daring quite to Live or Die.   (15–20)

Both "fair" and "brave," "strong" and "weak," the lady embodies obviously gendered oppositions. Her hermaphrodism becomes newly *productive*, however, in the highly impacted pun on the word "labour." First, and most literally, Crashaw likens the addressee's protracted conversion to a process of giving "birth" to herself – a process of "labour" in which she, as pregnant woman, brings herself into the world, alive with a new religious identity. But the word "labour" also likens her deferral of conversion to a man's sexual work before the culminative "dying" of orgasm. This use of "labour" occurs most notoriously in the opening couplet of John Donne's "Elegy 19": "Come madam, come, all rest my powers defy, / Until I labour I in labour lie." Donne's speaker "labours" in his unfulfilled desire to "labour" in bed with his lady. By contrast, when Crashaw's speaker accuses his addressee of lying in "labour of [her]self," he superimposes the two meanings of the word "labour," erotic and obstetric. Gesturing toward their respective ends, the "death" of male orgasm and the "life" produced by female childbirth, these two kinds of "labour" mark conversion as a paradoxically simultaneous process of self-annihilation, self-impregnation, and self-generation. The lines force us to imagine the addressee as doing both masculine and feminine work in the reproductive process, as well as likening her, in her converted state, to the child resulting from this peculiar union.

Crashaw provides other examples of such hermaphroditic self-generation in the natural world. The harvest of ripe fruit becomes part of another hermaphroditic economy of production, as Crashaw reminds us that while fruits are feminine, plants are grammatically masculine. Thus, in the process of ripening, "each mindfull Plant hasts to make good / The hope and promise of *his* bud" (35–6, my emphasis). Here again, Crashaw constructs an image of sexualized, instantaneous self-fertilization in which female fertility and male potency, "harvest" and "seed-time," occur simultaneously. Even the ocean demonstrates this phenomenon for Crashaw:

> Mark how the curl'd Waves work and wind,
> All hating to be left behind.
> Each bigge with businesse thrusts the other,
> And seems to say, Make haste, my Brother.   (41–4)

This clearly homoerotic vision of brotherly encouragement is, nonetheless, interwoven with a number of feminine associations. The waves are "curl'd," suggesting the ornamentation of feminine beauty; they "work and wind," suggesting the housewifely task of spinning; their "bigge" appearance might signify pregnancy as well as tumescence. Here again, Crashaw elaborates upon a natural metaphor to indicate a process of hermaphroditic self-reproduction.

Finally, this poem proposes that conversion bestows the ability to "wind" across erotic and gendered thresholds – seducing, impregnating, yielding to, and ultimately giving birth to a new self. This idea of conversion as a generative hybridity differs from the feminized devotion described by Crashaw's Capuchin and Laudian contemporaries alike. These writers, particularly the Catholics, use their spiritual direction to communities of women as a platform for advocating an eroticized mysticism for all worshipers. But the analogy, in such works, is stable: the soul (whether of a man or woman) must adopt a weak and thus "feminine" position, abandoning itself to the ravishment of the active "masculine" Godhead. Reducing Crashaw's gendered poetics to such a simplistic praise of feminine anti-heroics, Anthony Low, like Maureen Sabine, celebrates him for suggesting that "others should, like himself and the female saints he admired, cheerfully offer themselves up, in sacrifice, love, and suffering."[55] But such praise fails to acknowledge the self-reflexive quality of this particular sacrifice: "What fatall, yet fantastick, bands," Crashaw asks, "Keep the free Heart *from his own Hands!*" (13–14). The paradox, here, is not just that conversion gives the Heart the strength to surrender (that it is "want of courage not to yield"), but that it enables it to surrender *to itself,* to "his own Hands," once again playing both roles in the drama of seduction.

---

[55] Low, *Reinvention*, 131.

This kind of hermaphroditic conversion, in turn, differs from Crashaw's depictions of the hermaphroditically vulnerable body of Jesus himself, who, in Eugene Cunnar's words, Crashaw "conceived of as a nurturing mother, whose breasts/wounds provided spiritual nourishment."[56] Richard Rambuss has noted Crashaw's abiding interest in the "somatic possibilities" of the incarnation, particularly in the penetrability of Christ.[57] The gendered ambiguity Rambuss details, however, mainly involves the blending of two genders into one, so that Jesus and his worshipers interpenetrate, "mixing" wounds and tears, orifices and bodily fluids. While I am also interested in the somatic, gendered transgressions of Crashaw's religious imagination, I would suggest that this operates differently in the poems written to counsel contemporary women about religious choice. The "malleability of gender within the figural space of devotional expression," according to Rambuss, involves the miraculous fusion of genders in a sexually ambiguous incarnation.[58] The poems of conversion, by contrast, present not the blending of two into one, but the expansion of one into (at least) two: what Janel Mueller has called in another context "a hybrid consciousness, a supersensibility."[59] In terms of devotional subjectivity, this is not, *pace* Richard Strier, a poem that aims to "transmute flux into stillness," but rather a poem that works in precisely the opposite direction.[60]

But why should Crashaw describe conversion in terms of polymorphous gender identity at all? I have already proposed, in discussing the poem to Mrs. M. R., that Crashaw's erotics of conversion do not simply rehearse the "spiritual marriage" *topos*, but rather borrow from the descriptions of worldly seductions common in the controversial texts of a particular historical period, using this pervasive metaphoric system as a way to describe the peculiar dynamics of conversion. I would argue, further, that Crashaw's

---

[56] E. R. Cunnar, "Opening the Religious Lyric: Crashaw's Ritual, Liminal and Visual Wounds," in J. R. Roberts (ed.), *New Perspectives on the Seventeenth-Century English Religious Lyric* (Columbia: University of Missouri Press, 1994), 244. For the notion of Jesus as sacred hermaphrodite, see C. Bynum, *Jesus as Mother: Studies in the Spirituality of the High Middle Ages* (Berkeley: University of California Press, 1982). The medieval notion of Jesus as mother is nowhere more explicit than in Crashaw's notorious epigraph on Luke 11, "Blessed be the paps which Thou hast sucked":

> Suppose he had been tabled at thy teates
> Thy hunger feels not what he eates.
> Hee'l have his Teat e're long (a bloody one)
> The Mother then must suck the Son.

For a subtle reading of this poem, see S. Mintz, "The Crashavian Mother," *SEL* 39.1 (1999), 111–29.
[57] R. Rambuss, *Closet Devotions* (Durham, NC: Duke University Press, 1998), 26–32.   [58] *Ibid.*, 38.
[59] Mueller, "Women among the Metaphysicals," 151.
[60] R. Strier, "Crashaw's Other Voice," *SEL* 9 (1969), 135–51, 143. Strier significantly attends only to the first version of the poem, dismissing the 1653 revision as "inferior and far less interesting" (136 n. 3).

vision of the autoerotics of conversion finally enables him to articulate something more about the felt experience of religious change – something that seems, *prima facie*, counterintuitive. This is the idea that in conversion, one ceases to be a unified consciousness, and instead possesses, if only for an instant, a number of distinct and incommensurable identities at once.[61] Rather than proposing that conversion brings with it a newly synthesized *unity* of being, in other words, Crashaw suggests in his poetry that conversion creates an exalted variety or multiplicity within the self. The converting soul is not only Catholic and Protestant at this moment of crossing, but also "in and out," heart and soul, male and female, active and passive, old and new, rational and passionate, weak and strong, infant and mature. Crashaw's poems, particularly the lachrymal extravaganza "The Weeper," demonstrate his tendency toward aesthetic and sensual excess. I would suggest that in the poems on conversion, sensual excess – in the particular form of an excessive, overabundant "genderedness" – responds to Crashaw's earlier exhortation, in the *Hymn to the Name of Jesus*: "GO SOUL, out of thyself, and seek for More" (27). The female convert provides him with an imitable example of how this "More" can be found or forged within.

"READ HIM FOR HER AND HER FOR HIM": TROPING TERESA

In his series of poems inspired by the life of another exemplary woman, St. Teresa of Avila, Crashaw demonstrates how the capacity to exist as more or other than a single self is not limited to the temporary experience of conversion, but can become an essential and enduring element of the ensuing sanctified life. Like Donne's poem to the newly ordained Mr. Tilman, Crashaw's poems on Teresa draw on his earlier, more particular considerations of confessional choice and change. For Crashaw, Teresa exemplifies an achieved devotion that is nevertheless endlessly transformative; she is the model of a soul constantly doubling in order to "Labor of" itself.[62] By presenting Teresa's experiences in a sequence of poems, moreover, Crashaw shows this metamorphosis from a number of perspectives,

---

[61] So Karl Morrison has linked conversion and the experience of empathy in two related studies, *Understanding Conversion*, and *"I am You": The Hermeneutics of Empathy in Western Literature, Theology and Art* (Princeton University Press, 1988).

[62] Rambuss offers an eloquent description of the "shiftingly gendered, variously eroticized devotional tableaux" of the Teresa poems in *Closet Devotions*, 39–41; this gendered shifting, I propose, has much do with Crashaw's particular interest in confessional change.

detailing the experience of conversion and its aftermath, and finally associating that same multiplicity with his own voice as a converting poet.

Teresa, of course, did not leave one church for another, and so was not a convert in the manner of Olivia Porter or Elizabeth Cary. Her autobiography, however, captured the imagination of a number of early modern English Catholic converts, who seem to have envisioned her as a particularly apt spiritual exemplar. Donne's friend Sir Toby Matthew, for instance, followed his own conversion to Catholicism by producing the first translation of her *Vida*, entitled *The Flaming Hart, Or, the Life of the Glorious S. Teresa, Foundresse of the Reformation, of the Order of the All-Immaculate Virgin-Mother, our B. Lady, of Mount-Carmel* (Antwerp, 1642). In his dedicatory epistle, addressed to Queen Henrietta Maria, Matthew proposes Teresa's life as a model for those "Religious woemen of her Angelicall Order; whereof, the English Nation (which now enioyes the honour, to be also, yours) hath a Monastery at Antwerpe." Matthew proposes Teresa, in other words, as the patron saint of exiled English Catholics, including converted ladies such as the Lechford and Gerbier daughters, and converted men such as himself, Walter Montague, and Richard Crashaw. Similarly, Crashaw's series of poems on the saint does not only indicate an interest in the culture of Spanish mysticism.[63] In "A Hymn to the Name and honor of the Admirable Saint Teresa," he emphasizes details of the saint's childhood that recall the situation of English Catholic converts, particularly converting women. He notes, for example, that Teresa's embrace of a sanctified life led to a break with her family, recalling those English conversions that divided parents and children:

> Farewell what ever deare may bee,
> MOTHER's armes or FATHER's knee
> Farewell house, and farewell home!
> She's for the Moores, and MARTYRDOM.   (61–4)

Abandoning her home, Teresa journeys abroad seeking a purer life of devotion, in much the same way that the converted children of Protestants fled to Catholic religious communities on the continent.

As a convert, Teresa embodies for Crashaw those sexualized paradoxes of agency and identity familiar from his poems of counsel to contemporary English noblewomen. The "Hymn," for instance, begins with a discussion of the excessive innocence and vulnerability of the young Teresa, who has

---

[63] In *Richard Crashaw and the Spanish Golden Age* (New Haven: Yale University Press, 1982), R. V. Young describes Crashaw's debt to theories of *conceptismo* found in Gongora and Gracian.

"[s]carse … learn't to lisp the name / Of Martyr" when she resolves to become one (15–16). Crashaw underscores this immaturity with an obvious reference to sexuality: "Scarse has she Blood enough to make / A guilty sword blush for her sake" (25–6). Teresa is prepubescent and pre-sexual, innocent both of menstrual blood and the hymeneal blood that would cause a phallic "sword" to "blush." This spiritual and sexual inexperience, however, is coupled with a precocious yearning, as her "weake brest heaves with strong desire / Of what she may with fruitles wishes / Seek for amongst her MOTHER's kisses" (40–2). If we did not already know the end of the story, we might think that this girl's "strong desire" for more-than-maternal kisses looks forward to an imminent sexual awakening. Her departure "for the Moores, and MARTYRDOM," then, occurring precisely in the narrative position of an erotic coming-of-age, causes the reader to expect a depiction of Teresa's coming to sainthood that is also, metaphorically, an achievement of sexual adulthood.[64]

Crashaw does indeed describe Teresa's conversion in terms of erotic experience, but moreover depicts this maturation in terms of a miraculous sexual polyvalence. Envisioning her mission among the Moors, for instance, Crashaw notes that Teresa will be able to "teach them how to Dy" – the virginal innocent taking on the role of the more experienced sexual partner (54). When Crashaw tells us that the brave girl is willing "to leave amongst them sown / Her LORD's Blood; or at lest her own" (55–6), he is not only alluding to the longstanding adage that the "blood of martyrs is the seed of the Church," but is also deliberately placing the girlish saint in the role of male inseminator, "sowing" her holy seed in the souls of new converts. Only at the end of the poem does Crashaw suggest an alternative consummation, with Teresa occupying a different position with a different "Spouse." Rather than dying a martyr's death, Teresa is instead "loves victime; and must dy / A death more mysticall and high" (75–6). Crashaw represents this death-as-deflowering in the conventionally erotic terms of mystic rapture: "*His* is the DART must make the DEATH / Whose stroke shall tast thy hallow'd breath" (79–80, my italics). Crashaw's allusion to Teresa's eventual sexual rapture at the hands of her Lord, once again, echoes the devotional texts written by, among others, the Capuchins surrounding Henrietta Maria. Crashaw's prediction

> How kindly will thy gentle HEART
> Kisse the sweetly-killing DART!

---

[64] Discussing the poem's emphasis on affective "love," Anthony Low refrains from any mention of the specifically erotic nature of that love. Low, *Love's Architecture*, 146–9.

> And close in his embraces keep
> Those delicious Wounds   (105–8)

echoes the prefatory poem to the *Life of the Reverend Father Angel of Joyeuse, Capucin Preacher* (1623):

> For Christ thy lover from above
> Thy heart had pierced with fiery dart
> Which made thee like one drunk with love
> To languish in delightful smart.[65]

Like Father Angel, Teresa will become ideally sanctified in her erotic response to the amorous Godhead.

But Crashaw also predicts that Teresa will have more than one sexual partner in this culminative erotic scenario. In addition to the dart-wielding Christ himself, Crashaw warns Teresa that the "Blest Seraphim" will "leave their quire / And turn love's souldiers upon Thee / To exercise their archerie" (94–6). In addition to the masculine angels, described as "sons of fire" in a phrase repeated from the poem to Mrs. M. R., the "MOON of maiden starrs, thy white / MISTRESSE" will "dart / Her mild rayes through [Teresa's] melting heart" (123–4, 135–6). After all this strenuously androgynous sexual activity, Teresa will produce children of her own: "Sons of thy vowes / The virgin-births with which thy soveraign spouse / Made fruitfull thy fair soul" (167–9). With the word "virgin-births" (albeit slightly incongruous after all this talk of penetration), Crashaw indicates that Teresa will now assume the female role in the spiritual marriage, giving "birth" to new converts like the poet himself. Several years earlier, Crashaw had predicted that conversion would allow the Countess of Denbigh to become "more" than a mere woman, allowing her to become at once man, woman, and resulting child (the person new-born in religious life). Here, in the story of her early conversion to a spiritual vocation, Teresa takes on the *personae* of an innocently asexual child, a potent male warrior, and a fertile female object of sexual desire. Female conversion, once again, involves what Rambuss terms "a kind of gender ecstasy."[66]

Crashaw continues to explore the miraculous capacity of conversion to allow one to become, literally, more than a single self in the two ensuing Teresa poems. The "Apologie for the fore-going Hymne" reiterates the

---

[65] R. R. (trans.), *The Life of the Reverend Father Angel of Joyeuse, Capucin Preacher ... Together with the Lives of the Reverend Fathers, Father Bennet Englishman and Father Archangell Scotchman, of the Same Ordere* (Douai, 1623), sig. IV.

[66] Rambuss, *Closet Devotions*, 42.

convert's broader capacity for experience in both national and confessional terms:

> Souls are not SPANIARDS too, one freindly floud
> Of BAPTISM blends them all into a blood.
> CHRIST's faith makes but one body of all soules,
> And love's that body's soul, no law controwlls
> Our free traffique for heav'n, we may maintaine
> Peace, sure, with piety, though it come from SPAIN.
> What soul so e're, in any language, can
> Speak heav'n like her's is my soul's country-man.
> O 'tis not spanish, but 'tis heav'n she speaks! (15–23)

Crashaw reasserts Teresa as an imitable paragon of sanctity even for an Englishman who counts himself "still among the Protestantes." Her exemplarity, moreover, can effect a transformation without any effort on the part of the "wondering reader," who will, upon reading her autobiography, be suddenly and miraculously multiplied – "feel[ing] his warm HEART hatched into a nest / Of little EAGLES and young loves" (25–7). Speaking as such a reader himself, Crashaw cries,

> Change we too, our shape
> (My soul,) Some drink from men to beasts, o then
> Drink till we prove more, not lesse, then men,
> And turn not beasts, but Angels. (34–7)

According to Crashaw's editor, the poet here uses the medieval concept of "divine inebriation" to describe his own reading of Teresa's autobiography.[67] The imagery in these lines, however, is not simply that of drunkenness, but more specifically of expansion, of the reader becoming ever "more" than the man he once was.[68]

Crashaw turns to his own multiplied experience more explicitly at the end of the final and best-known poem of the series, adopting the title of Toby Matthew's translation of Teresa's *Vida*: *The Flaming Hart*. This poem returns to the gendered presentation of Teresa's sanctified shape-changing, opening with an elaboration on the earlier claim, made in the full title of the "Hymn to the Name," that Teresa can be considered "A WOMAN for Angelical heighth of speculation, for masculine courage of performance,

---

[67] See notes to Crashaw, *Complete Poetry*, 60. Williams gives a fuller account of Crashaw's use of the inebriation *topos* in *Image and Symbol in the Poetry of Richard Crashaw* (Columbia: University of South Carolina Press, 1963), 91–4.
[68] Young points out a "juxtaposition of apparently divergent kinds of experience" in the Teresa series as a whole, *Richard Crashaw and the Spanish Golden Age*, 69–70.

More then a woman" (my emphasis). If the first poem describes Teresa's conversion as a process of moving through gendered positions in succession, "The Flaming Hart" presents her post-conversion life as a self-elaborating androgyny, recalling the ambiguous undulation and vegetation of the Denbigh poem. The poem opens with a reference to the iconic image, reproduced on the frontispiece of Matthew's translation, depicting Teresa visited by the angel at the moment of her religious rapture. The opening apostrophe schools us in the proper appreciation of the scene:

> Well meaning readers! You that come as freinds
> And catch the pretious name this peice pretends;
> Make not too much hast t'admire
> That fair cheek't fallacy of fire.
> That is a SERAPHIM, they say
> And this is the great TERESIA.
> Readers, be rul'd by me; and make
> Here a well-plac't and wise mistake,
> You must transpose the picture quite,
> And spell it wrong to read it right[.]   (1–10)

Susan Stewart has called this passage an example of Crashaw's "rhetoric of transposition," indicative of hermeneutic transformations on a number of levels.[69] Although we are addressed as "readers," for instance, we have been transformed implicitly into viewers; the poem, meanwhile, is transformed into a "peice" of visual art. This transformation, in turn, begets others: "Reading" (or viewing) the picture (or poem) "right" means reading it perversely, "transposing" the male seraphic messenger with the female he addresses: "Read Him for her, and her for him; / And call the saint the SERAPHIM," Crashaw suggests (11–12).

Having addressed the reader in the first twelve lines, poet then turns to painter and requests complicity in this project of holy transvestism. "Undresse thy SERAPHIM into mine," he implores. "Redeem this injury of thy art: / Give HIM the vail, give her the dart" (41–2). This sartorial change, Crashaw imagines, will reveal the deeper truth of conversion by blurring the conventions of feminine reticence and masculine seduction. As in the earlier Denbigh poem, the "dart" metonymizes masculine prowess, both military and erotic. Possessing the seraphic "dart," Teresa will take on the role of the

---

[69] S. Stewart, *Poetry and the Fate of the Senses* (University of Chicago Press, 2002), 183. Stewart's main concern is with the poem's transpositions of "representation" and the "real," and with the consequently vertiginous effects of the "deictic representation of sensation" (190). While I share her focus on the "rhetorical gestures of being moved, moving, reversing and transposing" in these poems (185), I am here more interested in the dynamically metamorphic *content* of the images themselves.

male seducer/converter, actively targeting others for conquest. But Crashaw does not imagine this sexual transformation as terminal or uni-directional, since he immediately redescribes Teresa's heart as "not one loose shaft, but Love's whole quiver" (70). The replacement of "shaft" with "quiver" is, in essence, another sex change back from male to female, since a "quiver" is not only a metonym for arrows, but, literally, the receptacle into which they are put.[70] The following lines expand this notion of the heart as both phallic dart and vaginal destination:

> For in love's feild was never found
> A nobler weapon then a WOUND.
> Love's passives are his activ'st part
> The wounded is the wounding heart. (71–4)

Here, even more explicitly than in the Denbigh poem, Crashaw credits a converting lady with the miraculous ability to penetrate herself, to be both active and passive in an autoerotic experience of conversion. As a result of this erotic self-wounding, Teresa will be "Bigge alike with wounds and darts" (76) – here, again, the word "bigge" simultaneously suggests both female fertility and male arousal. A few lines later, Crashaw succinctly describes the converted saint's miraculous ability to "love and dy and kill / And bleed and wound; and yeild and conquer" interchangeably (79–80).

Throughout Crashaw's sequence, Teresa exemplifies the productively antithetical qualities of the ideal convert. The final twenty-four lines of this last poem, one of the only passages of Crashaw's poetry written in the first person, explicitly claim a similar miraculous hybridity for the converting poet. Returning briefly to the "Epistle to the Countess of Denbigh," we find an earlier instance of Crashaw asking us to "read him for her and her for him." This is not just in the depiction of the converting countess as hermaphrodite, but also in the androgynous effects of poetic voice. As the writer of a poem of counsel, Crashaw begins the poem by adopting a conventionally "masculine" voice of counsel, stressing his authority with imperatives: "Linger not," "Plead your Pretences," etc. The speaker's voice, however, becomes increasingly emotional over the course of the poem, mimicking some of the excessive affect commonly attributed to women in male-authored religious polemic. We see this not only in exclamations like "Yield then, O Yield!" but in the sweetly sentimental description of Jesus

---

[70] These metaphoric terms are not unique to Crashaw's devotional poetry; in "St. Peter's Complaint," Robert Southwell has his repentant speaker refer to Christ's eyes as "graceful quivers of loves dearest darts" (352). Crashaw's particular use of the metaphor, however, draws attention to the relationship between its two constituent parts.

"Leaping on the Hills, to be / The humble King of You and Me" (71–2). Anthony Low has expressed the view, shared by a number of critics, that Crashaw's late poetry demonstrates "an identification with, and a feeling through the viewpoint of, his subject."[71] What this tends to mean, though, again, is simply that Crashaw's speakers sound "like women." I would suggest, instead, that the poet "identifies" with his subject precisely because his poetic voice reflects the same gendered ambiguity he attributes to the female convert in her experience of transformation. If conversion allows the countess to assume the *personae* of man, woman, and child, so the poetry of conversion permits Crashaw to speak in three voices, expressing that same familial trinity.[72]

"The Flaming Hart" concludes with an explicit acknowledgment of the similarities between conversion and poetic composition, with the poet-convert taking on the multiple sexual identities he had elsewhere ascribed to converting women. Beginning his final apostrophe to the saint, Crashaw rephrases and redirects the plea for gender transformation with which the poem began. Where he once urged the reader to imaginatively invert the picture of the seraph penetrating the saint with a beam of holy light, here he asks the autobiographer Teresa to penetrate *him* with her writing:

> Let all thy scattered shafts of light, that play
> Among the leaves of thy larg Books of day,
> Combined against this BREST at once break in
> And take away from me my self and sin.   (87–90)

This plea surpasses Donne's famous request that God "batter [his] heart" in its sexual daring, since the ravisher here is not an omnipotent male God, but rather an androgynized human woman. Crashaw now possesses the "BREST" and Teresa the "shaft"; Crashaw is not merely feminized, but made the willing victim of Teresa's sexual aggression. If Rambuss has

---

[71] Low, *Reinvention*, 111. For the idea of male Renaissance poets identifying with female speakers more generally, see E. Harvey, *Ventriloquized Voices: Feminist Theory and English Renaissance Texts* (London: Routledge, 1992), and J. Goldberg, *Desiring Women Writing: English Renaissance Examples* (Stanford University Press, 1997).

[72] Leah Marcus suggests that the speakers in many of Crashaw's poems reflect how "an actual infant may experience the world around him": in a welter of confused images and sensations, occasionally yielding to the "warmth and safety of complete encirclement." Marcus, *Childhood and Cultural Despair: A Theme and Variations in Seventeenth-Century Literature* (University of Pittsburgh Press, 1978), 148, 150. Marcus sees poetic "infancy" as essentially conservative, a longing for the embrace of the mother as a respite from the confused strife of the adult world. I want to argue that Crashaw's depiction of spiritual infancy occurs within a more complicated erotic scheme; if he depicts himself as child, he also depicts himself as the male and female progenitors of that child. This scheme, furthermore, is part of Crashaw's engagement with and emphasis on confusion (religious and sexual), rather than an effort to escape from it.

helpfully reminded us that the erotic penetrability of a body does not necessarily make it a feminine body, here Crashaw insists that the convert- ing body is not only penetrated, but impregnated as well.[73] We have already seen his depiction of a conversion in which the countess must "labor of [her] self." Here, Crashaw suggests that his seminal inspiration by Teresa will allow him to bring himself forth, and then to "live" as a newly converted soul.

But he will also bring forth the poetry that is, for him, a corollary to the new life of the convert. The ensuing lines of the apostrophic invocation provide an unparalleled example of Crashaw's particular poetics of conver- sion, in which lines pregnant with paradox seem to give birth to more paradoxes, in a process of fecund poetic multiplicity:

> O thou undanted daughter of desires!
> By all thy dowr of LIGHTS and FIRES;
> By all the eagle in thee, all the dove;
> By all thy lives and deaths of love;
> By thy large draughts of intellectuall day
> And by thy thirsts of love more large then they ...   (93–8)

With these anaphoras Crashaw is, on one level, doing nothing more than invoking Teresa. But the technical virtuosity of the interlocking paradoxes creates a sense of accumulation, rendering poetically the kind of generative antitheses that Crashaw had described earlier in erotic terms. The passage starts out by invoking Teresa's contrasting qualities of eagle and dove, describing her as predator and prey, active and passive principles. Then – as if triggered by the word "dove" – Crashaw calls upon her "love." This "love," in turn, will involve both living and dying simultaneously (recalling, of course, the earlier puns on "labor" and "die"). Crashaw doesn't rest with the reference to Teresa's "love," however, but immediately invokes her contrasting enlightened reason: "large draughts of intellectuall day." The plenitude suggested by these draughts, however, immediately invites qual- ification in the next line, which refers to the enduring "thirsts of love" that these draughts fail to slake. The relentless energy of this description, the paradoxical excess of its strategies, create a poetic corollary of Teresa's religious experience – an experience that is dynamically multiform not only at the particular moment of conversion, but for ever after.

We have seen William Alabaster conclude a sonnet on his conversion with a plea for continued rapture: "that fire may draw forth blood, blood

---

[73] Rambuss, *Closet Devotions*, Chapter 1 *passim*.

extend fire, / Desire possession, possession desire." Crashaw's apostrophe to
Teresa echoes this idea of generative antithesis. But if Alabaster imagined
conversion as a perpetually unresolved alternation ("possession" yielding to
"desire" and vice versa), Crashaw imagines a potentially endless process of
accumulation and expansion, of both soul and poem. This is not to suggest
that Crashaw celebrates the "undifferentiated oneness" of the soul, in
contrast to, for example, Alabaster's vision of constant mutability.[74]
Crashaw's poetry – and its representation of the convert's subjectivity – is
no less complex than Alabaster's. Its complexity results not from self-
division, however, but finally from self-*multiplication*. The notion of
Crashaw's self-multiplying poetry of conversion finally can provide a way
back to Mario Praz's influential description of Crashaw's synaesthetics, or to
Sabine's recent discussion of the "mixed metaphors, the strange shifts in
tone, the coercive union of conceptual opposites and the gender interchangeability" of Crashaw's poetry – both of these comments restating
Alexander Pope's early criticism that it lacks "exactness, or consent of
parts."[75] Having considered these poems in light of other early modern
discussions of female conversion, I would suggest that this mixing and
multiplying is not only deliberate, but is indeed – particularly in its erotic
register – the key characteristic of Crashaw's devotional poetics.[76]

The "Song" appended to the end of "The Flaming Hart" can be read as a
final statement of those miraculous hybridities – of male and female, human
and divine, poet and saint – which have marked the poem thus far.

> LORD, when the sense of thy sweet grace
> Sends up my soul to seek thy face
> Thy blessed eyes breed such desire,
> I dy in love's delicious Fire.
>   O love, I am thy SACRIFICE.
> Be still triumphant, blessed eyes.
> Still shine on me, fair suns! that I
> Still may behold, though still I dy.   (1–8)

The repetition of the word "still" in the last three lines is slyly ironic; the
song in fact is anything but "still," moving through a series of rapid-fire
erotic and religious paradoxes in its second part:

[74] Sabine, *Feminine Engendered Faith*, 118.
[75] Praz understands this multiplicity as an illustration of Tesauro's concept of *acutezza*, or wit. Mario
Praz, *The Flaming Heart* (New York: Doubleday, 1958), 245 and *passim*; cf. Sabine, *Feminine
Engendered Faith*, 113.
[76] See L. Roberts, "Crashaw's Sacred Voice, 'A Commerce of Contrary Powers,'" in Roberts (ed.), *Life
and Art of Richard Crashaw*, 66–79.

> Though still I dy, I live again;
> Still longing so to be still slain,
> So gainfull is such losse of breath,
> I dy even in desire of death.
>   Still live in me this loving strife
> Of living DEATH and dying LIFE.
> For while thou sweetly slayest me,
> Dead to my selfe, I live in Thee.   (9–16)

The chiastic crossings create motion not just on the level of trope and image (the oscillations implicit in "living DEATH" and "dying LIFE" etc.), but on the level of voice as well. Literally, this song is meant to be understood as Teresa's, the first-person voice that of an ecstatic female worshiper declaring her submission to her male Lord (and using familiar Petrarchan oxymorons to do so). But it also comes immediately after Crashaw's own first-person apostrophe addressed to the saint – and recalls his motto, printed as an epigraph to *Steps to the Temple*: "Live, Jesus, Live, and let it bee / My life to dye for love of thee." In the final lines "while thou sweetly slayest me, / Dead to my selfe, I live in Thee," then, we hear three voices simultaneously, each envisioning a transformative spiritual ravishment: Teresa speaking to Jesus, Crashaw speaking to Jesus, and, finally, Crashaw speaking to Teresa.[77] The final couplet exemplifies Crashaw's poetry of conversion, poetry in which a variety of erotic perspectives and a variety of amorous voices combine to reflect the multiplied experience of subject, speaker, and poet.

---

[77] A. F. Allison notes, in addition, an echo of Car's translation of Sales's *Traité*: "To love or to die! To die and to love! To die to all other love in order to live to Jesus's love!" Allison, "Crashaw and St. François de Sales," 296.

CHAPTER 4

Versing and reversing in the poetry of John Dryden

The Aesopian pastoral of *The Hind and the Panther* might seem an unlikely endpoint for a book on the early modern poetics of conversion, for a number of reasons. First, Dryden's poem is late: composed and published soon after his conversion to Catholicism in 1685, it appeared in print almost four decades after the death and posthumous publication of Richard Crashaw's *Carmen Deo Nostro*. It is also long: a three-part beast fable, amounting to some 1,300 lines of heroic couplets. But most importantly, the poem seems to offer a clear and unequivocal statement of its author's religious position, precisely the kind of statement rejected, in various ways, by Alabaster, Donne, and Crashaw.[1] We have seen how Alabaster's sonnets express the volatility of belief, how Donne's early satires and late lyrics insist upon the inexpressibility of belief, how Crashaw's hymns and verse epistles demonstrate the hybridizing of belief. In contrast, Dryden's theological fable – idealizing Catholicism in the serene figure of the Hind, and lampooning the Protestant churches as a motley menagerie – seems definitive and single-minded, celebrating the sufficient end of its author's devotional uncertainty.[2] "My doubts," the poet triumphantly announces toward the beginning of his fable, "are done" (1.78).

Acknowledging Dryden's devotional convictions, however, should not lead us to dismiss their poetic expression as either simple or straightforward. In this chapter, I will suggest that *The Hind and the Panther* demonstrates a

---

[1] T. P. Fujimura describes the poem as "an intensely personal confession of faith." Fujimura, "The Personal Drama of Dryden's *The Hind and the Panther*," *PMLA* 87 (1972), 406–16, 406.

[2] Louis Bredvold thus reads *The Hind and the Panther* as both the final phase of, and the sufficient end to, the skepticism of *Religio Laici*. Bredvold, *The Intellectual Milieu of John Dryden: Studies in Some Aspects of Seventeenth-Century Thought* (1934; Ann Arbor: University of Michigan Press, 1956), 128 and *passim*. Elias Chiasson takes issue with Bredvold's reading, suggesting that *Religio Laici* in fact belongs to the "tradition of Christian humanism." Chiasson, "Dryden's Apparent Skepticism in *Religio Laici*," in H. T. Swedenberg (ed.), *Essential Articles for the Study of John Dryden* (Hamden, CT: Archon, 1966), 245–60. But even while questioning the "skepticism" of *Religio Laici*, Chiasson implicitly accepts Bredvold's fideistic reading of *The Hind and the Panther*.

poetics of conversion that is not simply continuous with the tradition I have been tracing, but more thoroughgoing than that of any other poet I have discussed. Beneath the regularity of its couplets, this poem is built on numerous paradoxes of argument and allusion. Behind the superficial clarity of its Catholic position, this poem also acknowledges the specific and contingent circumstances of religious adherence, and the possibility that the terms of any credo can change meaning in context and over time. *The Hind and the Panther* thus displays its particular poetics of conversion precisely in those moments that have irritated Restoration satirists and modern critics alike.[3] In their early "transversal" of *The Hind and the Panther*, for instance, Matthew Prior and Charles Montague mock Dryden for violating "the Rules and Examples of all Fables," chastising him for "shifting the scene at every Line."[4] Dryden's most recent biographer concurs with this assessment, explaining that "his failure to control the poem was an inevitable consequence of trying to do too many things at once … too many inventions, too many styles, too many conflicting purposes."[5] I want to suggest that these and other moments of conflict are precisely *not* lapses in poetic judgment, or evidence of Dryden's "failure to control the poem." They are instead strategic and deliberate, revealing Dryden's awareness, even as a confirmed Catholic, that religious positions can be firmly held and at the same time profoundly unstable. In its narrative and descriptive contents and formal construction, *The Hind and the Panther* finally depicts a contingency exemplified by, but not limited to, the subjective experience of the convert himself. This seemingly ahistorical, "personal" Catholic fable in fact offers a complex rumination upon the centrality of conversion to English religious and literary history.

RATIONALIZING CONVERSION IN RESTORATION ENGLAND

When Charles II accepted a gift of "a very rich Bible" upon landing at Dover in 1660, proclaiming it to be "the thing he loved above all things in the world," he indicated the central role that a Protestant settlement would play in the Restoration of the English monarchy.[6] After the

---

[3] See H. Macdonald, "The Attacks on Dryden," in Swedenberg (ed.), *Essential Articles*, 41–2.

[4] [Charles Montague and Matthew Prior], *The Hind and the Panther Transvers'd To the Story of the Country-Mouse and the City-Mouse* (London, 1687), A3r.

[5] J. A. Winn, *John Dryden and His World* (New Haven: Yale University Press, 1987), 425.

[6] Entry for May 25, 1660, in John Warrington (ed.), *The Diary of Samuel Pepys in Three Volumes* (London: Dent, 1971), vol. 1, 65.

sectarian trauma of the civil wars and the breakdown of the Cromwellian holy commonwealth, the success of the restored Stuart government would depend on the confirmation and consolidation of a single Reformed church. Strategies for achieving such religious consensus, however, varied. A number of the younger Anglican clergy, inspired by the conciliatory tone of Charles's Declaration of Breda, proposed a moderate ecclesiology as the least contentious way to guard against the Protestant sectarianism that had so recently divided England.[7] In his 1661 *Irenicum*, Edward Stillingfleet attempted to articulate grounds for a more broadly defined Protestant church.[8] Fellow irenicists, slandered as "latitude-men" by their more zealous Protestant detractors, saw this new Anglicanism as a positive *via media*, one which by avoiding theological excesses would comprehend the vast majority of Christians in England.[9] So John Dryden himself, in *Religio Laici*, describes the Anglican church as the crowning achievement of English ecclesiology, offering respite from both the Puritanism of the interregnum and the Roman Catholicism of the continent, "waving each Extreme, / The Tides of Ignorance and Pride to stem" (427–8).[10] In the ensuing decades, however, even the latitude-men began to acknowledge the potential unassimilability of Protestant dissent. Stillingfleet would finally refer to toleration as a "Trojan Horse, which brings in our enemies without being seen."[11] His rhetoric of "enemies," here, echoes the harder line taken from the beginning by those who advocated a strictly enforced

---

[7] See W. M. Spellman, *The Latitudinarians and the Church of England, 1660–1700* (Athens: University of Georgia Press, 1993). Spellman details the philosophical origins of irenic religion (11–32), and discusses the role of these moderate churchmen in the Anglican settlement (33–53). In the Declaration itself, Charles expressed his desire that "all notes of discord, separation and difference of parties be utterly abolished," and that the English Christian community achieve "a perfect union among themselves." See P. Seaward, *The Cavalier Parliament and the Reconstruction of the Old Regime 1661–1667* (Cambridge University Press, 1989), 162.

[8] Edward Stillingfleet, *Irenicum: A Weapon-Salve for the Church's Wounds* (1661). For a discussion of Stillingfleet in the context of "liberal churchmen," see J. Tulloch, *Rational Theology and Christian Philosophy in the Seventeenth Century*, 2 vols. (Hildesheim: Georg Olms, 1966), vol. I, 411–63.

[9] See J. Spurr, "'Latitudinarianism' and the Restoration Church," *HJ* 31 (1988), 61–82. According to Spurr, the term was originally leveled by dissenters against "what they saw as the self-interested conformity, the fraudulent moderation, and the theological moralism of some of the younger churchmen," 68. See also J. A. I. Champion, *The Pillars of Priestcraft Shaken: The Church of England and its Enemies 1660–1730* (Cambridge University Press, 1992), 5–14.

[10] So Donald Benson describes *Religio Laici* as "an attempt to … destroy the religious foundations of political extremism." Benson, "Theology and Politics in Dryden's Conversion," *SEL* 4 (1964), 393–412, 396. For the poem's syncretism, see V. Hamm, "Dryden's *The Hind and the Panther* and Roman Catholic Apologetics," *PMLA* 83 (1968), 400–15.

[11] Stillingfleet, *The Mischief of Separation* (1680), 58. For the evolution of Stillingfleet's attitude toward dissent, see Champion, *Pillars*, 63.

conformity, producing the stringent Clarendon Code and the renewed Conventicle Act.[12]

By the 1670s, however, a common enemy united English Protestants more successfully than conciliatory theological schemes or draconian penal codes: this was, of course, the faithful foe, Roman Catholicism. John Spurr has described the events of 1673 as the "greatest outbreak of anti-popery since the 1640s."[13] This outbreak, and its virulence, had a number of connected causes. First, the start of the Anglo-Dutch war coincided with a newly acute fear of French Catholic influence on Stuart policy.[14] This fear had to do with English diplomatic strategies abroad, but was intensified by the fact that the king's immediate family was largely Catholic: his mother, Henrietta Maria, still attended by Capuchin chaplains; his sister, Henriette, raised in Catholic France; his wife, Catherine of Braganza; and his mistress, Lady Castlemaine.[15] Charles's Declaration of Indulgence of 1672, which declared an end to "the execution of all and all manner of penal laws in matters ecclesiastical, against whatsoever sorts of nonconformists or recusants," seemed to many proof of his Catholic sympathies.[16] Most disturbingly, the Test Act of 1673, meant to discover crypto-Catholics at home, revealed that Charles's brother James, Duke of York, could no longer conform to the English Church in good conscience.[17] James had quietly stopped receiving Anglican communion the year before, but the Test Act ensured that his Catholic conversion could no longer be dissembled.[18] While James made no immediate public declaration of his Catholicism, by 1676 he, and his second wife Mary of Modena, were openly refusing to attend Protestant services. As his claim to the English throne became ever stronger, the old fear that England might be converted back to Catholicism received a new infusion of energy.[19] "Philanax Verax," writing to James "touching his revolt from and Return to the Church of England" in 1681,

---

[12] Tim Harris points out that under the Clarendon Code in the 1660s "it was mainly the Quakers and Baptists who suffered," while the 1670 Conventicle Act targeted Presbyterians and Independents. Harris, *London Crowds in the Reign of Charles II: Propaganda and Politics from the Restoration until the Exclusion Crisis* (Cambridge University Press, 1987), 70.

[13] J. Spurr, *The Restoration Church of England 1646–1689* (New Haven: Yale University Press, 1991), 65.

[14] See S. Pincus, "From Butterboxes to Wooden Shoes: The Shift in English Popular Sentiment from Anti-Dutch to Anti-French in the 1670s," *HJ* 38 (1995), 333–61.

[15] This shared Catholicism was not necessarily a guarantee of family harmony, however; in his diary entry for December 22, 1663, Samuel Pepys claimed to "hear for certain that my Lady Castlemaine is turn'd Papist, which the Queen for all do not much like, thinking that she do it not for conscience sake." Pepys, *Diary*, vol. 1, 470.

[16] Spurr describes the circumstances and consequences of the Declaration in *The Restoration Church*, 62–4.

[17] Aveling, *The Handle and the Axe*, 195.

[18] F. C. Turner, *James II* (London: Eyre and Spottiswoode, 1948), 87–106.   [19] Turner, *James II*, 125–6.

summed up this position: "'Tis generally reported, that you are long since turn'd Papist; and so far believed, that every day many Hundred Thousand Protestants are melted into tears and Horror … and lament the same, as one of the greatest Calamities that has happened in our Age."[20] This same statement of "horror" refers to the "subtle Sophisters … *which are always croaking about Persons of Quality, whom they have perverted to their Idolatries.*"[21] Evidently, the Duke of York's conversion was one of many rumored to have taken place at the restored Stuart court.[22] If the number of actual Catholic conversions during the reign of Charles II was relatively small, high-profile court Catholicism helped to provoke a new spate of controversial writings addressing the subject.[23]

The specific doctrinal objections to Catholicism were, by the late seventeenth century, perhaps too familiar to need rehearsing. Newly striking, however, is a polemical focus on the dangerous implications of religious change *per se* – targeting not the papist so much as the convert. In a satiric poem written after 1685, one author announces: "Of earls, of lords, of knights I'll sing / That chang'd their faith to please their King."[24] But this fear of "trimmers" antedated the accession of an openly Catholic monarch. Over a decade earlier, an anonymous satiric broadside offered *A Politique Confession of Faith Calculated for the Meridian of Both Churches*, printed in two columns. The columns, read in succession, constitute a "Catholic" credo; read across the page, however, they produce a "Protestant" prayer – poetic form facilitating the handy modification of outward confessional identity according to the exigencies of circumstance.[25] On the first lines of

---

[20] [Anon.], *A Letter to his Royal Highness the Duke of York, Touching his Revolt from or Return to the Protestant Religion. By an Old Cavalier, and Faithful Son of the Church of England, as Established by Law* (1681), A1r.

[21] *A Letter to his Royal Highness*, 2.

[22] Aveling, *The Handle and the Axe*, 181. According to Aveling, the wave of post-1685 Catholic conversions included those of Lord Sunderland, the Earl of Yarmouth, Sir Thomas Stradling, Sir Nicholas Butler, Sir Thomas Wright, Lady Theophila Nelson, the printers Stephen Bulkeley and Henry Hills, Mathew Tindal, Obadiah Walker, John Massey, Robert Charnock, Joshua Basset, James Cecil the 4th Earl of Salisbury, the Countess of Tyrconnell, the 2nd Earl of Peterborough, and the Duke of Richmond. *The Handle and the Axe*, 230–2.

[23] J. Miller discusses the statistics in *Popery and Politics in England, 1660–1688* (Cambridge University Press, 1973), 49–50, suggesting that "even in the three years 1669–71, when the clergy enjoyed freedom from persecution, the Society reconciled a total of less than 2000 persons to the faith." Conversion nevertheless loomed large in the polemical writing of the period; see T. Jones (ed.), *A Catalogue of the Discourses for and against Popery*, Chetham Society 48 and 64 (London, 1859 and 1865), and Edward Gee (ed.), *The Catalogue of all the Discourses Published Against Popery, During the Reign of King James II* (London, 1689).

[24] *The Converts: Or, the Folly of Priestcraft. A Comedy* (1686), 9–10.

[25] The pamphlet proclaims that it was "composed for the assistance of weak Catholicks, in the necessary art of Equivocation," but taken generally it parodies the ease with which individual worshipers could move between Catholic and Protestant self-identification (1673).

the 1681 *Dialogue Between Monmouth-Shire and York-Shire, about cutting Religion according to Fashion*, two characters – representing the Protestant Duke of Monmouth and the Catholic Duke of York – discuss the ease with which the trappings of religious identity can be altered or modified. Monmouthshire exclaims that "this Religion … is a very Seasonable Garment; cool in Summer, hot in Winter, and Suits with Spring and Autumne both," and Yorkshire concurs, adding that "a man in a Religious Cloak may walk incognito, carry Vice on with Virtues face, present his Friend a Dagger, when he expects but a How d'you Do."[26] Satires like these suggest that, across the theological spectrum, religious difference was ultimately less troubling than religious instability itself.[27] So, in marked contrast to the desire to "reclaim" apostates so common in polemics from earlier in the century, Restoration writers often suggest that reconversion would only make the linked problems of heterodoxy and hypocrisy more acute.[28] In a letter written in reply to the Catholic convert Serenus Cressy, for instance, the Bishop of Winchester noted "how impossible it is for the world to know whether what such men write or assert in Print, be not indeed quite contrary to what themselves do really believe, or noe."[29] The king himself occupied such an impossible position; one anonymous pamphleteer, even while urging James to return to the Protestant fold, acknowledges that "the grand difficulty will be to satisfie the prejudiced world of your *sincerity* herein … though you should go never so duly to Church, receive the sacrament a *thousand times*, and take Oaths all the way from Holy-Rood House to Saint James's, yet the people would scarce believe the reality of your Conversion."[30]

Responding to such allegations, Catholic converts defended their new church as a source of theological and political stability. Exposed by the 1673 Test Act, the Earl of Bristol reassured Parliament that "I am … a Catholic of the Church of Rome, not a Catholic of the Court of Rome," adding that he will prove "a faithful member of a Protestant Parliament" precisely because he is a faithful member of the Catholic Church, and "none

---

[26] *Dialogue Between Monmouth-Shire and York-Shire, about cutting Religion according to Fashion* (1681), 1.
[27] So one anonymous pamphlet warned of *The Great Danger of Continuing in and the Greater of Apostatizing To, the Romish Religion* (1669), while John Bryan proposed *The Nonsuch Habitation, or Dwelling with God, the Interest and Duty of Believers; in opposition to the Complemental, Heartless and Reserved Religion of the Hypocrite* (1670).
[28] See the pamphlet by "T. B." which alleges *The General Inefficacy and Insincerity of a Late or Deathbed Repentance* (1670).
[29] BL Additional MS 21630, fo. 14r. This exchange, from 1662, centers on Cressy's own *Exomologesis*, an autobiographical text of motives for conversion, first published in Paris in 1647.
[30] *A Letter to his Royal Highness*, 7–8.

of those wherry-men in religion who look one way and row another."[31] The idea that Catholicism best teaches submission to authority, and thus political obedience in general, had been a popular argument among Catholic loyalists in England since the Elizabethan period, and James's accession as a Catholic monarch made this line of argument still more potent.[32] The old notion of Catholicism as the faith of obedience, meanwhile, drew additional force from the notion of religious stability as a unanimous post-Cromwellian *desideratum*. So, Edward Sclater assures his readers that his conversion to Catholicism in fact reflects *Anglican* teachings, particularly the established Church's insistence on the necessity of "unanimity and peace" during mid-century turmoil. "I have lived to see too much mischief in our own, as yet unhappy Nation" produced by private judgment in matters of religion, writes Sclater. Catholicism, he comes to realize, is the best ecclesiological expression of the "common reason" he has always valued; his turn becomes, then, not a turn at all but rather the logical consequence of a firm purpose.[33]

Sclater's insistence that his conversion was grounded in "reason" further draws on the discourse of rational religion gaining currency among Catholic and Protestant thinkers alike.[34] Writing in hopes of converting the Catholic Earl of Shrewsbury back to Protestantism in 1679, John Tillotson insists on the "reasonableness of Mens examining their religion and the grounds of it." Conversion, Tillotson suggests, need not signify "instability" in belief but precisely the reverse; his argument couches in "reasonable" terms the arguments for "suspension of belief" seen in Jacobean texts of resolution. Opposition to conversion *per se*, meanwhile, "is evidently unreasonable … for at this rate every man that hath once embraced an error and a false Religion must for ever continue in it, because if he be not allowed to

---

[31] George Digby, *Two Speeches of George, Earl of Bristol, With Some Observations upon them* (London, 1674), 2, 5.

[32] Mark Knights argues that "between 1685 and 1688, the Catholics argued more vigorously and more freely than ever that their Church was politically preferable as well as theologically true." Knights, "'Meer religion' and the 'church-state' of Restoration England," in A. Houston and S. Pincus (eds.), *A Nation Transformed: England after the Restoration* (Cambridge University Press, 2001), 41–70, 62.

[33] [Edward Sclater], *Consensus Veterum: Or, the Reasons of Edward Sclater, Minister of Putney, for his Conversion to the Catholic Faith and Communion* (1686), 3. For a riposte, see Edward Gee, *Veteres Vindicati: In an Expostulatory Letter to Mr. Sclater of Putney, upon his Consensus Veterum* (1687).

[34] For a taxonomy of different kinds of theological "rationalism," see Spurr, "'Rational Religion' in Restoration England," *Journal of the History of Ideas* (1988), 563–85. R. D. Tumbleson connects the emphasis on reason in Anglican controversial writings with late seventeenth-century scientific experimentalism. Tumbleson, "'Reason and Religion': The Science of Anglicanism," *Journal of the History of Ideas* 57 (1996), 131–56. For Catholic rationalism, see K. Campbell, *The Intellectual Struggle of the English Papists in the Seventeenth Century: The Catholic Dilemma* (Lewiston, NY: Edwin Mellen, 1987), 127–56, and P. Harth, *Contexts of Dryden's Thought* (University of Chicago Press, 1968), 246–60.

examine it, he can never have reason to change, and to make a change without reason is unreasonable and mere levity and inconstancy."[35] The Restoration debate over conversion drew on texts and arguments from earlier decades of the seventeenth century, returning again and again to ideas of stability and authority. Catholic and Protestant converts alike constantly asserted that their religious change did not undermine these principles, as their opponents alleged, but instead reaffirmed them. With a new emphasis on "reasonableness," moreover, both defended their changes, not as the result of casuistical argument, but as a turn toward straightforward, "plain," and easily comprehended truth.

THE DUCHESS AND THE LAUREATE

Each strand of this complex debate can be seen in the controversy surrounding the Catholic conversion of the Duchess of York – a controversy that gave the newly Catholic John Dryden his first occasion to address the subject of religious change in print. The conversion of Anne Hyde was revealed to the public only posthumously, in 1686, when her widowed husband, now James II, printed a letter of some years earlier in which Anne explained the reasons for her change.[36] But rumors of the duchess's Catholic sympathies had circulated long before James's accession, rumors which had proved politically unfortunate for James and his brother Charles, both keen to deflect allegations of crypto-Catholicism. In a letter written around this time, Anne's father, the Earl of Clarendon, advised James that "your Wife is generally believed to have so perfect Duty & entire resignation to the Will of Your Highness, that any Defection in her from Her Religion will be imputed to want of Circumspection in you, & not using your Authority; or To your connivance. I need not tell you the ill consequence that such a Mutation would be attended with in Reference to your R. H: & even the King Himself, whose greatest Security (under God) is the Affection & Duty of His Protestant Subjects."[37] The masculine fear of female Catholic conversions, so common in the decades of Charles I's reign, had evidently not abated; indeed, the responses to the

---

[35] Tillotson to Shrewsbury, BL Additional MS 69396, fos. 90–6.
[36] *Copy of a Paper written by the Late Duchess of York* (1686). All citations from this document come from Dryden, *Works*, vol. xvii, gen. ed. Swedenberg, vol. ed. S. H. Monk, where it is reprinted as Appendix B on 519.
[37] Edward Hyde, Earl of Clarendon, *Two Letters Written by the Right Honourable Edward Earl of Clarendon, Late Lord High Chancellour of England: one to His Royal Highness the Duke of York: the Other to the Dutchess, Occasioned by her Embracing the Roman Catholic Religion* (1679), 1. Cf. BL Egerton MS 1533, fo. 58r.

duchess's letter suggest a culmination of anxieties about queenly conversions that had been building since the Catholic conversion of James I's wife Anna.

Clarendon wrote still more candidly to his daughter, objecting to her conversion on several grounds. First, he argued, such a move is political dissidence: "they who desert the Church of England, of which they are Members … become thereby disobedient to the Ecclesiastical and Civil Laws of their Country." Second, it is domestic rebellion:

if you change your Religion you renounce all obedience & affection to your Father, who loves you so tenderly that such an odious Mutation would break his heart … you bring irreparable dishonour, scandal, & prejudice to the Duke your Husband, to whom you ought to pay all imaginable Duty … & all possible ruin to your Children, of whose Company & Conversation you must look to be deprived; for God forbid that after such an Apostacy you should have any power in the Education of your Children.

Above all, though, it is a failure of reason. Those who have scruples about the Protestant church, according to Clarendon, "ought rather to suspect that their Understanding hath forsaken them, and they are become mad, then that the Church which is replenished with all Learning and Piety requisite, can betray them to Perdition." This is particularly true of Anne, who, in her father's opinion, was particularly ill-equipped to make a reasonable investigation of religion. "I presume," Clarendon writes, "you do not entangle yourself with the particular Controversies between the Romanists & us, or think yourself a competent Judge of all Difficulties which occur therein."[38] Were he not banished, Clarendon suggests, he would be able to advise her "that there are many Absurdities in the Roman Religion, inconsistent with your Judgement and Understanding … so before you can submit to the Obligations of Faith, you must divest yourself of your Natural Reason, and common sense, and captivate the dictates of your own conscience, to the Impositions of Authority which hath not any pretence to oblige or advise you."[39] Clarendon here couples the familiar rhetoric of the "papist seducer" with the newly widespread idea that religion ought to be based on "Natural Reason and common sense," as his daughter's conversion evidently had not been.

This part of Clarendon's analysis was more or less confirmed by the duchess's reply, defending her conversion in decidedly unintellectual terms. "I choose," she writes, "rather to endeavor to satisfie my Friends … than to

---

[38] Clarendon, *Two Letters*, 2–3.   [39] *Ibid.*, 4.

have the trouble to answer all the Questions that may daily be asked me." She admits that her Catholic turn did not result from theological investigation, but "is a blessing I wholly owe to Almighty God, and I hope the hearing of a Prayer I daily made him." While Anne admits to reading Heylyn's *History of the Reformation*, she describes it as a record of Protestants' failed sympathy rather than their false doctrine. She finds Henry VIII's treatment of Catherine of Aragon, for instance, among the "horridest Sacriledges in the world" for pity's sake, not religion's. In general, the duchess's self-justification substitutes affect for argument: "I take God to Witness I would never have [changed my religion] if I had thought it possible to Save my Soul otherwise." Such an irreducibly subjective statement would seem to foreclose the possibility of a controversial response, but Edward Stillingfleet offered one anyway. His *Answer to Some Papers Lately Printed* (1686) echoes some elements of Clarendon's letter to his daughter. Stillingfleet reasserts Anglican reason and authority, and points out the lack of intellectual grounds for the duchess's religious change:

The way of her Satisfaction must needs appear very extraordinary; for towards the Conclusion she confesses, *She was not able, nor would she enter into Disputes with any Body.* Now where the difference between the two Churches lies wholly in matters of dispute, how any one could be truly satisfied, as to the Grounds of leaving one Church and going to the other, without *entring into matter of Dispute with any body* is hard to understand … what *Satisfaction* is to be had in this manner of proceeding?[40]

After subjecting each of the duchess's timidly proffered claims to indignant logical scrutiny, Stillingfleet sums up: "from all these things laid together I can see no imaginable Reason of any force to conclude, that *she could not save her soul otherwise*, than by embracing the Communion of the Church of Rome."[41] Her conversion cannot be taken seriously, he implies, since it lacks both ample reasons and adequate Reason.

It is precisely this anti-intellectualism, however, that formed the basis for Dryden's contribution to the anonymous pamphlet *Defence of the Papers Written by the Late King of Blessed Memory, and Duchess of York.*[42] Four years earlier, in *Religio Laici*, the Protestant Dryden had indicted the "rust and ignorance" of the Catholic congregations, whose "want of learning" made

---

[40] [Edward Stillingfleet], *An Answer to Some Papers Lately Printed, concerning the Authority of the Catholic Church in Matters of Faith and the Reformation of the Church of England* (1686), 57. Stillingfleet addresses the duchess's paper in particular on pages 56–72.

[41] *Ibid.*, 72.

[42] *Defence of the Papers* is reprinted in Dryden, *Works*, vol. XVII, 291–323. For Dryden's authorship, see Winn, *Dryden*, 420.

them vulnerable to the deceptions of a corrupt clergy (372). In this pamphlet, by contrast, the Catholic Dryden praises the sincerity of Anne's conversion precisely on the basis of its lack of theological sophistication. According to Dryden, the statement in which she confesses her new faith contains such a "Spirit of Meekness, Devotion and Sincerity" that its truth cannot be doubted. Anne's devotional honesty is commensurate with the simplicity of her writing: "moving, plain, without Artifice, and discovering the Piety of the Soul from which it flowed." Dryden continues, "Truth has a Language to it self, which 'tis impossible for Hypocrisie to imitate: Dissimulation could never write so warmly, nor with so much life." Stillingfleet's attack, by contrast, is the work of a man whose "peculiar Talent is that of subtle Calumny and sly Aspersion, by which he insinuates into his Readers an ill Opinion of his Adversaries, before he comes to Argument."[43] Dryden decries the author's wish "to make that difficult, which she found easie: for every thing becomes hard by chopping Logic upon it." He praises, by contrast, simple belief expressed in plain language:

I am sure enough, that the Wall before me is White, and that I can go to it: but put me once upon unriddling Sophisms, I shall not be satisfied of what colour the Wall is, nor how 'tis possible for me to stir from the place in which I am. Alas, if People would be as much in earnest as she was, and read the Scriptures with the same disposition, the same unprejudic'd sincerity in their Hearts, and docility in their Understanding, seeking to bend their Judgments to what they find, not what they find to their Judgments, more I believe would find things as easie as she did.[44]

Dryden praises Anne for refusing "to become an Experiment of the perfection to which the Art of Learned Obscurity is improv'd in this our Age." He credits her conversion precisely because her reasons for it are uncomplex, reflecting an admirable intellectual "docility." If Clarendon and Stillingfleet cast doubt upon the "reasonableness" of the duchess's conversion, Dryden's *Defence* turns the tables, suggesting that her critics demonstrate "Learned Obscurity" instead of Christian reason. Examining ideas of rational theology in the Restoration, John Spurr has pointed out an "unacknowledged incongruity" between two concepts of "reason": "logical coherence" on the one hand, and "moral rectitude" ("right reason") on the other.[45] Dryden defends the duchess's conversion as "reasonable" in the latter sense, and objects to those who focus only on the former, maintaining too-stringent standards of intellectual justification.

[43] *Defence of the Papers*, in *Works*, vol. XVII, 292–3.   [44] *Ibid.*, 321–2.
[45] Spurr, "'Rational Religion,'" 580–1.

Stillingfleet, of course, responded, accusing Dryden of sophistry himself. "The Words of the Royal Paper are plain," he writes, "but these Interpretations of them so forced and unnatural" that they fail to make their case. According to Stillingfleet, Dryden couples unnatural argument with unnecessary *ad hominem* attacks – both of which undermine his own sincerity as a convert to the Catholic Church:

> Is this indeed the Spirit of a *New Convert*? Is this the Meekness and Temper you intend to gain Proselites by, and to convert the Nation? He tells us in the beginning, that *Truth has a Language* peculiar to it self; I desire to be informed whether these be any of the Characters of it? And how the language of Reproach and Evil-speaking may be distinguished from it? But Zeal in a New Convert is a terrible thing; for it not only burns but rages, like the Eruptions of Mount Aetna, it fills the Air with noise and smoak; and throws out such a torrent of liquid fire that there is no standing before it.[46]

Dryden's *Defence*, according to Stillingfleet, shows a distinct lack of both theological sophistication ("This Gentleman talks like a meer Novice as to matters of Faith, as tho' Believing were *a new thing* to him") and verbal clarity ("the plain truth is: Controversie is quite another thing from Courtship and Poetry").[47] Dryden pointedly responded, several months later, with a poem. *The Hind and the Panther*, a work which Margaret Doody calls "the great, the undeniable *sui generis* poem of the Restoration era," had, in fact, a clear genealogy in Restoration polemic: it was written as Dryden's further attempt to justify his and Anne's Catholic conversions, and as an attempt – *contra* Stillingfleet – to assert the compatibility of "Controversie" and "Poetry."[48]

The Hind and the Panther

Even before its first couplet, *The Hind and the Panther* revisits some of the central claims of the *Defence*. In a preface to the reader, Dryden reiterates his praise of the sanctified simplicity of Catholicism, in contrast both to the "logic-chopping" of its detractors and the generally chaotic "Ferment" of religious affairs in England.[49] Just as Dryden had earlier insisted that the

---

[46] [Edward Stillingfleet], *A Vindication of the Answer to Some Late Papers concerning the Unity and Authority of the Catholic Church, and the Reformation of the Church of England* (1687), 102.

[47] *Ibid.*, 107–8.

[48] M. Doody, *The Daring Muse: Augustan Poetry Reconsidered* (Cambridge University Press, 1985), 77. Doody's analysis of the poem's "odd structure and mode of proceeding" is part of her larger characterization of post-Restoration poetry as dynamic, turbulent, and expressive of conflict.

[49] Dryden, Preface to *The Hind and the Panther*, in *Works*, vol. III, gen. ed. Swedenberg, vol. ed. E. Miner, 119–122, 119.

duchess intended the account of her conversion for "no one but her friends," so he now claims that his own poem "was neither impos'd on me, nor so much as the subject given me by any man."[50] His preface thus declares its own argumentative superfluity: "What I desire the *Reader* should know concerning me, he will find in the Body of the Poem; if he have but the patience to peruse it."[51] Dryden announces that "one Design of the Poem" itself was to argue "That the Church of *England* might have been perswaded to have taken off the *Penal Lawes* and the *Test*," an argument that he promises to offer in the poem's third part.[52] In the preface, however, he avoids adumbrating any of these particular arguments, suggesting instead that the poem will demonstrate, will literally *embody*, the straightforward truth of his new Catholic beliefs.[53]

As in his *Defence* of the duchess, Dryden here implies that style can, itself, indicate religious sincerity, implicitly rejecting Stillingfleet's opposition between piety and poetry. Contemporary satirists responded with skepticism: one commentator wonders "what kind of Champion the Roman Catholicks have now gotten; for they have had divers ways of *representing* themselves; but this way of *Rhiming* us to death, is altogether new … take away the *Railing* and no *Argument* remains."[54] He concludes by advising Dryden that "it had been more edifying, if you had written *in Prose*."[55] Such complaints miss one of the crucial argumentative tactics of the poem: to develop a poetic style that can mirror, and thus celebrate, a church which is

> One in herself not rent by schism, but sound,
> Entire, one solid shining Diamond […]
> As undivided, so from errours free,
> As one in faith, so one in sanctity.   (II.526–32)

In *The Hind and the Panther*, Dryden implies that the clarity of his new Catholic beliefs can best be conveyed through a corresponding clarity of poetic diction.

This effort to construct a poetics of simplicity is evident even in the opening eight lines of Book I, where Dryden reincarnates the docile believer Anne Hyde as the (near-homonymic) Catholic Hind, "Milk white … immortal and unchang'd" (I.I). The two adjectives "immortal" and

---

[50] Dryden, Preface, 121; Dryden, *Defence*, 338.   [51] Dryden, Preface, 119.   [52] Dryden, Preface, 121.

[53] Dryden thus admits in advance that, as Harth points out, "Neither [the Defence of the Duchess's Papers nor *The Hind and the Panther*] is an attempt to explain his reasons for becoming a Catholic." Harth, *Contexts*, 230.

[54] M. Clifford, *Notes upon Mr. Dryden's Poems in Four Letters, to which are annexed some Reflections on the Hind and Panther, by another Hand* (1687), 17, 19.

[55] *Ibid.*, 34.

"unchang'd" in the poem's first line neatly summarize decades of controversial literature asserting the eternal and immutable qualities of Catholic tradition.[56] The syntactic balances in lines 3 and 4, moreover, both reassert and reflect the Hind's miraculous, unchanging faith: "Without unspotted, innocent within / She fear'd no danger, for she knew no sin" (1.3–4). Past and future, inner and outer become stable approximations of each other for Dryden's eternally mild, preternaturally innocent Hind. Her "plain simplicity"(III.31) becomes clearer still when juxtaposed with the rest of the "drossy [and] divisible" bestiary (1.320).[57] Here again, poetic diction underscores polemical argument, as Dryden depicts Protestant sectarianism with abruptly divided, grammatically restless lines.

> The bloudy *Bear*, an *Independent* beast,
> Unlick'd to form, in groans her hate expressed.
> Among the timorous kind the *Quaking Hare*
> Profess'd neutrality, but would not swear.
> Next her the *Buffoon Ape*, as atheists use,
> Mimick'd all Sects and had his own to chuse:
> Still when the *Lyon* look'd, his knees he bent,
> And pay'd at Church a Courtier's Complement. (1.35–42)

Rapid transitions and short clauses cram a large and motley crew into a small space, while the succession of enjambments suggest the promiscuous and rapid mingling of Protestant kinds. In contrast to the nominative calm of the Hind's description, Dryden's presentation of these sectarians centers on their verbal actions – they "groan" and "quake," "mimick" and "chuse." While the innocent Hind seems to inhabit the timeless green world of fable, these beasts belong to Dryden's world: a corrupt world of calumny, flattery, mutability, and oath-flouting hypocrisy.

These antic animal non-conformists prepare us to encounter the Hind's arch-enemy, the Panther, representing the English Protestant establishment. This animal's corruption lies not so much in sinful action, but in flawed essence: "Her faults and virtues lye so mix'd, that she / Nor wholly stands condemn'd nor wholly free" (1.333–4). Here, the verbs "lye" and "stand" indicate states of being rather than actions; the antonymic relationship between them, however, underscores the Panther's fatal lack of internal

---

[56] See the Hind's discourse at II.305 ff. for a discussion of the conveyance of "Eternal truth" through the apostolic succession, and the function of Church authority to "prevent surprise" in doctrine (II.365).

[57] Harth has surveyed the evidence of Dryden's discomfort with the "excesses of private judgement" permitted by Protestantism. He suggests a number of contemporary Catholic sources for the Hind's claim that the Catholic Church offers an infallible and corporate standard of interpretation (*Contexts*, 232–44).

coherence. In contrast to the mirroring clauses in the description of the Hind, the elegantly balanced division of the couplet's second line expresses the smoothness of Anglican compromise. Later, Dryden will describe the Panther as similarly divided:

> neither loved nor fear'd,
> A meer mock Queen of a divided Herd ...
> Now, mixing with a salvage crowd, she goes
> And meanly flatters her invet'rate foes.
> Ruled while she rules, and losing every hour
> Her wretched remnants of precarious pow'r.   (1.497–511)

The Anglican church, for Dryden, is marked by inconsistency and weakness of will. His initial description of the Panther has, however, already made this point more subtly; even in the syntax of their respective descriptions, the "mix'd" and "spotted" lady neatly foils the miraculous wholeness and coherence of her Catholic enemy.

Yet, as satirists of the poem observed more than three hundred years ago, Dryden's explicit praise and practice of simplicity – the "limpid stream" or "seamless coat" of both poem and faith – conceals crucial discontinuities. Early critics were fond of noting that Dryden's praise of an irrefutable Catholic truth in fact contradicts not only the anti-Catholic slanders of *Absalom and Achitophel* and *The Spanish Fryar*, but also the earlier Anglican rationalism of *Religio Laici*, which roundly condemned the "partial papists" (356). In the preface to *The New Atlantis*, Thomas Heyrick quips that "*Religio Laici* ... indeed is a Confutation of [the] *Hind and the Panther* before hand."[58] Another satirist, Thomas Brown, dramatizes Dryden's self-division by presenting "a Dialogue between Crites, Eugenius, and Mr. Bays," or a dialogue between the two interlocutors of Dryden's own *Essay of Dramatic Poetry* and the author of *The Hind and the Panther*.[59] By reanimating Dryden's own characters, and allowing them to object to his later Catholic poem, the satirist suggests that Dryden's error is aesthetic as well as theological; the conversion of "Mr. Bays" is an inconsistency that violates his own principles of decorum in art and in life.

A number of modern critics have defended Dryden by identifying a coherent line of philosophical or theological commitment extending from

---

[58] [Thomas Heyrick], *The New Atlantis. A Poem in Three Books, with some Reflections on the Hind and the Panther* (1687), A2v.

[59] [Thomas Brown], *The Reasons of Mr. Bays Changing his Religion, Considered in a Dialogue between Crites, Eugenius, and Mr. Bays* (1688).

Religio Laici to *The Hind and the Panther*.[60] This seems, strictly speaking, unnecessary. Dryden acknowledges, and indeed insists, that his convictions *did* in fact change. In one of the most famous passages of the poem, Dryden interrupts his fable with an autobiographical aside:

> My thoughtless youth was wing'd with vain desires,
> My manhood, long misled by wand'ring fires,
> Follow'd false lights; and when their glimps was gone,
> My pride struck out new sparkles of her own.
> Such was I, such by nature still I am,
> Be Thine the glory, and be mine the shame. (1.72–7)

The poet's admission of his enduring sinfulness ("such by nature still I am") does not qualify his larger description of a fundamentally altered life. If the Catholic Church is itself "unchanged," Dryden has changed in order to embrace it. *The Hind and the Panther* is thus a statement of the poet having "reviewed and revised" his earlier Anglican convictions – having, in other words, converted.[61] Inconsistencies between this poem and Dryden's earlier work are thus not only permissible, but necessary proofs of this self-conscious "self-correction."[62]

A more troubling mutability or inconsistency, however, occurs not so much between Dryden's Catholic fable and his earlier writings as a Protestant, but within *The Hind and the Panther* itself. Margaret Doody notes that the poem moves "from level to level and from style to style" as it moves from book to book.[63] But even the first twenty lines of the poem, lines that seem to present the allegory of the Catholic Church in its most "plain simplicity," contain subtly jarring disruptions of tone and sense. The first line's insistence on the Hind's eternity and immutability, first of all, is immediately qualified by an admission in the second line that she "fed on the lawn and in the forest rang'd" – details that locate her in a particular time and place. This contextualization, moreover, contains an implicit

---

[60] Hamm, "Dryden's *The Hind and the Panther*," 400–15.

[61] S. Budick, *Dryden and the Abyss of Light: A Study of "Religio Laici" and "The Hind and the Panther"* (New Haven: Yale University Press, 1970), 172.

[62] Harth, *Contexts*, 227; P. Hammond, *John Dryden: A Literary Life* (Basingstoke: Macmillan, 1991), 133. I follow Steven Zwicker's suggestion that "the drive to discover consistency of belief" in Dryden's work "is misguided." Zwicker, "How Many Religions Did John Dryden Have?," in J. Lewis and M. E. Novak (eds.), *Enchanted Ground: Reimagining John Dryden* (University of Toronto Press, 2004), 178.

[63] Doody, *The Daring Muse*, 78. Doody concludes that Dryden is asking his reader "to remain skeptical about all styles and genres," although she does not consider the theological implications of such an attitude. I agree with her basic suggestion that "Dryden knew his poem was odd and difficult," and intended it as such (79).

paradox: a deer who grazes on a lawn is socialized, tamed, domesticated, while a deer who ranges in the forest is contrastingly wild. After claiming that the Hind is essentially "unchanged," Dryden admits that she has in fact already wandered into transformative, antithetical contexts. The poem's ambiguous first couplet already flirts with contingency, its initial tautology immediately followed by an implicit disjunction between stasis and errancy.

The second four lines qualify the linked simplicity of Hind and poem still further. Dryden tells us that his heroine is "Without unspotted, innocent within," and that this state of innocence prevents her from worrying about harm: "[s]he fear'd no danger, for she knew no sin" (1.4). Immediately, however, the assertion of ahistorical inexperience is undercut: "Yet," he admits, "had she oft been chas'd with horns and hounds / And *Scythian* shafts" (1.5–6). The "immortal and unchang'd" Hind, it seems, has had a lively history after all: she *has* in fact been subject to danger, and *has* known others' sin, if not her own, before the start of the poem. Dryden's description of the hunt as a trinity of alliterative assaults on the Hind continues this temporal distortion – particularly his reference to the "winged wounds / Aim'd at her heart" (1.6–7). Each element of this metonymic phrase indicates a different moment of the attack: the arrows are at once "winged," suggesting suspension in flight, "aim'd," indicating their state prior to their release, and, of course, "wounds," implying that they have in fact already arrived at their target. The ensuing line only adds to the confusion, since the Hind's "doom" is "death," while her "fate" is "not to die" (1.8). The Hind's ambivalent future casts doubt on Dryden's initial declaration of the Hind's "immortal and unchang'd" innocence. By elaborating the dangers and dramas of the hunt, Dryden makes the Hind's miraculous, extratemporal endurance seem all the more improbable.

The phrase "*Scythian* shafts," metonymically describing the Hind's pursuers, introduces another complication, on the level of allusion. Dryden's editor notes that the phrase likely refers to the "*scythia sagitta*" [*sic*] in Book 10 of Ovid's *Metamorphoses*, retelling the story of Atalanta.[64] This source seems likely; Dryden maintained a lively poetic interest in Ovid, and especially Ovid's representations of women's suffering, throughout his career.[65] This particular Ovidian allusion, to a virginal maiden fleeing her rapacious suitors, seems at first an appropriate analogy for Dryden's depiction of a

---

[64] Dryden, *Works*, vol. III, 353.
[65] See D. Hopkins, "Dryden and Ovid's 'Wit out of Season'", in Charles Martindale (ed.), *Ovid Renewed: Ovidian Influences on Literature and Art from the Middle Ages to the Twentieth Century* (Cambridge University Press, 1988), 167–90.

feminized and victimized church. Comparing Dryden's description of the
Hind's flight with the original passage in Ovid, however, reveals a number
of troubling implications. First, the "Scythian shafts" in Dryden's poem
are weapons that have been aimed at the Hind. In Ovid, by contrast, the
phrase is an ablative of comparison: "*Quae quamquam Scythica non setius ire
sagitta / Aeonio visa est iuveni, tamen ille decorem / Miratur magis*" ["Though
she seemed to the Aeonian youth to go not less swiftly than a Scythian
arrow, yet he admired her beauty still more"].[66] Ovid's Atalanta is not the
victim of "Scythian shafts," but likened to one herself. The comparison
associates her flight, superficially a sign of her feminine chastity, with a proud
and cruel sexual withholding. Hardly running in fear from her pursuers,
Ovid's proud huntress in fact leads her suitors on a doomed chase that will
send most of them to their deaths. Second, even if Dryden had intentionally
used the story of Atalanta to indicate the chaste Catholic Hind's eventual
eluding of her pursuers, he also necessarily invokes another moment in Ovid's
narrative: Atalanta's eventual capture by the apple-tossing Hippomenes,
which – if we maintain the analogy – would suggest that the triumph of
Catholicism is only provisional. Finally, but perhaps most obviously of all, the
Metamorphoses seems an extremely peculiar intertext to use in a description of
an "unchanged" heroine.

Another problematic allusion might lurk behind Dryden's unexplained
choice of species for his heroine. To borrow a question from *The Hind and
the Panther Transvers'd*, why is Catholicism a *Hind* in the first place?
Sanford Budick suggests an allusion to the central stag of the Legend of
St. Chad; Anne Barbeau Gardiner argues that the Hind represents the
Church as "bride of Christ," described as a "deer" in Canticles.[67] But the
figure of the maidenly, hunted Hind could also call to mind another secular
source: the tradition of romantic venery popularized in the sixteenth-
century English love lyric, where "deers" and "harts" embody an erotic
paronomasia. The appearance of a feminized deer ranging in the forest of the
sovereign may even allude to one of the most notorious Tudor hind-poems,
Sir Thomas Wyatt's translation of Petrarch's *Rime Sparse* 190 as "Whoso list
to hount," a sonnet in which the wearied speaker declares his decision to

---

[66] Ovid, *Metamorphoses*, Books IX–XIV, ed. and trans. F. J. Miller, rsd. G. P. Goold, 2nd edn.
(Cambridge, MA: Harvard University Press, 1984), x.588–90.
[67] Budick, *Dryden and the Abyss of Light*, 181. A. B. Gardiner, *Ancient Faith and Modern Freedom in John
Dryden's "The Hind and the Panther"* (Washington, DC: The Catholic University Press, 1998), 12–95.
Gardiner sees Canticles as the key to the fable, the source for the Hind's status as holy spouse, and a
text that implicitly comments on Dryden's conversion, representing the poet's "ascent" along with
that of the Bride herself (96–110). For a fuller survey of traditions of hind-imagery, see the note in
Dryden, *Selected Poems*, ed. P. Hammond and D. Hopkins (London: Longman, 2007), 386–7.

"leave off" his pursuit of an unattainable Hind.[68] Wyatt's sonnets did not circulate widely in the Restoration, and although Dryden prided himself on his command of English literary history, it is difficult to establish with any certainty that he knew this poem. But a central and striking similarity links Wyatt's Hind with Dryden's: both deer are fair and feminized, and both are defended from molestation by the particular power and favor of the male monarch. Wyatt explains that his chase is doomed to frustration because the Hind wears a diamond collar marking her as "Caesar's," while Dryden refers to his Hind's "sov'reign" protection from harm. Dryden clearly refers to the Catholicism of James II; in the England of 1687, the Catholic Church was, indeed, "Caesar's." The specter of Wyatt, however, points in precisely the opposite ecclesiological direction; the Hind of this sonnet is an allegory of Anne Boleyn, whose ill-fated marriage to Henry VIII inaugurated the English Reformation a century and a half earlier.[69]

While the echo of Wyatt's poem may be no more than a tantalizing possibility, Dryden's use of the adjective "milk-white" to describe the Hind introduces a clearer but no less troubling English poetic allusion: to the *Faerie Queene*. We know that Dryden had Spenser in mind as he wrote this poem; he mentions *Mother Hubberd's Tale* explicitly at the beginning of Book III as a model for his own beast fable.[70] But the initial characterizations of Hind and Panther also recall the first canto of Spenser's epic, in which we meet Redcrosse Knight and his companion: a "louely Ladie," "whiter" than the Ass "more white then snow" on which she rides (1.1.4–5). This fair lady, Una, is accompanied, in turn, by a "milk-white Lambe," to whom she is compared: she is "so pure an Innocent, as that same lambe." Una has been "expeld" from her lands by "that infernall feend," from whom she must be guarded (1.1.5). Spenser's Una and Dryden's Hind, in other words, share more than milk-whiteness. They are both vulnerable, "innocent" exiles, and royal ones as well: Una "by descent from Royall lynage

---

[68] R. Sylvester (ed.), *English Sixteenth-Century Verse: An Anthology* (New York: Norton, 1984), 163. For the Petrarchan original, see R. Durling (ed.), *Petrarch's Lyric Poems* (Cambridge, MA: Harvard University Press, 1976), 336–7.

[69] For the relation of this poem to Anne in particular, see G. Walker, *Writing under Tyranny: English Literature and the Henrician Reformation* (Oxford University Press, 2005), 287–8. The popularity of John Banks's 1682 tragedy *Anna Bullen, or Virtue Betray'd* suggests that Restoration audiences had an ongoing interest in the story of Anne and Henry. See J. Marsden, *Fatal Desire: Women, Sexuality and the English Stage 1660–1720* (Ithaca, NY: Cornell University Press, 2006), 79.

[70] Imagining men who will "censure this mysterious writ," Dryden retorts, "Let Aesop answer, who has set to view / Such kinds as Greece and Phrygia never knew; / And Mother Hubbard in her homely dress / Has sharply blam'd a British Lionesse … Led by those great examples, may not I / The wanted organs of their words supply?" (III.6–13). See A. Patterson, *Fables of Power: Aesopian Writing and Political History* (Durham, NC: Duke University Press, 1991), 94–109.

came / Of ancient Kings and Queenes, that had of yore / Their scepters stretcht from East to Westerne shore" (1.i.5), while the tragically dispossessed Hind wanders "in kingdoms once her own" (1.6). Unlike the allusion to the imperious Atalanta, this literary reference seems to support Dryden's characterization of the meek and mild Catholic Church seeking safety from harm. Except, that is, for the obvious fact that Spenser's white lady seems allegorically to embody an embattled *Protestantism*. Indeed, it is Una who warns Red Crosse about Errour, a monstrous creature intended to represent specifically religious error, and most likely Catholic error. For Spenser, Catholicism is hardly "unspotted," but is instead a grotesquely hybrid figure: "the vgly monster plaine, / Halfe like a serpent horribly displaide / But th'other halfe did womans shape retaine, / Most lothsom, filthie, foule, and full of vile disdaine" (1.i.14). The opening allegory of *The Hind and the Panther* seems to invoke the opening allegory of *The Faerie Queene* in order to invert it; Spenser's gentle Protestant lady becomes the Catholic Hind, while the hybrid Errour surfaces in the half-breed Anglican Panther.

From the very beginning of his poem, then, Dryden gestures – overtly or obliquely – toward sources that trouble, or even flatly contradict, his poem's "plain" or "simple" surface meaning, putting allusion at cross-purposes with argument. Perhaps we are simply not meant to notice these difficulties; in the words of Prior and Montague in *The Hind and the Panther Transvers'd*, "the Author can play with words so well, that this and twenty such [contradictions] will pass off at a slight reading" (A3v). But why include such contradictions at all? Why should Dryden fashion his poetic affirmation of an immortal, unchanged church from such problematic sources? Perhaps by allowing his reader to find evidence against his own declarations of belief – even inserting such evidence into the text itself – Dryden makes those declarations seem all the more grounded upon simple, miraculous conviction (the kind for which he had earlier praised Anne Hyde). In other words, perhaps the contradictory claims in the description of Catholicism are not to be explained, but rather pre-empted, carefully embedded in the poem in order to demonstrate eternal truth's supervention of logic. Sanford Budick reads the poem as Dryden's confrontation of an "abyss of light," a move which he sees as an outgrowth of the rational mysticism of the Cambridge Platonists.[71] Dryden's faith, for Budick, exists precisely in "the planned leap or gap itself – the architectonic void supported between proposition and conclusion."[72] Anne Cotterill suggests that this movement toward "mystery" allowed Dryden "to express his complex feelings of vulnerability, of

[71] Budick, *Dryden and the Abyss of Light*, 72–3, 85–94. [72] *Ibid.*, 174, 235–6.

disappointment and anger" at his king.[73] Offering a similarly pragmatic explanation, Steven Zwicker proposes that *The Hind and the Panther*, "newly concerned with mysteries and enigmas, with the difficulties and uncertainties of interpretation and application, and with the multivalence of language itself," reflects Dryden's conflicted political stance at the time of the poem's composition.[74]

I want to suggest that the poem's ambiguities and contradictions do not merely reflect Dryden's mysticism on the one hand, or his particular "vulnerability and dilemmas" in the spring of 1687 on the other.[75] Instead, taken together, these poetic cruxes comprise Dryden's subtle reading of English ecclesio-political history more broadly conceived. This reading, in turn, centers on the subject of conversion, both personal and national. Through the problematic allusions of Book I, coupled with the more oft-noted dialogic ambiguities of Books II and III, Dryden emphasizes the centrality of change as a theme both in his own poetry and in his understanding of his nation's past. *The Hind and the Panther*'s equivocations not only evoke its particular religious and political moment, but also ask us to consider the kinds of evasion, inversion, and ambiguity that had consistently characterized English political and theological discourse throughout the foregoing century. In this sense, *The Hind and the Panther* is not only a poem about England's history of conversion, but it is an attempt to render that history poetically.

CONVERSION, RETROSPECTION, AND POETIC LANGUAGE

If Zwicker has put us on our guard against language as "disguise" in the Restoration, other historians have cautioned that even the most undisguised

---

[73] A. Cotterill, "Parenthesis at the Center: The Complex Embrace of *The Hind and the Panther*," *Eighteenth Century Studies* 30 (1996–7), 139–40. Similarly, A. Patterson connects the poem's ambiguity with its particular historical context, as part of her larger discussion of the literary strategies with which writers confronted persecution and censorship. The "ambiguous rhetorical effect" of the poem, for Patterson, shows us that "Dryden in this poem was fascinated by problems of interpretation in scripture, and in the technical meaning of 'equivocation' as saying something, under pressure, other than what one believes" (*Fables of Power*, 105). Patterson elaborates on this argument in *Censorship and Interpretation: The Conditions of Reading and Writing in Early Modern England* (Madison: University of Wisconsin Press, 1984).

[74] S. Zwicker, *Politics and Language in Dryden's Poetry: The Arts of Disguise* (Princeton University Press, 1984), 124–5. In "The Paradoxes of Tender Conscience," *ELH* 63 (1996), 851–69, Zwicker suggests that "the mixed motives and mixed modes of this text project both the ironies and paradoxes in which the poet was caught and the larger puzzles and paradoxes of the [political] moment itself" (852).

[75] Zwicker, "Paradoxes," 854.

expressions of seemingly irreconcilable religious or political positions can sound confusingly similar in the period. This is, at least in part, because of an inherited language of crisis; indeed, representations of popery and arbitrary government from this period frequently refer to earlier crises as shorthand for their own contemporary ones.[76] In the flood of texts on the subject of conversion printed after the lapse of the Licensing Act in 1679, for instance, many moderate Anglican writers played on the longstanding association of popery and radical Protestantism, linking Catholic conversions to the sectarian mayhem of the civil wars. However, the debates were retrospective not only in content, but also in form. The Term Catalogues show that a preponderance of the works on "Divinity" published between 1668 and 1685 were in fact reprintings of earlier controversial texts.[77] New texts appeared, to be sure, but almost always as variations on genres that had been invented earlier in the century, including the statement of motive, the guide to resolution, and the letter of counsel.[78]

A key difference, however, in the controversial literature of the Restoration, and particularly the literature on the subject of conversion, exists on the level of style. Often, for example, the process of polemical debate speeds up into a kind of stichomythic shorthand. Earlier in the century, printed statements of motives for conversions would often occasion lengthy replies, the author taking up each motive advanced by the convert and responding at considerable length (the responses to Alabaster's *Seven Motives* are here a case in point). In the Restoration, and especially by the accession of James II, quasi-dramatic dialogues about religious conversions present

[76] J. Miller notes the "anachronism" of anti-Catholic writing in the Restoration, *Popery and Politics in England*, 86–9. In numerous books and articles, most recently in *England's Troubles 1603–1702: Seventeenth-Century English Political Instability in European Context* (Cambridge University Press, 2000), Jonathan Scott advances a bolder version of this idea, arguing that Restoration writers were "prisoners of memory," trapped in a recurrent fear of "popery and arbitrary government." Mark Knights suggests that the retrospective nature of political and religious rhetoric was in fact deliberate; Restoration writers were manipulators of memory, not its prisoners. Knights, *Politics and Opinion in Crisis, 1678–81* (Cambridge University Press, 1994), 11 and *passim*.

[77] *The Term Catalogues, 1668–1709 A.D.: A Contemporary Bibliography of English Literature in the Reigns of Charles II, James II, William and Mary, and Anne* (London, 1903–6). See also the *Catalogues* edited by Jones and Gee.

[78] Other representative examples of such writings about conversion, in addition to the discussions of the Duke and Duchess of York, include John Tillotson, *The Protestant Religion Vindicated* (1680); Vincent Alsup, *Melius Inquirendum* (1678); Serenus Cressy, *Fanaticism Fanatically Imputed* (1674); William Barlow, *A Few Plain Reasons Why a Protestant Should Not Turn Catholic* (1688); [William Lloyd], *Papists No Catholics* (1679); Christopher Musgrave, *Motives and Reasons for Dissevering from the Church of Rome* (1688); Nicholas French, *The Dolefull Fall of Andrew Sall, a Jesuit of the fourth vow, from the Roman Catholick apostolick faith lamented by his constant friend, with an open rebuking of his imbracing the confession, contained in the XXXIX Articles of the Church of England* (Louvain, 1674); [Anon.], *The Great Danger of Continuing in and the Greater of Apostatizing To, the Romish Religion* (1669).

interlocutors who seem to anticipate each other's positions before hearing them, responding with mimicry and mockery rather than argument.[79] In texts like Serenus Cressy's *I. Why are You a Catholic? The Answer follows. II. Question: But Why are You a Protestant?* (1686), the back-and-forth of theological debate comes close to self-parody. In others, dialogues answer other dialogues, the titles forming a kind of meta-dialogue that teeters on the edge of the ridiculous: *A Dialogue between a New Catholic Convert and a Protestant, Shewing the Doctrine of Transubstantiation to be as Reasonable to be Believ'd as the Great Mystery of the Trinity* (1686) is no sooner published than answered by the dialogic *Answer to a Dialogue between a New Catholick Convert and a Protestant, to Prove the Mystery of the Trinity to be as absurd a Doctrine as Transubstantiation* (1686). Restoration authors accuse each other of insincerity and instability, but they use nearly identical calumnies to do so – Patrick Pastgrace can sound a lot like Peter Pleadwell.[80] Add to this the vogue for explicitly satiric "transversals" and "transprosings," and Restoration polemic becomes still harder to interpret with any degree of confidence.[81]

Before his conversion, Dryden had joined the chorus that associated "fanaticism" equally with Catholicism and radical Protestantism. In the postscript to his 1684 *History of the League*, for instance, Dryden describes the "agreement of principles" between Jesuits and Presbyterians, asserting that "besides the names of the Countreys, France and England, and the Names of Religions, Protestant and Papists, there is scarcely to be found the least difference, in the project of the whole, and in the substance of the articles."[82] He offers that he "might advise a *Dutch* maker of Emblemes, he shou'd draw a Presbyterian in Arms on one side, a Jesuit on the other, and a crowned head betwixt them," with the English monarchy hanging in the balance between these two interchangeable threats.[83] In the deliberate confusions and contradictions of *The Hind and the Panther*, we can see that Dryden did not abandon this idea of interchangeability after his conversion, but instead refined and elaborated it. Instead of focusing on the unstable extremes of Jesuit and Presbyterian, Dryden's poem paints a fuller picture of the unstable and retrospective qualities of religious and political culture in

---

[79] In this sense, what Doody has called "generic self-consciousness" in Augustan poetry can also be seen in the controversial literature of the period. See *The Daring Muse*, Chapter 3.

[80] These names come from the title of one of the earliest instances of such satiric printed debates: *A New Way of Conference, being a Dialogue between Patrick Pastgrace, a Papist, and Peter Pleadwell, a Protestant, Fild with Mirth and varnisht with Modesty* (1641).

[81] For a discussion of "epistemological uncertainty" in terms of Restoration political discourse, see M. Knights, *Representation and Misrepresentation in Later Stuart Culture: Partisanship and Political Culture* (Oxford University Press, 2005), 278 and Part 2 *passim*.

[82] Dryden, *History of the League* (1684), in *Works*, vol. XVIII, 402.   [83] *Ibid.*, 403.

late seventeenth-century England – acknowledging, moreover, his own complicity in that unstable culture as a convert to Catholicism. In Book I's allusions to Protestant poetry of the preceding century, for example, Dryden connects contemporary English religious and political conflicts to a longer history of instability. Writing in the aftermath of the Exclusion Crisis, Dryden reminds his readers of earlier crises that put the English throne in jeopardy: the divorce of Henry VIII, the death of Mary, and accession of his daughter Elizabeth. Rather than referring immediately and directly to recent Catholic conversions (either his own or the Duchess of York's), Dryden's allusions point the reader to England's earlier religious alterations under successive Tudors. Fashioned, at least in part, out of poetic descriptions of Protestant heroines, the Hind becomes less a representative Catholic than a representative *convert*. Rather than proposing the Hind as a harbinger of a future (Catholic) denominational stability, then, Dryden uses allusion to turn her into an emblem of England's religious unrest.

Acknowledging Dryden's interest in the contingency of doctrinal positions and their polemic expression leads to a new way of understanding Books II and III, in which Hind and Panther retire for lengthy theological debates. Critics have argued over which elements of doctrine were uppermost in Dryden's mind as he composed the arguments that comprise these books. Anne Barbeau Gardiner and Donald Benson have both contended that the disagreement between the Hind and the Panther centers on the status of the Real Presence in the sacrament.[84] T. A. Birrell claims that the Hind's position is largely informed by the modified Gallicanism of Benedictines like Father James Maurus Corker, while Victor Hamm has argued for the influence of the skeptical Catholic epistemology of the Blackloists.[85] Against such "clarificatory" readings, Margaret Doody has suggested that Dryden gives us a "recreation of poetic crisis in his poem; elements [of style and doctrine] are mixed up and stood on their heads," while Philip Harth points out that the particular topics debated by the Hind and the Panther – for instance, the proper relation between scripture and tradition – were not current subjects of theological debate in 1685, but in fact belong to earlier episodes of religious conflict.[86] All this suggests that

---

[84] A. B. Gardiner, "A Witty French Preacher in the English Court, Dryden, and the Great Debate on the Real Presence," *ELH* 65 (1998), 593–616. Benson's analysis attempts to connect the issue of sacramental presence with Dryden's poetics: "Dryden's *The Hind and the Panther*: Transubstantiation and Figurative Language," *Journal of the History of Ideas* 43 (1982), 195–208.

[85] See T. A. Birrell, "James Maurus Corker and John Dryden's Conversion," *SEL* 4 (1964), 461–8; Hamm, "Dryden's *The Hind and the Panther*," *PMLA* 83 (1968), 400–15.

[86] Doody, *The Daring Muse*, 76; P. Harth, "Religion and Politics in Dryden's Poetry and Plays," *MP* 70 (1973), 236–42.

The Hind and the Panther is, finally, not so much a work of controversial poetry as it is a poem *about* controversy, and particularly about its intersecting qualities of equivocation and retrospection at the end of the seventeenth century. The debate between the Hind and Panther is meant precisely to dramatize the kinds of ambivalent exchange that characterize the controversial literature of the time.

Dryden stresses the resemblance between the Catholic Hind and Anglican Panther from the opening lines of Book II. Here, the Panther congratulates the Hind on having "'scap'd" the "toils" of the Philistians – having avoided persecution after the Popish Plot (II.1–16). The Hind reminds her guest that the targets of persecution were not only Catholics, but Anglicans as well. "As I remember ... / Those toils were for your own dear self design'd, / As well as me" (II.18–20). This initial acknowledgment of the interchangeability of the Hind and the Panther in the eyes of their enemies – expressed in a neatly balanced exchange – sets a precedent for the rest of the section, in which the interlocutors trade places as often as they trade insults. The Hind accuses the Panther of altering her view of the sacraments: "There chang'd your faith, and what may change may fall. / Who can believe what varies every day, / Nor ever was, nor will be at a stay?" (II.35–7). In response to the Panther's swift denial of such changes, the Hind retorts "not only Jesuits can equivocate" (II.45). Here, as Zwicker has pointed out, the Hind "raises the very charges raised against [Dryden] and turns them against the Anglicans." The Panther's defense, in turn (that "men may err" (II.486)), is "exactly the same admission of change and the same defense of fallibility that the poet himself had earlier rehearsed" in the lines about his own conversion.[87] "If that common principle be true," the Panther adds, "The Cannon, Dame, is level'd full at you" (II.62–3). Indeed, the Panther's deflection of slanderous charges, in its echo of Dryden's own self-defense, points to the poem's diagnosis of the more persistent cultural tendency toward denominational change. Hind and Panther are equally liable to change, to "err" and to correct themselves; the frequency with which they borrow each other's language to defend themselves only reinforces that fact. Later in the poem, the Hind reminds the Panther that their disagreements are often masked by superficial verbal resemblance:

> By various texts we both uphold our claim,
> Nay, often ground our titles on the same:
> After long labour lost and time's expence,
> Both grant the words, and quarrel for the sense.   (II.198–201)

---

[87] Zwicker, *Politics and Language*, 141.

This idea of shared "words" but debated "sense" could be a description of the latter two parts of the poem, as well as a description of a culture in which antagonists battled over the same concepts using identical terms.

Book III wittily dramatizes the protagonists' tendency toward argumentative reversals in their debate on the very subject of reversal – and, more specifically, on the subject of religious conversion. Like many of Dryden's contemporaries (and like Dryden himself in the *Defence* of the duchess), both the Hind and the Panther claim that converts to their respective churches exemplify sincerity, reason, and constancy, while converts to their opponent's churches possess both inferior faith and ulterior motives. The Hind suggests that the politics of conformity produced mercenary converts to Protestantism, which she compares to "those *Swisses* [who] fight on any side for pay, / And 'tis the living that conforms, not they" (III.177–8). He continues,

> Your sons of breadth at home, are much like these,
> Their soft and yielding metals run with ease,
> They melt, and take the figure of the mould,
> But harden, and preserve it best in gold.   (III.187–90)

Immediately, the Panther retorts with the kind of equal-and-opposite accusation by now familiar in the poem:

> Your *Delphick* sword, the *Panther* then repli'd,
> Is double edg'd, and cuts on either side.
> Some sons of mine who bear upon their shield,
> Three steeples argent in a sable field,
> Have sharply tax'd your converts, who unfed
> Have follow'd you for miracles of bread;
> Such who themselves of no religion are,
> Allur'd with gain, for any will declare.   (III.191–8)

For decades, English Catholics had slandered Protestant converts for the hypocrisy and political ambition potentially animating their turns. After the accession of the Catholic James, and his promotion of Catholic favorites, Protestants made eager use of this same rhetoric. Here, Dryden points out this equivalence by placing almost identical sentiments in the mouths of his interlocutors, juxtaposing them so that the reader cannot fail to see their similarities. When he notes "to [them] the Hind and Panther are the same" (I.326), we partially sympathize with that view.

Finally, and perhaps still more surprisingly, Dryden refuses to consolidate the Hind's position against the Panther without qualification, allowing the Panther to score some valid argumentative points against his seemingly "innocent" antagonist. When the Panther accuses the Hind's fellow Catholics of time-serving, the Hind retorts that new Catholics – like Dryden himself – received no material advantages under James II ("the Lion buys no converts" (III.225)).[88] But the Panther's other accusation – that Catholic converts hypocritically slander the conversion that resulted from "our eighth *Henry's* marriage" (III.203) – is less easily deflected, since it has been proven by an earlier passage in the poem itself. Here, in Book I, Dryden describes the Panther's conception and birth:

> A *Lyon* old, obscene, and furious made
> By lust, compress'd her mother in a shade;
> Then, by a left-hand marr'age weds the Dame,
> Cov'ring adult'ry with a specious name:
> So schism begot; and sacrilege and she,
> A well-match'd pair, got graceless heresie. (I.351–6)

This Catholic convert's account of Henry VIII's courtship of Anne Boleyn could hardly be more slanderous, corroborating the Panther's accusation of libel even before he makes it.

 Dryden's ambivalent presentation of his interlocutors reaches the apex of its complexity, finally, in the fables-within-a-fable of Book III. Dryden mentions these meta-fabular interludes in his Preface, using terms that prepare the reader for further equivocations: "In both of these," he admits, "I have made use of the Common Places of *Satyr*, whether true or false, which are urg'd by the Members of the one Church against the other."[89] He concludes this extremely ambivalent description of the inset fables by wishing that "no reader of either party will be scandalized" by them. But, by presenting "either party" in ambiguous terms, Dryden may well have offended both – even as he expresses elements of his own religious beliefs *in utramque partem*. This becomes clearest in the fable of the Martin and the Swallows (III.427–638). The Panther begins by describing the innocence of the Swallows, meant to represent the English Catholics, and their deception by the Martin, a figure meant to represent the unscrupulous advisors of James II. While the fable is told from the perspective of an Anglican opponent of corrupt Catholic rule, the fable is remarkable not only for its sophisticated Virgilian echoes, but for its sympathy to the deceived Swallows, who are

---

[88] In "The Paradoxes of Tender Conscience," Zwicker suggests that such moments in Book III reflect Dryden's own bitter disappointment over not receiving such advantages, and his partial disillusionment with James – who had begun a program to actively court the favor of precisely those dissenters who had opposed his reign (the dissenters that Dryden disparages in Book I).

[89] Dryden, *Works*, vol. III, 122.

finally left "an undefended prey" (III.626) after the Martin's cowardly flight. This satire of bad advisors further undermines the stability of the identification between the Hind's position and Dryden's own, and thus the opposition between the Panther and his Catholic interlocutor.

When the Hind responds with another parable, things become still less clear. She presents a figure that seems to be a version of James II:

> A Plain good Man, whose Name is understood,
> (So few deserve the name of Plain and Good)
> Of three fair lineal Lordships stood possess'd,
> And liv'd, as reason was, upon the best;
> Inur'd to hardships from his early Youth,
> Much had he done, and suffered for his truth:
> At Land and Sea, in many a doubtfull Fight[.]   (III.906–12)

The Hind introduces this simple farmer in simple terms, and her syntax and meter closely echoes Dryden's initial description of the heroine herself: "a milk-white Hind" becomes "a Plain Good Man." But the equivocal force of "doubtful" in that last line (is it a fight whose outcome was in doubt, or a fight conducted on dubious grounds?) cannot be ignored, particularly when, several lines later, the Hind offers another backhanded compliment: this farmer was "Slow to resolve, but in performance quick; / So true, that he was awkard at a trick" (III.921–2). If the Panther's criticism of the Catholic Swallows seemed surprisingly sympathetic, the Hind's "praise" of the Catholic king seems surprisingly unsympathetic – imputing to the "Plain good man" either a bluff simplicity or an idiotic haplessness.[90] The fable seems intended to satirize the Anglican tendency to choose malicious champions – selecting as their king a Buzzard whose motives are decidedly suspect. But the fable also implicitly takes the "Plain good Man" to task for failing to control the barnyard, placing Catholic and Protestant birds in equal danger. Finally, King Buzzard himself seems as equivocal in his rapacity as the Hind did in her docility, a character who could represent either Gilbert Burnet, or William of Orange.[91] The ambiguous fable at the end of the poem, then, recalls the equivocal fable at its beginning.

In general, the dialogic relationship between the Hind and the Panther in these books does not resemble the stark *psychomachia* described by Thomas Fujimura, who claims that the figures "symbolize the conflicting tendencies

---

[90] A point made both by Patterson, *Fables of Power*, 104, and by Zwicker, "Paradoxes," 857–8.
[91] E. Miner offers an exhaustive survey of the readings linking the Buzzard to both William and Gilbert Burnet in his notes to *The Hind and the Panther* in Dryden, *Works*, vol. III, gen. ed. Swedenberg, vol. ed. Miner, 448–54.

in Dryden himself," with the Hind symbolizing Christian charity and the Panther proud arrogance.[92] Nor is the equivocation that marks the poem as a whole simply evidence that Dryden "loved to engage in the two-sidedness of religious issues" for argument's own sake.[93] Rather, the poem is Dryden's carefully calibrated depiction of the equivocal nature of both religious identity and religious controversy in the late seventeenth century, dramatizing its tendency toward ever-harsher designations and ever-neater inversions. By making Hind and Panther occasionally difficult to tell apart, Dryden does not wish simply to show the "common ground he shares with his antagonists."[94] Instead he dramatically demonstrates how committed theological antagonists can offer similar or even identical statements of doctrine, and how frequently they can voice their opposing positions in similar terms.

TOWARD A POETICS OF TOLERATION

I have suggested that Dryden's equivocations, pursued in various ways throughout the three parts of the poem, schematize the deep contingency of late Stuart religion, a contingency with a long and difficult history. Yet, even as Dryden presents this instability as pervasive and ongoing, he refuses to characterize it as entirely cataclysmic or destructive. As he diagnoses a long history of religious change, in other words, Dryden also identifies a kind of intelligible, shared pattern in the phenomenon of conversion itself. In *The Hind and the Panther*, individual conversion is not an anomaly, but instead a way of participating in an English religious tradition of several generations' standing. K. G. Hamilton has suggested that this is Dryden's "great ratiocinative poem ... intended to sway public opinion," and partic-ularly, as Dryden announces in the preface, to sway opinion to favor the repeal of the Test.[95] But if the poem attempts to sway opinion, it does so not by engaging in contemporary religious controversy, but rather by emphasiz-ing the equal instability of the positions that comprise that controversy. In making a larger point about Catholic and Protestant interchangeability,

---

[92] Fujimura, "Personal Drama," 408–9.

[93] R. Salvaggio, *Dryden's Dualities* (University of Victoria Press, 1983), 80. Cf. M. Price, *To the Palace of Wisdom: Studies in Order and Energy from Dryden to Blake* (New York: Doubleday, 1964), 29, 28–78 *passim*. Price specifies that in *The Hind and the Panther* this "dialectical" imagination can be seen in "the conflict between faith and the senses, a conflict in which the control of reason is at stake" (72). I suggest, here, that the dialectic is less abstract, and instead reflects the structure of contemporary theological debates.

[94] J. Sloman, *Dryden: The Poetics of Translation* (University of Toronto Press, 1985), 19.

[95] K. G. Hamilton, *John Dryden and the Poetry of Statement* (Ann Arbor: University of Michigan Press, 1969), 160.

Dryden implicitly registers his objection to the use of religious penalties like the Test to guarantee an artificially static uniformity.

Dryden thus offers not just a history of conversion, but also and perhaps most originally, a critical history of the *language* of conversion. *The Hind and the Panther* does more than simply versify an account of the Reformation, something that Dryden had already done, virtuosically, in *Religio Laici*. There, he described the decline of Catholicism and the coming of Protestantism with outspoken bias:

> In times o'ergrown with Rust and Ignorance,
> A gainful Trade their Clergy did advance:
> When want of Learning kept the *Laymen* low,
> And none but *Priests* were *Authorized* to *know* ...
> In those dark times they learn'd their knack so well,
> That by long use they grew *Infallible*:
> At last, a knowing age began t'enquire
> If *they* the *Book*, or *That* did *them* inspire[.]   (370–3, 386–9)

Dryden goes on to narrate a clear linear history of error and correction: he explains that the welcome skepticism of the "knowing age" soon degenerated into a "common rule" under which "the Book [was] put in every vulgar hand" (400), causing an interpretive chaos that Anglican orthodoxy brought to a happy end. By contrast, the history of religious change presented in *The Hind and the Panther* is neither linear nor teleological, but instead marked by potentially endless echoes, equivocations, and repetitions. The unity of shared belief is, for Dryden, no longer an imaginable outcome; instead, he sees individual convictions as potentially sincere, but nevertheless subject to qualification and inversion. If *Religio Laici* envisioned England's religious future as a shared middle way, *The Hind and the Panther* presents England's religious past and present as something akin to what, in a different context, Wyatt described as "busily seeking with a continuall change."

Dryden depicts the paradox of constant change, as we have seen, in allusion and equivocal dialogue. But he reiterates the point even on the level of particular poetic figures. Dryden's expert use of the couplet becomes, for example, a mechanism for expressing simultaneous repetition and transformation. Earl Miner has drawn our attention to the speed of Dryden's couplets, in contrast to the balance and stasis of Pope's.[96] Elaborating on this notion, Ruth Salvaggio argues that Dryden's couplets, like Shakespeare's,

---

[96] E. Miner, Introduction to *Selected Poetry and Prose of John Dryden*, ed. E. Miner (New York: Modern Library, 1985), xxvi.

make us aware of *time*; "the sequential thrust completes the message, brings us from point to point," even as "sometimes a Dryden couplet forces us to move backwards momentarily," so that "to reread a Dryden couplet is to re-experience the dynamics of sequential flow."[97] Returning to the opening couplet of the poem, we see this temporal effect clearly: the incomplete syntax of the first line draws us on to the next, only to find that the conclusion of the couplet qualifies our sense of the Hind's true essence. The line "[f]ed on the lawns, and in the forest rang'd," in other words, forces us to return to the foregoing line, "A Milk white Hind, immortal and unchang'd," and to understand the figure it describes differently – now seeing the Hind as somehow both unchanged *and* contextualized in time and place. The couplet's unfolding in time – like Dryden's sense of English history – is marked by fitful and incomplete revision rather than linear progress. Yet, even as it draws our attention to movement and change, the couplet by definition regularizes that energy, creating a predictable and ongoing sequence.[98] The regularity of the couplet also links the central antagonists of this poem, who share a discursive style despite their theological differences, and still further connects the poem as a whole back to many of Dryden's earlier Protestant poems, where allegiance to an entirely different church found expression in an identical verse form.

Even more than the couplet, though, one particular figure enables Dryden to express his larger sense of England's ongoing history of conversion, and he uses it to great effect throughout *The Hind and the Panther*. That figure is, appropriately, the chiasmus. Puttenham's "Counterchange" has surfaced at key poetic moments throughout this study, from Alabaster's "Desire possession, possession desire" to Crashaw's "Read him for her and her for him." Dryden, however, uses the chiastic line more frequently and more subtly than either of these poets, using the figure at once to evoke the movement of crossing or change and to create a poised, legible equilibrium. Returning to Book I, we find the Catholic Hind described as "[w]ithout unspotted, innocent within" (1.3). In this neatly chiastic asyndeton, two antonymic adverbs, "without" and "within," surround two synonymous adjectives, "innocent" and "unspotted" (i.e. unpolluted or pure). We might expect chiasmus to invert a phrase's syntax to rearrange its sense – AB,

---

[97] R. Salvaggio, "Time, Space and the Couplet," *Philological Quarterly* 82 (1983), 95–108, 101–2.

[98] J. P. Hunter has discussed the Augustan couplet as both an instantiation of and a challenge to "binary" thinking; his notion that the couplet "breaks down and redefines easy oppositions" has obvious relevance to my reading of Dryden. Hunter, "Binarism and the Anglophone Couplet," *MLQ* 61 (2000), 109–28. The classic study remains W. B. Piper, *The Heroic Couplet* (Cleveland, OH: Case Western Reserve University Press, 1969).

even though BA; AB, *and yet* BA; AB, *but then* BA.[99] By contrast, Dryden
here uses chiastic crossing to reaffirm a relationship of complementarity,
even iteration. An adversative structure conveys an identity of sense: the
Hind's lack of outward spots is replicated in her lack of inward moral flaws.
In this descriptive chiasmus, antonyms like inner and outer, self and other,
past and future, become stable approximations or doublings of each other.
But Dryden does not reserve the figure for his Catholic heroine; the
Panther, as well, merits chiastic description: she is "least deform'd, because
reform'd the least" (1.409). Dryden mocks Anglican theological instability
with a devastating chiasmus: "Where one for substance, one for sign
contends, / Their contradicting terms she strives to join, / *Sign shall be
substance, substance shall be sign*" (1.411–13, my italics). Here, the chiasmus
works as a more conventional inversion, illustrating the Panther's ability to
reverse doctrine for the sake of expedience. But the fact that Dryden uses the
same rhetorical figure for both antagonists finally links them stylistically as
well. It suggests, moreover, that the relationship of the Hind and Panther
itself forms a kind of structural chiasmus in the poem at large, their
positions perennially crossing and intersecting in order to create what is,
in the end, the poem's only stable subject.

The figure of chiasmus thus offers a schematic iteration of Dryden's
central insight, one expressed in other ways throughout *The Hind and the
Panther*, and one that is implied or adumbrated in the poetics of conversion
as practiced by Dryden's predecessors. Its crossings indicate, in formal
terms, that the contested experience of confessional identity in early modern
England, the tendency of Protestant positions to yield to Catholic, and vice
versa, finally produces a legible, recognizable pattern. The constituent
elements may be reversed, and reversed again, but the pattern only grows
more deeply etched: X, as it were, marks the spot. As is often the case, it is
a satirist who best summarizes Dryden's position. In an anonymous broadside presenting a short "Heroic Scene," "Johnny" (the Dryden figure)
responds ingenuously to charges of religious fickleness: "A windmill is not
fickle, for we find / That it is always constant to the wind" (lines 43–4).[100]
The satirist intends this response to be absurd. But Dryden does, in fact,
imply something very like this in his use of chiasmus and in his poem as a

[99] For a survey of chiastic possibilities, see S. Budick, "Cross-Culture, Chiasmus, and the Manifold of
Mind," in S. Budick and W. Iser (eds.), *The Translatability of Cultures: Figurations of the Space
Between* (Stanford University Press, 1996), 224–44.
[100] "A Heroic Scene," reproduced in G. deF. Lord (gen. ed.), *Poems on Affairs of State: Augustan Satirical
Verse 1660–1714*, vol. IV: 1685–8, ed. G. M. Crump (New Haven: Yale University Press, 1963–75),
80–90, 82.

whole; he represents a constancy created through a process of change: both endlessly transformative and stably figurative. In this way, *The Hind and the Panther* not only invokes the history of conversion, but also reinscribes its poetic traces.

But it also indicates a history, and a poetics, in its final phase. In the decades after Dryden's poem, English religious polemical discourse over intra-Christian conversion would lose its urgency. With the accession of William and Mary, Catholicism ceased to be a live political threat and, in this climate of relief, differences within Christianity might have seemed less pressingly dangerous. In his account of religious culture in the period, John Spurr surveys the passage of various acts legislating religious toleration, and quotes the telling response of one Protestant clergyman, who complains that "there is not one of a thousand of [his parishioners] that knows what schism means, or will believe that they are guilty of the crime, since they are freed by the laws from the penalty of it."[101] This clergyman persuasively attributes the creeping apathy of his parishioners to the relaxation of the penal laws. But it is also possible to see in this new religious climate a kind of controversial fatigue, an exhaustion stemming from decades upon decades of polemicists' attempts to pin down the location of the true church. By the end of the seventeenth century, more and more English Christians might have come to acknowledge the truth that the poets in this book fought to articulate: that the rhetoric of finality and clarity used by controversialists on either side of the Reformation is, precisely and merely, rhetorical. The constant and ambivalent confessional antagonism that Dryden describes and represents in *The Hind and the Panther* restates a lesson that was becoming ever clearer: that all roads might lead not to Rome, but to Damascus. Conversion, Dryden seems to suggest, has not only shaped England's religious past, but continues to mark its present.

This sense of the historical inevitability of conversion might be at least part of the reason why the end of the seventeenth century witnesses a new, more relaxed English attitude toward denominational variety. Starting in the final years of James's reign, in Spurr's evocative summary, "religious duties, sermon-tasting, and church visiting took their place as leisure activities alongside coffee-houses, political clubs, self-improving societies, newspapers, plays and taverns."[102] The idea that worship could be reclassified as a "leisure activity" is remarkable enough, but the particular

---

[101] Spurr, *Restoration Church*, 377 (Lambeth Palace MS 933, 9.3 Edward Bowerman to Tenison, Dec. 17, 1692).
[102] Spurr, *Restoration Church*, 384.

description of "sermon-tasting" and "church visiting" suggests a distinct lack of cultural anxiety at the prospect of religious difference and change. We can see a similarly urbane attitude in an anonymous *Letter of Advice to a Young Gentleman of an Honourable Family Now in his Travels Beyond the Seas ... By a True Son of the Church of England* (1688). The "True Son" advises this young gentleman on practical matters, including "well husbanding and management of your time," "moralls and civil deportment," and finally "the business of religion," which, according to the author, ought to be conducted along Reformed lines. Rather than a matter of eternal damnation or life everlasting, however, this choice of churches has here become merely another piece of "business," an aspect of a cultivated gentleman's education in virtue. Other sermons and religious tracts would continue to address the subject of conversion, and anti-Catholicism would never entirely lose its force. Yet, by the end of the century, the English religious imagination had become increasingly focused on counteracting a tendency toward "irreligion" in general. A rough century after William Alabaster described his conversion from Protestantism with images of sacrificial blood and fire, and a half-century after William Laud dreamed of being involuntarily, scandalously converted to the Church of Rome, London audiences enjoyed *The Pilgrims, or the Happy Converts*, a comedy in which a prostitute and a "debauched Atheistical person" are comically converted from vice to virtue – with no mention of what particular church they will ultimately join.

For Whig historians especially, this development of a qualified toleration for Christian heterodoxy seems a happy conclusion to an era of heated confessional disagreement, one that would relieve over a century of individual anxieties about the conversions of friends and family, kings and queens. Describing the 1689 Toleration Act, Macaulay wonders whether there has been any law "which has so much diminished the sum of human unhappiness, which has done so much to allay bad passions, which has put an end to so much petty tyranny and vexation, which has brought gladness, peace and security to so many private dwellings."[103] Perhaps not. And yet, this same era of "passion" and "vexation," in which church rivalry dominated the English religious imagination, was also a time of extraordinary innovation and experiment in English religious poetry. I have argued that

[103] Quoted in H. Trevor-Roper, "Toleration and Religion after 1688," in O. Grell, J. Israel, and N. Tyacke (eds.), *From Persecution to Toleration: The Glorious Revolution and Religion in England* (Oxford: Clarendon, 1991), 389–408, 389. Trevor-Roper goes on to qualify Macaulay's terms, discussing the limits of tolerationism in the period.

this was no coincidence. For some of the most inventive poets of the early modern period, the turns and tropes of English verse provided the best vehicle to convey the redefinitions of the believing self in a world of violently competing discourses and vexingly persistent possibilities. The English would, in later generations, confront different questions about identity and community, and later English writers would turn to correspondingly different literary genres in order to face those questions. Such turns, however, I must leave for other readers to follow.

Afterword: Eliot's inheritance and the criticism of conversion

In basic terms, this has been a book about poetry and change, and the relationship between them. It has centered on four poets who meditate, artfully and often, on the mutability of even the firmest-seeming convictions. As Christians in post-Reformation England, Alabaster, Donne, Crashaw, and Dryden inhabited a culture of conversion, a culture that asked them – and at times even required them – to reconsider the forms in which self and soul were understood and expressed, especially the rival forms of Catholicism and Protestantism. Unlike most of their contemporaries, these four converts used poetry as part of that process of reckoning. The verse they produced – knotty, opaque, self-qualifying – registers its authors' reconsiderations, and also invites its closest readers to re-examine the forms through which they understand themselves and their place in the world. To read such poetry with care, to pay attention to its turns and returns, is to hear a call to conversion. This is not to suggest that any of these poems advocate particular articles of belief; again, a central claim of this study has been that the poetics of conversion conspicuously avoids statements of dogmatic certainty. What this poetry does, instead, is encode and encourage reconsideration itself; in Alabaster's words, it "stirs the reader up to [some] estimation of what [its author] felt at the time" of conversion. It moves the reader to imagine, to admire, and even to emulate the work of self-scrutiny and self-revision.

One reader who seems to have been so stirred is, perhaps surprisingly, T. S. Eliot. Eliot's theories of the "impersonality" of the artist and the "autotelic" nature of art have long been understood as cornerstones of a New Criticism that sees poetry as hermetic and self-sustaining, its value lying outside the realms of history or ideology. Eliot's Anglophilia and conversion to Anglicanism, meanwhile, suggest a mind increasingly enthralled by orthodoxy. The preface to his 1929 collection of essays, *For Lancelot Andrewes*, makes the link between aesthetic and cultural conservatism clear: he is, he declares, "classicist in literature, royalist in politics, and

anglo-Catholic in religion."[1] The stridency of this statement, however, is
belied by Eliot's deep critical interest in the particular "decisions and
revisions" made by devotional poets in earlier historical contexts – especially
the English metaphysicals, and most especially the converts Donne and
Crashaw.[2] In seventeenth-century England, Eliot argues, "every man was a
theologian" – but, in the wake of the Reformation, theology was a source of
distress and debate, of uncertainty and self-interrogation, giving rise to the
"catabolic tendency, the tendency toward dissolution ... in Donne's
poetry," and the "deliberate, conscious perversity" of Crashaw's hymns.[3]
Eliot's famous description of the metaphysical poets stresses their "unified
sensibility," by which he means an ideal fusion of thought and feeling. But
Eliot also acknowledges that the divisive and contentious nature of belief in
the age of Donne also produced a significant aesthetic *dis*unity. "[The]
maintenance in suspension of a number of philosophies, attitudes, and
theories," he argues, can result in an "affected, tortuous, and often over-
elaborate and ingenious manner of speech."[4] Eliot sees Donne's style in
particular as a reflection of his divided allegiances and his penchant for self-
revision. In short, he associates Donne's poetic complexity – his "metaphy-
sicality" – with his intellectual and spiritual mutability. For Eliot, the
metaphysical poets are no mere craftsmen of well-wrought urns; instead,
they are bellwethers of a deeply divided historical moment, one that
presages the "disintegration" of modern European culture.[5]

Eliot contrasts such moments of cultural catabolism with, for example,
the relative calm of the Italian *trecento*. In the age of Dante and Cavalcanti,
he writes, "the Church was one; it was not occupied with polemic or
defence against other churches." Once again, poetic style reflects its historical moment; "the acceptance of one orderly system of thought and feeling
results ... in a simple, direct, and even austere manner of speech."[6] Longing
for such an "orderly system" might have motivated Eliot's conversion to a
traditional "anglo-Catholicism" in the mid-1920s. And yet the poems he
wrote at the time of this conversion, the "Ariel" series and especially *Ash-
Wednesday*, do not demonstrate a "simple" or "direct" mode of expression.
Instead, they are marked by a style as "tortuous" as that of the metaphysicals
he was reading at the time, full of hesitations and doubts, protracted

[1] T. S. Eliot, *For Lancelot Andrewes: Essays on Style and Order* (London: Faber and Gwyer, 1929), vii.
[2] Eliot's main works of criticism on the metaphysicals, including his 1926 Clark Lectures, are collected in T. S. Eliot, *The Varieties of Metaphysical Poetry*, ed. R. Schuchard (New York: Harcourt Brace, 1994).
[3] Eliot, *Varieties*, 74–6; *For Lancelot Andrewes*, 135.   [4] Eliot, *Varieties*, 120.
[5] *Ibid.*, 43.   [6] *Ibid.*, 120.

journeys and abrupt reversals. Some years later, in "Little Gidding," Eliot would eulogize a place "[w]here prayer has been valid"; these earlier poems record something like the search for such a place.[7] In "The Journey of the Magi," for example, the speaker describes the "cold coming" of faith, and the difficulty in abandoning an "old dispensation." In "Marina," he looks forward to "the hope, the new ships," only to represent this desired end in imprecise and indefinite terms. Although the speaker of *Ash-Wednesday* "do[es] not hope to turn again," the poem ends "wavering between the profit and the loss," "between birth and dying," repeating and revising its lines with no certainty in sight. In his prose and later poetry, Eliot would describe his conversion as the successful achievement of conviction (he simply *is* "anglo-Catholic" in 1929). His early devotional poems, by contrast, evoke the disorientation and reorientation implicit in that achievement – what, in "East Coker," he would term "the intolerable wrestle / With words and meanings." This "wrestle," as Eliot well knew, had a long history – and these poems thus do more than reflect his own changing faith. They also comprise one of the most sensitive modern readings of the early modern poetics of conversion, one that both heeds and echoes its message of reconsideration.

Such a critical example is difficult to follow; scholarly monographs rarely end with a turn to verse. But what if I attempted to "sing a recantation" of another sort? What if I were to end this study by changing my mind on the page, openly reconsidering some of my own scholarly presumptions, and imagining the other kinds of study I might have written instead? I could, for example, "confess" that my historical purview has been too broad. Perhaps, in order to explore in adequate detail the phenomenon of conversion and its literary consequences, I ought to have limited myself to the years around the Jacobean settlement, or the marriage of Charles I, or the accession of James II. Alternatively, I might "confess" that my generic focus has been too narrow; perhaps, by concentrating on a few poems written by a few poets, I have neglected other important literary representations of conversion: dramatic, diaristic, epistolary, epic. Or, in a still more profound critical palinode, I might renounce my more basic methodology. I have throughout this book considered a large cultural development through the close reading of individual poems. In recanting this approach, I might claim a belated conversion to the bosom of a singular critical orthodoxy, promising to abide more faithfully by the tenets of historical or formal analysis. A version of this book written in the former vein would not privilege the works of four (elite,

---

[7] Peter Ackroyd describes the context of these transitional poems in *T. S. Eliot: A Life* (New York: Simon and Schuster, 1984), 160–1.

male) poets, but would consider equally all manner of textual artifacts that shed light on early modern denominational change, from sonnets to recusant rolls, from plays to acts of parliament. A version of this book written in the latter vein, by contrast, might claim that the lines and stanzas of a poem can enact various kinds of turn, quite apart from surrounding cultural pressures, and that a careful exploration of such aesthetic patternings is finally its own reward.

I have drawn these imaginary critical "conversions" with the broad strokes of caricature. I do, however, want to reaffirm my scholarly commitment to a different kind of conversion, more akin to the conversions described and exemplified by the poets I have here considered: namely, a galvanizing, potentially ongoing movement between "churches" of criticism. I have argued that Alabaster, Donne, Crashaw, and Dryden gathered poetic energy by moving across the commonly accepted denominational boundaries that separated believing Christians, particularly the boundary between Catholic and Reformed. By following these crossings, I have sought to challenge any literary history that would, in Donne's words, "immure" all early modern devotional poetry either in "a *Rome*, or a *Wittemberg*, or a *Geneva*." The poetry I have considered does not attempt to ignore or transcend denominational difference. Unlike Herbert's poetry of grace, or Southwell's poetry of repentance, this poetry always represents conversion as a choice of churches, adopting the language of polemic and controversy to do so. But this poetry also presents such choice as rarely straightforward, and often reversible. In seeking to highlight this interest in choice and change, shared by converts to and from Rome, I have repeatedly crossed the critical boundary separating early modern Catholic and Protestant poetics.

But I have also repeatedly crossed another, analogous boundary, one as entrenched in contemporary critical discourse as the separation between "Catholic" and "Reformed" was in early modern polemic. This is the boundary between two interpretive modes defined decades ago by Wellek and Warren as the "extrinsic" and the "intrinsic," more familiar to us now as "historicism" and "formalism." In the study of early modern poetry in particular, these two modes still seem to maintain virtually separate critical spheres.[8] And yet, in the poetry of conversion I have considered, even the

---

[8] In recent decades, these separate spheres have been anything but equal, with the new historicism holding far greater sway over early modern studies (resulting in the marginalization of lyric, still seemingly tainted with the New Critical brush of Eliot and Brooks). For an eloquent discussion of this development, see R. Strier, "How Formalism became a Dirty Word, and Why We Can't Do Without

smallest "intrinsic" details of poetic form – the chiasmus, for instance, or the couplet, or the turn from octave to sestet – are placed in productive dialogue with "extrinsic" matters of individual biography, community formation, and even ecclesiastical politics. In the four chapters of this book, I have tried to explore this dialogue in a correspondingly dynamic way, turning from cultural history to formal explication and back again, rather than positing either mode of criticism as a means or an end. I have, in Crashaw's words, allowed myself to "transpose the picture quite" in order to see it better or more whole, refusing to "immure" myself in one critical position even at the risk of occasional confusion or error. If the resulting study has at times seemed less a happily irenic blend of methodologies than a jarringly ambivalent oscillation between them, I hope it has also demonstrated some of the incidental virtues of a criticism – as well as a poetics – of conversion.

It," in M. D. Rasmussen (ed.), *Renaissance Literature and Its Formal Engagements* (London: Palgrave, 2002), 107–15. For an overview of the recent "new formalism," see M. Levinson, "What is New Formalism?," *PMLA* 122.2 (2007), 558–69. For a practical example of "new formalist" criticism, see H. Dubrow, "Guess Who's Coming to Dinner? Reinterpreting Formalism and the Country House Poem," *MLQ* 61.1 (2000), 59–77.

Bibliography of printed sources
(see also Note on the text)

PRIMARY SOURCES

(Place of Publication is London unless otherwise indicated)

Abbott, W. C. (ed.), *The Writings and Speeches of Oliver Cromwell*, 4 vols. (Oxford: Clarendon, 1937–47, reissued 1988).

Alabaster, William, *Apparatus in Revelationem Jesu Christi* (Antwerp, 1607).

Ecce Sponsus Venit (1633).

Elisaeis, ed. and trans. Michael McConnell, *Studies in Philology* 76 (1979).

Roxana (1632).

Unpublished Works of William Alabaster, ed. Dana Sutton, Salzburg Studies in English Literature, Elizabethan and Renaissance Studies 126 (University of Salzburg, 1997).

Alsup, Vincent, *Melius Inquirendum* (1678).

Askew, Anne, *The Examinations of Anne Askew*, ed. Elaine Beilin (Oxford University Press, 1990).

St. Augustine, *The Confessions*, ed. and trans. Henry Chadwick (1991; paperback edn. Oxford University Press, 1998).

Avignon, Bertrand, *Declaration présenté en la Faculté de Théologie et Sorbonne, par laquelle il deduict les raisons qui l'ont meu de quitter la Religion Romaine, pour embrasser la verité de l'Évangile* (Paris, 1605).

[B., T.], *The General Inefficacy and Insincerity of a Late or Deathbed Repentance* (1670).

Bacon, Francis, *Works*, ed. J. Spedding, R. Ellis, and D. Heath, 14 vols. (London: Longmans, 1862–74).

A Few Plain Reasons Why a Protestant Should Not Turn Catholic (1688).

Bedell, William, *An Examination of Certain Motives to Recusancie* (Cambridge, 1628).

Bell, Thomas, *Thomas Bels Motives* (Cambridge, 1593).

Bernard of Clairvaux, *Selected Works*, ed. G. R. Evans. (New York: Paulist Press, 1987).

Sermons on Conversion, ed. and trans. M.-B. Saïd (Kalamazoo, MI: Cistercian Publications, 1981).

Birchley, William [pseud. John Austin], *The Christian Moderator: The Second Part, or Persecution for Religion Condemned ... whereto there are New Additions since the Octavo was Printed*, revised edn. (1652–3).

Braden, G. (ed.), *Sixteenth-Century Poetry: An Annotated Anthology* (Oxford: Blackwell, 2005).

Breton, Nicholas, *Mary Magdalen's Love* (1595).
  The Ravish't Soul and the Blessed Weeper (1601).

Bristow, Richard, *A Briefe Treatise of Divers Plaine and Sure Waies to Finde Out the Truthe in this Doubtfull and Dangerous Time of Heresie* ([Antwerp,] 1574, rpt. 1599).

Broughton, Richard, *An Apologicall Epistle: Directed to the Right Honorable Lords, and Others of her Maiesties Privie Counsell. Serving as Well for a Preface to a Booke Entituled, A Resolution of Religion* (Antwerp, 1601).

[Brown, Thomas], *The Reasons of Mr. Bays Changing his Religion, Considered in a Dialogue between Crites, Eugenius, and Mr. Bays* (1688).

Bryan, John, *The Nonsuch Habitation, or Dwelling with God, the Interest and Duty of Believers; in opposition to the Complemental, Heartless and Reserved Religion of the Hypocrite* (1670).

Burton, E. (ed.), *Douai Diaries* (London: Publications of the Catholic Record Society, 1911).

Calvin, John, *New Testament Commentaries*, vol. VIII: *The Epistles of Paul the Apostle to the Romans and Thessalonians*, trans. R. Mackenzie, ed. D. and T. Torrance (Edinburgh: Oliver and Boyd, 1960).
  New Testament Commentaries, vol. X: *Epistles of Paul the Apostle to the Galatians, Ephesians, Philippians and Colossians*, trans. T. H. L. Parker, ed. D. and T. Torrance (Edinburgh: Oliver and Boyd 1965).

Carier, Benjamin, *A Missive to His Majesty of Great Britain King James* (Paris, 1649).
  A Treatise written by Mr. Doctor Carier (Brussels, 1614).

Carleton, George, *Directions to Know the True Church*, 2nd edn. (1615).

Cary, Elizabeth, *The Tragedy of Mariam, The Fair Queen of Jewry, with The Lady Falkland, her Life, by One of Her Daughters*, ed. B. Weller and M. Ferguson (Berkeley: University of California Press, 1994).

Clarendon, Edward Hyde, Earl of, *Two Letters written by the Right Honourable Edward Earl of Clarendon, Late Lord High Chancellour of England: one to his Royal Highness the Duke of York; the other to the Dutchess, occasioned by her Embracing the Roman Catholic Religion* (1679).

Clifford, M., *Notes upon Mr. Dryden's Poems in Four Letters, to which are annexed some Reflections on the Hind and Panther, by another Hand* (1687).

The Confession and Publike Recantation of thirteene learned personages, lately converted in France, Germanie and the Lowe-Countreys, from Poperie to the Churches Reformed: wherein they have zealously and learnedly set downe the reasons that moved them therunto (1602).

Constable, Henry, *The Poems*, ed. J. Grundy (Liverpool University Press, 1960).

The Converts: Or, the Folly of Priestcraft. A Comedy (1686).

Cosin, John, *Private Devotions* (1627).

Crashaw, William, *The Bespotted Jesuit* (1641).
  Falsificationum Romanarum (1606).
  The Jesuites Gospel (1610).

Cressy, Serenus, *Exomologesis, or, A faithfull narration of the occasion and motives of the conversion unto Catholique unity of Hugh-Paulin Cressy* (Paris, 1647).

Fanaticism Fanatically Imputed (1674).

[Cressy, Serenus], *I. Why are You a Catholic? The Answer follows. II. Question: But Why are You a Protestant?* (1686).

Crowley, Robert, *A Breefe Discourse, concerning the Foure Usuall Notes, whereby Christes Catholique Church is Knowen* (1581).

A Dialogue Between Monmouth-Shire and York-Shire, About cutting Religion according to Fashion (1681).

Digby, George, Earl of Bristol, *Two Speeches of George, Earl of Bristol, with Some Observations upon Them* (1674).

Digby, Kenelm, *A Conference with a Lady about Choice of Religion* (1638).

Donne, John, *The Complete Poetry*, ed. J. T. Shawcross (New York: Anchor, 1967).

The Divine Poems, ed. H. Gardner, 2nd edn. (Oxford: Clarendon, 1978).

Essays in Divinity, ed. E. Simpson (Oxford: Clarendon, 1952).

Letters to Severall Persons of Honour, ed. C. E. Merrill (New York: Sturgis and Walton, 1910).

Poetical Works, ed. H. J. C. Grierson, 2 vols. (Oxford University Press, 1912, rpt. 1980).

Pseudo-Martyr, ed. A. Raspa (Buffalo: McGill-Queen's University Press, 1993).

The Satires, Epigrams, and Verse Letters, ed. W. Milgate (Oxford: Clarendon, 1967).

The Sermons, ed. G. R. Potter, and E. M. Simpson, 10 vols. (Berkeley: University of California Press, 1953–62).

Donne, John, Jr. (ed.), *A Collection of Letters Made by Sir Tobie Matthews, KT. With a Character of the Most Excellent Lady, Lucy Countesse of Carleile. To which are Added many Letters of his own, to severall Persons of Honour, who were contemporary with him* (1660).

Dryden, John, *Selected Poems*, ed. P. Hammond and D. Hopkins (London: Longman, 2007).

Selected Poetry and Prose, ed. E. Miner (New York: Modern Library, 1985).

Durling, R. (ed. and trans.), *Petrarch's Lyric Poems* (Cambridge, MA: Harvard University Press, 1976).

Fairlambe, Peter, *The Recantation of a Brownist; Or: A Reformed Puritan* (London, 1606).

Fazzari, Clara (ed.), *Alabaster's Conversion (anno 1598)* (Florence: Università degli Studi di Firenze, 1983).

Fenton, Roger, *Answer to William Alablaster [sic] His Motives* (1599).

Fitzsimon, Henry, *A Catholike Confutation of M. John Riders Clayme of Antiquitie* (Rouen, 1608).

Floyd, John, *A Secure and Prudent Choice of Beliefe* (St. Omer, 1639).

Foxe, John, *Acts and Monuments*, ed. G. Townsend (New York: AMS Press, 1965).

French, Nicholas, *The Dolefull Fall of Andrew Sall, a Jesuit of the fourth vow, from the Roman Catholick apostolick faith lamented by his constant friend, with an open rebuking of his imbracing the confession, contained in the XXXIX Articles of the Church of England* (Louvain, 1674).

Fulke, William, *A Retentive to Stay Good Christians* (1580).

Fuller, Thomas, *History of the Worthies of England* (1662).

Gage, Thomas, *The English-American: A New Survey of the West Indies (1648)*, ed. A. P. Newton (London: Routledge, 1928).

The Tyranny of Satan Discovered in the Tears of a Converted Sinner (1642).

Gee, Edward, *Veteres Vindicati: In an Expostulatory Letter to Mr. Sclater of Putney, upon his Consensus Veterum* (1687).

Gerard, John, *Autobiography of a Hunted Priest,* ed. P. Caraman (New York: Image Books, 1955).

Gerbier, Balthasar, *A Letter from Sir Balthazar Gerbier, Knight, to his Three Daughters Inclosed in a Nunnery at Paris* (Paris, 1646).

The Great Danger of Continuing in and the greater of Apostatizing To, the Romish Religion (1669).

Gualdo Priorato, Galeazzo, *The History of the Sacred and Royal Majesty of Christina Alessandra, Queen of Swedland. With the Reasons of her late Conversion to the Roman Catholique Religion* (1658).

Hamilton, A. (ed.), *The Chronicle of the English Augustinian Canonesses Regular of the Lateran, at St. Monica's in Louvain*, vol. I (1548–1625) and vol. II (1625–44) (London: Sands, 1904–6).

Harding, John, *A Recantation Sermon Preached in the Gatehouse at Westminster* (1620).

Haren, John, *The Repentance of John Haren, Priest, and his Return to the Church of God* (1610).

Harpsfield, Nicholas, *The Life and Death of Sir Thomas Moore, Knight, sometimes Lord High Chancellor of England, written in the time of Queene Marie*, ed. E. V. Hitchcock (Oxford University Press, 1932).

Hawkins, Henry, *Partheneia Sacra* (1633).

"A Heroic Scene," reproduced in G. deF. Lord (gen. ed.), *Poems on Affairs of State: Augustan Satirical Verse 1660–1714*, vol. IV: *1685–8*, ed. G. M. Crump (New Haven: Yale University Press, 1963–75), 80–90.

[Heyrick, Thomas], *The New Atlantis. A Poem in Three Books, with some Reflections on the Hind and the Panther* (1687).

Hieron, Samuel, *Answer to a Popish Ryme, lately scattered abroad in the West Parts, and much Relyed upon by some simply-seduced* (1608).

[Higgons, Theophilus], *The Apology of Theophilus Higgons, lately Minister now Catholique* (Rouen, 1609).

The First Motive of T. H. Maister of Arts and Lately Minister, to suspect the integrity of his Religion, With an Appendix intituled, Try Before You Trust (Douai, 1609).

Hoby, Edward, *Letter to Mr. T. H. late Minister now Fugitive* (1609).

[Hungerford, Anthony], *Advise of a Sonne, now professing the religion established in the present Church of England, to his deare mother, yet a Roman Catholike* (Oxford, 1616).

The Holie Bible faithfully translated into English, out of the authentical Latin (Douai, 1609–10).

Instructions for your Search into Religion, with Reasons why the truth once founde, further conference is not to be admitted (Douai, 1607).

Johnson, Samuel, *Lives of the Poets*, ed. A. W. Waugh, 2 vols. (Oxford University Press, 1955–6).

Jonson, Ben, *Works*, ed. C. H. Herford, P. Simpson, and E. Simpson, 11 vols. (Oxford: Clarendon, 1925–52).

Kenny, Anthony (ed.), *Responsa Scholarum of the English College, Rome*, Publications of the Catholic Record Society 54–5 (London: Catholic Record Society, 1962).

[King, Edward], *The Bishop of London his Legacy, Or: Certain Motives of Dr. King, Late Bishop of London, for his Change of Religion* (1623).

The King's Cabinet Opened (1645).

Laud, William, *The Autobiography of Dr. William Laud, Collected from his Remains* (Oxford: J. H. Parker, 1839).

   Works, ed. J. Bliss and W. Scott, 7 vols. (Oxford: J. H. Parker, 1847–60).

Legenda Lignea: with an Answer to Mr. Birchley's Moderator, Pleading for a Toleration of Popery. And a Character of some Hopefull Saints Revolted to the Church of Rome (1653).

Lessius, Leonardus, *A Consultation what Faith and Religion is Best to be Imbraced*, 2nd edn. (St. Omer, 1621).

   Quae Religio Sit Capessenda (Paris, 1609).

Letter to his Royal Highness the Duke of York, Touching his Revolt from or Return to the Protestant Religion. By an Old Cavalier, and Faithful Son of the Church of England, as Established by Law (1681).

Letter Written by a Learned and Reverent Divine to William Laud, now Lord Bishop of Canterbury: Concerning his Inclination to Popery, perswading him not to halt betweene two opinions, but to be stedfast to the Protestant Religion (1643).

Letters Between the Ld George Digby, and Sr Kenelm Digby Kt Concerning Religion (1651).

[Lloyd, William], *Papists No Catholics* (1679).

Locke, Anne, *A Meditation of a Penitent Sinner: Written in the maner of a Paraphrase upon the 51. Psalme of David* (1560).

Lodge, Thomas, *Prosopopoeia, Containing the Teares of the Holy Marie* (1596).

Lok, Henry, *Sundry Christian Passions, contained in two hundred Sonnets* (1597).

Luther, Martin, *Complete Works*, ed. H. Lehmann (Philadelphia: Muhlenberg Press, 1960).

Magdalens Lamentations (1601).

Martz, Louis (ed.), *The Meditative Poem: An Anthology of Seventeenth-Century Verse* (New York University Press, 1963).

Matthew, Sir Toby, *A True Historical Relation of the Conversion of Sir Tobie Matthew to the Holy Catholic Faith*, ed. A. H. Mathew (London: Burns and Oates, 1904).

Matthew, Sir Toby (trans.), *The Confessions of the Incomparable Doctour S Augustine, translated into English* (Paris, 1620).

   The Flaming Hart, Or, the Life of the Glorious S. Teresa, Foundresse of the Reformation, of the Order of the All-Immaculate Virgin-Mother, our B. Lady, of Mount-Carmel (Antwerp, 1642).

Montague, Charles and Matthew Prior, *The Hind and the Panther Transvers'd To the Story of the Country-Mouse and the City-Mouse* (1687).

Montague, Walter, *The Coppy of a Letter by Mr. Walter Mountagu to his father the Lord Privie Seale, with his answer therunto, also a Second Answer to the Same Letter by the Lord Faukland* (1641).

More, Gertrude, *The Holy Practises of a Devine Lover, or the Sainctly Ideot's Devotions* (Paris, 1657).

   The Inner Life and Writings of Dame Gertrude More, ed. B. Weld-Blundell, 2 vols. (London: Washbourne, 1910–11).

Morton, Thomas, *A Direct Answer unto the Scandalous Exceptions, which Theophilus Higgons hath lately obiected* (1609).

Munday, Anthony, *English Roman Life*, ed. P. J. Ayres (Oxford: Clarendon, 1980).

Musgrave, Christopher, *Motives and Reasons for Dissevering from the Church of Rome* (1688).

N. N., *An Epistle of a Catholike Young Gentleman to his Father a Protestant* (Douai, 1623).

Neile, Richard, *M. Ant. De Dnis. Archbishop of Spalato, his Shiftings in Religion* (1624).

A New Way of Conference, being a Dialogue between Patrick Pastgrace, a Papist, and Peter Pleadwell, a Protestant, Fild with Mirth and varnisht with Modesty (1641).

Nouwen, H. (ed.), *Letters of Spiritual Direction by Francis de Sales and Jane de Chantal*, trans. P. M Thibert (New York: Paulist Press, 1988).

Parr, Susanna, *Susanna's Apology Against the Elders: Or, a Vindication of Susanna Parr* (Oxford, 1659).

Persons, Robert, *Discouerie of I. Nicols minister, Misreported a Jesuite, Lately Recanted in the Tower* (1581).

   Memoirs, printed by the Catholic Record Society as *Miscellanea II* (London: Arden, 1906).

Pepys, Samuel, *The Diary of Samuel Pepys in Three Volumes*, ed. J. Warrington, 3 vols. (London: Dent, 1971).

A Politique Confession of Faith Calculated for the Meridian of Both Churches (1673).

Prynne, William, *Rome's Master Peece* (1644).

Puttenham, George, *The Art of English Poesy*, ed. F. Whigham and W. Rebhorn (1589; Ithaca, NY: Cornell University Press, 2007).

Questier, M. (ed.), *Newsletters from the Caroline Court 1631–8: Catholicism and the Politics of the Personal Rule* (Cambridge University Press, 2005).

R., R. (trans.), *The Life of the Reverend Father Angel of Joyeuse, Capucin Preacher … Together with the Lives of the Reverend Fathers, Father Bennet Englishman and Father Archangell Scotchman, of the Same Order* (Douai, 1623).

Racster, John, *A Booke of the Seven Planets, Or, Seven Wandring Motives, of William Alablaster's Wit, Retrograded or Removed* (1598).

[Radford, John], *A Directorie teaching the Way to the Truth, Whereunto is Added a Short Treatise Against Adiaphorists, Neuters, and Such as Say they May be Saved in Any Sect or Religion, and Would Make of Many Divers Sects One Church* (1605).

The Satisfactorie Epistle of a Late Converted English Protestant, Unto the Catholike Religion (1630).

Rainolds, William, *A Refutation of Sundry Reprehensions* (Paris, 1583).

The Revolter: A Trage-Comedy acted between The Hind and the Panther and Religio Laici (1687).

de Sales, Francis, *Traité de l'Amour de Dieu* (1616).

Sandys, Edwin, *A View or Survey of the State of Religion in the Western Parts of the World* (1599, rpt. 1632).

Savage, Francis, *Conference betwixt a Mother a Devout Recusant and her Sonne, a Zealous Protestant* (1600).

[Sclater, Edward], *Consensus Veterum: Or, the Reasons of Edward Sclater, Minister of Putney, for his Conversion to the Catholic Faith and Communion* (1686).

Sharland, E. Cruwys (ed.), *The Story Books of Little Gidding* (New York: Dutton, 1899).

Sheldon, Richard, *The Motives of Richard Sheldon, Pr. For his iust, voluntary, and free renouncing of Communion with the Bishop of Rome, Paul the 5th, and his Church* (1612).

Sidney, Philip, *An Apology for Poetry* (New York: Palgrave, 2002).

Southwell, Robert, *Marie Magdalenes Funeral Tears* (1591).

Mary Magdalen's Complaint at Christ's Death (1596).

Stafford, Anthony, *Femall Glory* (1635).

Stillingfleet, Edward, *An Answer to Some Papers Lately Printed, concerning the Authority of the Catholic Church in Matters of Faith and the Reformation of the Church of England* (1686).

Irenicum: A Weapon-Salve for the Church's Wounds (1661).

The Mischief of Separation (1680).

[Stillingfleet, Edward], *A Vindication of the Answer to Some Late Papers concerning the Unity and Authority of the Catholic Church, and the Reformation of the Church of England* (1687).

Sutcliffe, Matthew, *The Unmasking of a Masse-monger, who in the counterfeit habit of S. Augustine hath cunningly crept into the closets of many English ladies. Or, the Vindication of Saint Augustines Confessions, from the calumniations of a late noted Apostate* (1626).

[Sweet, John], *Monsignor Fate'Voi. Or: a Discovery of the Dalmatian Apostata, M. Antonius de Dominis* (1617).

Sylvester, Richard (ed.), *English Sixteenth-Century Verse: An Anthology* (New York: Norton, 1984).

The Reclaimed Papist (1655).

Tillotson, John, *The Protestant Religion Vindicated* (1680).

Vitkus, D. (ed.), *Three Turk Plays from Early Modern England [Greene's Selimus, Massinger's Renegado, and Daborne's A Christian Turned Turk]* (New York: Columbia University Press, 2000).

The Voluntarie Recantation of foure great Learned Men, Professed Fryers in Sundry Monasteries in France, latelie converted from Poperie to the True Religion (1611).

Walsingham, Francis, *A Search Made into Matters of Religion* (St. Omer, 1609).

Walton, Izaak, *The Lives of John Donne, Sir Henry Wotton, Richard Hooker, George Herbert and Robert Sanderson (1640)*, ed. G. Saintsbury (Oxford University Press, 1947).
Watts, William, *Saint Augustines Confessions translated: and with some marginall notes illustrated. Wherein, Diuers Antiquities are explayned; and the marginall notes of a former Popish Translation, answered* (1631).
Weston, Edward, *The Triall of Christian Truth ... The Second Parte* (Douai, 1615).
Weston, William, *The Autobiography of an Elizabethan*, ed. P. Caraman (London: Longman, 1955).
Willet, Andrew, *An Antilogie or Counterplea to an Apologicall (he should have said) Apologeticall epistle published by a favorite of the Romane Separation* (1603).
[Williams, John], *The Protestant's Answer to the Catholic's Letter to the Seeker. Or, a Vindication of the Protestant's Letter to the Seeker's Request* (1688).
Wilson, Thomas, *The Art of Rhetoric (1560)*, ed. P. E. Medine (University Park, PA: Pennsylvania State University Press, 1994).
[Woodward, Philip], *The Dolefull Knell of Thomas Bell* (Rouen, 1607).

SECONDARY SOURCES

Ackroyd, P., *T. S. Eliot: A Life* (New York: Simon and Schuster, 1984).
Agamben, G., *The Time that Remains: A Commentary on the Letter to the Romans*, trans. P. Dailey (Stanford University Press, 2005).
Alabaster, J. S., *A Closer Look at William Alabaster (1568–1640): Poet, Theologian and Spy?* (Oxford: Alabaster Society, 2003).
Albion, G., *Charles I and the Court of Rome: A Study in Seventeenth-Century Diplomacy* (Louvain: Bureaux du Recueil, Bibliothèque de l'Université, 1935).
Allison, A. F., "Crashaw and St. François de Sales," *Review of English Studies* 96 (1948), 295–302.
Andrews, S. and T. Springall, *Hadleigh and the Alabaster Family* (Ipswich: Sue Andrews, 2005).
Aveling, J. H., *The Handle and the Axe: The Catholic Recusants in England from Reformation to Emancipation* (London: Blond and Briggs, 1976).
Bald, R. C., *John Donne: A Life* (Oxford University Press, 1970).
Barbour, R., *Literature and Religious Culture in Seventeenth-Century England* (Cambridge University Press, 2002).
Barroll, J. L., *Anna of Denmark, Queen of England: A Cultural Biography* (Philadelphia: University of Pennsylvania Press, 2001).
Beales, A. C. F., *Education under Penalty: English Catholic Education from the Reformation to the Fall of James II* (London: Athlone, 1963).
Bell, I., "Circular Strategies and Structures in Jonson and Herbert," in Maleski (ed.) *Fine Tuning*, 157–70.
  "'Setting Foot into Divinity': George Herbert and the English Reformation," *MLQ* 38 (1977), 219–41.

Benson, D., "Dryden's *The Hind and the Panther*: Transubstantiation and Figurative Language," *Journal of the History of Ideas* 43 (1982), 195–208.

"Theology and Politics in Dryden's Conversion," *SEL* 4 (1964), 393–412.

Birrell, T. A., "English Counter-Reformation Book Culture," *RH* 22.2 (1994), 113–21.

"James Maurus Corker and John Dryden's Conversion," *SEL* 4 (1964), 461–8.

Blackstone, B. (ed.), *The Ferrar Papers* (Cambridge University Press, 1938).

Bligh, E. W., *Sir Kenelm Digby and his Venetia* (London: Sampson Low, 1932).

Booth, S., *Precious Nonsense* (Berkeley: University of California Press, 1998).

Bossy, J., *The English Catholic Community, 1570–1850* (London: Longman, 1975).

Bouwsma, W. J., *John Calvin: A Sixteenth-Century Portrait* (Oxford University Press, 1988).

Bredvold, L., *The Intellectual Milieu of John Dryden: Studies in Some Aspects of Seventeenth-Century Thought* (1934; Ann Arbor: University of Michigan Press, 1956).

Studies in Shakespeare, Milton, and Donne (New York: Haskell House, 1964).

Bridgett, T. E., *Blunders and Forgeries: Historical Essays* (London: K. Paul, Trench, Trubner, 1890).

Bromley, D. (ed.), *The Politics of Religious Apostasy* (Westport, CT: Praeger, 1998).

Brown, F. B., *Transfigurations: Poetic Metaphor and the Languages of Religious Belief* (Chapel Hill: University of North Carolina Press, 1983).

Brown, M. L., *Donne and the Politics of Conscience in Early Modern England* (Leiden: Brill, 1995).

Brown, N. P., "Paperchase: The Dissemination of Catholic Texts in Elizabethan England," *English Manuscript Studies 1100–1700* 1 (1989), 120–43.

Brunning, A., "'Thou art damn'd for altering thy religion': The Double Coding of Conversion in City Comedy," in D. Mehl (ed.), *Plotting Early Modern London*, 145–62.

Budick, S., *Dryden and the Abyss of Light: A Study of 'Religio Laici' and 'The Hind and the Panther'* (New Haven: Yale University Press, 1970).

Budick, S. and W. Iser (eds.), *The Translatability of Cultures: Figurations of the Space Between* (Stanford University Press, 1996).

Bynum, C., *Jesus as Mother: Studies in Spirituality of the High Middle Ages* (Berkeley: University of California Press, 1982).

Metamorphosis and Identity (New York: Zone, 2005).

Caldwell, P., *The Puritan Conversion Narrative: The Beginnings of American Expression* (Cambridge University Press, 1993).

Campbell, K., *The Intellectual Struggle of the English Papists in the Seventeenth Century: The Catholic Dilemma.* (Lewiston, NY: Edwin Mellen, 1987).

Campbell, L., *Divine Poetry and Drama* (New York: Gordian Press, 1972).

Carey, J., *John Donne: Life, Mind, and Art* (Oxford University Press, 1981).

Caro, R., "William Alabaster: Rhetor, Meditator, Devotional Poet," *RH* 19 (1988), 62–79, 155–70.

Carrafiello, M., *Robert Parsons and English Catholicism, 1580–1610* (London: Associated University Presses, 1998).

Champion, J. A. I., *The Pillars of Priestcraft Shaken: The Church of England and its Enemies 1660–1730* (Cambridge University Press, 1992).

Citron, B., *New Birth: A Study of the Evangelical Doctrine of Conversion in the Protestant Fathers* (University of Edinburgh Press, 1951).

Clancy, T. H., *Papist Pamphleteers* (Chicago: Loyola University Press, 1964).

"Papist – Protestant – Puritan: English Religious Taxonomy 1565–1665," *RH* 13 (1975–6), 227–53.

Clark, I., *Christ Revealed: The History of the Neotypological Lyric in the English Renaissance*, University of Florida Monographs in the Humanities 51 (Gainesville: University of Florida Press, 1982).

Coldeway, J. C., "William Alabaster's *Roxana*: Some Textual Considerations," in Schoeck (ed.), *Acta*, 413–19.

Collinson, P., *The Birth-pangs of Protestant England* (New York: St. Martin's Press, 1988).

The Religion of Protestants (Oxford: Clarendon, 1982).

Corthell, R., F. Dolan, C. Highley, and A. Marotti (eds.), *Catholic Culture in Early Modern England* (University of Notre Dame Press, 2007).

Cotterill, A., "Parenthesis at the Center: The Complex Embrace of *The Hind and the Panther*," *Eighteenth Century Studies* 30.2 (1996–7), 139–58.

Cousins, A. D., *The Catholic Religious Poets from Southwell to Crashaw: A Critical History* (London: Sheed and Ward, 1991).

Coutts, E. J., "The Life and Works of William Alabaster, 1568–1640" (Ph.D. thesis, University of Wisconsin, 1956).

Craig, J., "Reformers, Conflict and Revisionism: The Reformation in Sixteenth-Century Hadleigh," *HJ* 42 (1999), 1–23.

Crawford, P., *Women and Religion in England 1500–1720* (London: Routledge, 1993).

Crowley, J. P., "'He took his religion by trust': The Matter of Ben Jonson's Conversion," *Renaissance and Reformation* 22 (1998), 53–70.

Cummings, B., *The Literary Culture of the Reformation: Grammar and Grace* (Oxford University Press, 2002).

Cunnar, E. R., "Opening the Religious Lyric: Crashaw's Ritual, Liminal and Visual Wounds," in Roberts (ed.), *New Perspectives on the Seventeenth-Century English Religious Lyric*, 237–67.

Cunnar, E. R. and J. Johnson (eds.), *Discovering and (Re)covering the Seventeenth-Century Religious Lyric* (Pittsburgh: Duquesne University Press, 2001).

Cuthbert, C., *The Capuchins: A Contribution to the History of the Counter-Reformation* (London: Sheed and Ward, 1928).

Davidson, P., *The Universal Baroque* (Manchester University Press, 2007).

Delany, P., *British Autobiography in the Seventeenth Century* (London: Routledge, 1969).

Delatte, P., *Commentary on the Rule of St. Benedict*, trans. J. McCann (London: Burns, Oates and Washburn, 1921).

Devlin, C., "An Unwilling Apostate: The Case of Anthony Tyrrell," *The Month* 6 (1951), 346–58.

Docherty, T., *John Donne, Undone* (London: Methuen, 1986).

Dodaro, R. and M. Questier, "Strategies in Jacobean Polemic: The Use and Abuse of St. Augustine in English Theological Controversy," *JEH* 44.3 (July 1993), 432–49.

Dolan, F., *Whores of Babylon: Catholicism, Gender, and Seventeenth-Century Print Culture* (Ithaca, NY: Cornell University Press, 1999).

Donaldson, I., *Jonson's Magic Houses* (Oxford: Clarendon, 1997).

Donaldson-Evans, L. K., "Two Baroque Devotional Poets: La Ceppède and Alabaster," *Comparative Literature Studies* 12 (1975), 21–31.

Doody, M., *The Daring Muse: Augustan Poetry Reconsidered* (Cambridge University Press, 1985).

Dubois, E., "Conversions à la cour de la reine Henriette-Marie," in *La Conversion au xxiième Siècle: Actes du XXe Colloque de Marseille* (Marseille: CMR, 1983), 201–8.

Dubrow, H., *Echoes of Desire: English Petrarchism and its Counterdiscourses* (Ithaca, NY: Cornell University Press, 1995).

"Guess Who's Coming to Dinner? Reinterpreting Formalism and the Country House Poem," *MLQ* 61.1 (2000), 59–77.

Duffy, E., *The Stripping of the Altars: Traditional Religion in England c.1400–c.1580* (New Haven: Yale University Press, 1992).

Ebner, D., *Autobiography in Seventeenth-Century England: Theology and the Self* (Paris: Mouton, 1971).

Eliot, T. S., *For Lancelot Andrewes: Essays on Style and Order* (London: Faber and Gwyer, 1929).

The Varieties of Metaphysical Poetry, ed. R. Schuchard (New York: Harcourt Brace, 1994).

Ellrodt, R., *Seven Metaphysical Poets* (Oxford University Press, 2000).

Evans, G. R., "A Change of Mind in Some Scholars of the Eleventh and Twelfth Centuries," *Studies in Church History* 15 (1978), 27–38.

Bernard of Clairvaux (Oxford University Press, 2000).

Feil, J. P., "Sir Tobie Matthew and his Collection of Letters" (Ph.D. thesis, University of Chicago, 1962).

Ferrell, L. A. and P. McCullough (eds.), *The English Sermon Revised* (Manchester University Press, 2000).

Ferry, A., *The "Inward" Language: Sonnets of Wyatt, Sidney, Shakespeare, Donne* (University of Chicago Press, 1983).

Fish, S. "Masculine Persuasive Force: Donne and Verbal Power," in Maus and Harvey (eds.), *Soliciting Intepretation*, 223–52.

Self-Consuming Artifacts: The Experience of Seventeenth-Century Literature (Berkeley: University of California Press, 1972).

Flynn, D., "Donne's Catholicism," *RH* 13 (1975), 1–17.

John Donne and the Ancient Catholic Nobility (Bloomington: Indiana University Press, 1995).

Freccero, J., *Dante: The Poetics of Conversion* (Cambridge, MA: Harvard University Press, 1986).

Freinkel, L., *Reading Shakespeare's Will: The Theology of the Figure from St. Augustine to the Sonnets* (New York: Columbia University Press, 2002).

Frontain, R.-J. and F. Malpezzi (eds.), *John Donne's Religious Imagination: Essays in Honor of John T. Shawcross* (Conway: University of Central Arkansas Press, 1995).

Fujimura, T. P., "The Personal Drama of Dryden's *The Hind and the Panther*," *PMLA* 87 (1972), 406–16.

Gardiner, A. B., "A Witty French Preacher in the English Court, Dryden, and the Great Debate on the Real Presence," *ELH* 65 (1998), 593–616.

  Ancient Faith and Modern Freedom in John Dryden's "The Hind and the Panther" (Washington, DC: Catholic University Press, 1998).

Goldberg, J., *Desiring Women Writing: English Renaissance Examples* (Stanford University Press, 1997).

Graef, H., *Mary: A History of Doctrine and Devotion*, vol. II (New York: Sheed and Ward, 1965).

Green, M. A. E. (ed.), *Letters of Queen Henrietta Maria* (London, 1857).

Grell, O., J. Israel, and N. Tyacke (eds.), *From Persecution to Toleration: The Glorious Revolution and Religion in England* (Oxford: Clarendon, 1991).

Grierson, H., *Metaphysical Lyrics and Poems of the Seventeenth Century, Donne to Butler* (Oxford University Press, 1959).

Guibbory, A. (ed.), *The Cambridge Companion to John Donne* (Cambridge University Press, 2006).

Guilday, P., *The English Catholic Refugees on the Continent 1558–1795* (London: Longmans, 1914).

Haigh, C., *English Reformations: Religion, Politics and Society under the Tudors* (Oxford: Clarendon, 1993).

Haigh, C. (ed.), *The English Reformation Revised* (Cambridge University Press, 1987).

Halewood, W., *The Poetry of Grace: Reformation Themes and Structures in English Seventeenth-Century Poetry* (New Haven: Yale University Press, 1970).

Hamilton, D., *Anthony Munday and the Catholics 1560–1633* (Aldershot: Ashgate, 2005).

Hamilton, D. and R. Strier (eds.), *Religion, Literature and Politics in Post-Reformation England, 1540–1688* (Cambridge University Press, 1996).

Hamilton, K. G., *John Dryden and the Poetry of Statement* (Ann Arbor: University of Michigan Press, 1969).

Hamm, V., "Dryden's *Religio Laici* and Roman Catholic Apologetics," *PMLA* 80 (1965), 190–8.

  "Dryden's *The Hind and the Panther* and Roman Catholic Apologetics," *PMLA* 83 (1968), 400–15.

Hammer, P., "Essex and Europe: Evidence from Confidential Instructions by the Earl of Essex 1595–6," *English Historical Review* III (1996), 380–1.

  The Polarisation of Elizabethan Politics: The Political Career of Robert Devereux, 2nd Earl of Essex 1585–1597 (Cambridge University Press, 1999).

Hammond, P., *John Dryden: A Literary Life* (Basingstoke: Macmillan, 1991).

Hardie, P. (ed.), *The Cambridge Companion to Ovid* (Cambridge University Press, 2002).

Harpham, G. G., *The Ascetic Imperative in Culture and Criticism* (University of Chicago Press, 1987).

Harran, M., *Luther on Conversion: The Early Years* (Ithaca, NY: Cornell University Press, 1983).

Harris, T., *London Crowds in the Reign of Charles II: Propaganda and Politics from the Restoration until the Exclusion Crisis* (Cambridge University Press, 1987).

Harris, Tim, Paul Seaward, and Mark Goldie (eds.), *The Politics of Religion in Restoration England* (Oxford: Blackwell, 1990).

Harth, Philip, *Contexts of Dryden's Thought* (University of Chicago Press, 1968).

"Religion and Politics in Dryden's Poetry and Plays," *Modern Philology* 70 (1973), 236–42.

Harvey, E., *Ventriloquized Voices: Feminist Theory and English Renaissance Texts* (London: Routledge, 1992).

Haskin, D., "Is There a Future for Donne's 'Litany'?," *John Donne Journal* 21 (2002), 51–88.

Hawkins, A. H., *Archetypes of Conversion: The Autobiographies of Augustine, Bunyan and Merton* (Lewisburg, PA: Bucknell University Press, 1985).

Healy, T., *Richard Crashaw* (Leiden: Brill, 1986).

Hester, M. T., *Kind Pitty and Brave Scorne: Donne's Satires* (Durham, NC: Duke University Press, 1982).

Hibbard, C., *Charles I and the Popish Plot* (Chapel Hill: University of North Carolina Press, 1983).

Hill, G., *The Lords of Limit* (Oxford University Press, 1984).

Hirschfeld, Heather, "'We all expect a gentle answer, Jew': *The Merchant of Venice* and the Psychotheology of Conversion," *ELH* 73.1 (Spring 2006), 61–81.

Holmes, P., *Resistance and Compromise: The Political Thought of the Elizabethan Catholics* (Cambridge University Press, 1982).

Hopkins, D., "Dryden and Ovid's 'Wit out of Season'", in C. Martindale (ed.), *Ovid Renewed: Ovidian Influences on Literature and Art from the Middle Ages to the Twentieth Century* (Cambridge University Press, 1988), 167–90.

Houston, A. and S. Pincus (eds.), *A Nation Transformed: England after the Restoration* (Cambridge University Press, 2001).

Hunter, J. P., "Binarism and the Anglophone Couplet," *MLQ* 61 (2000), 109–28.

Jackson, K. and A. Marotti, "The Turn to Religion in Early Modern English Studies," *Criticism* 4.1 (2004), 167–90.

James, W., *The Varieties of Religious Experience*, ed. R. Niebuhr (New York: Touchstone, 1997).

Janelle, P., *Robert Southwell, the Writer* (London: Sheed and Ward, 1935).

Javitch, D., *Poetry and Courtliness in Renaissance England* (Princeton University Press, 1978).

Johnson, J., *The Theology of John Donne* (Cambridge: D. S. Brewer, 1999).

Jones, R. F. (ed.), *The Seventeenth Century: Studies in the History of English Thought from Bacon to Pope* (Stanford University Press, 1951, rpt. 1969).

King, J., *English Reformation Literature: The Tudor Origins of the Protestant Tradition* (Princeton University Press, 1982).

Kneidel, G., "John Donne's *Via Pauli*," *Journal of English and Germanic Philology* (2001), 224–46.

Knights, M., *Politics and Opinion in Crisis, 1678–81* (Cambridge University Press, 1994).

    Representation and Misrepresentation in Later Stuart Britain: Partisanship and Political Culture (Oxford University Press, 2005).

Kristeller, P. O., *Iter Italicum* (London: Warburg, 1963–97).

Kuchar, G., *Divine Subjection: The Rhetoric of Sacramental Devotion in Early Modern England* (Pittsburgh: Duquesne University Press, 2005).

    "Henry Constable and the Question of Catholic Poetics: Affective Piety and Erotic Identification in the *Spiritual Sonnettes*," *Philological Quarterly* 85.1 (2006), 69–89.

    The Poetry of Religious Sorrow in Early Modern England (Cambridge University Press 2008).

Lacey, R., *Robert: Earl of Essex* (New York: Atheneum, 1971).

Lake, P., *Anglicans and Puritans?* (London: Unwin, 1988).

Lake, P., with M. Questier, *The Anti-Christ's Lewd Hat: Protestants, Papists and Players in Post-Reformation England* (New Haven: Yale University Press, 2002).

    Moderate Puritans and the Elizabethan Church (Cambridge University Press, 1982).

Lander, J., *Inventing Polemic: Religion, Print and Literary Culture in Early Modern England* (Cambridge University Press, 2006).

Lauritsen, J., "Donne's *Satyres*: The Drama of Self-Discovery," *SEL* 16 (1976), 117–30.

Leiner, W., *La Metamorphose dans la poésie baroque française et anglaise* (Paris: Éditions Jean-Michel Place, 1979).

Levinson, M., "What is New Formalism?," *PMLA* 122.2 (2007), 558–69.

Lewalski, B., *Protestant Poetics and the Seventeenth-Century Religious Lyric* (Princeton University Press, 1979).

Lewis, J. and M. E. Novak (eds.), *Enchanted Ground: Reimagining John Dryden* (University of Toronto Press, 2004).

Loomie, A. J., "A Catholic Petition to the Earl of Essex," *RH* 7 (1963), 1–37.

Low, A., *Love's Architecture: Devotional Modes in Seventeenth-Century English Poetry* (New York University Press, 1978).

    The Reinvention of Love: Poetry, Politics, and Culture from Sidney to Milton (Cambridge University Press, 1993).

Lupton, J. R., *Citizen-Saints: Shakespeare and Political Theology* (University of Chicago Press, 2005).

Malcolm, N., *De Dominis (1560–1624): Venetian, Anglican, Ecumenist and Relapsed Heretic* (London: Strickland and Scott, 1984).

Maleski, M. (ed.), *Fine Tuning: Studies of the Religious Poetry of Herbert and Milton* (Binghamton, NY: Medieval and Renaissance Texts and Studies, 1987).

Marcus, L. S., *Childhood and Cultural Despair: A Theme and Variations in Seventeenth-Century Literature* (University of Pittsburgh Press, 1978).

Marius, R., *Thomas More* (New York: Knopf, 1985).

Marotti, A., *John Donne: Coterie Poet* (Madison: University of Wisconsin Press, 1986).

Manuscript, Print and the English Renaissance Lyric (Ithaca, NY: Cornell University Press, 1999).

Religious Ideology and Cultural Fantasy: Catholic and Anti-Catholic Discourses in Early Modern England (University of Notre Dame Press, 2005).

Marotti, A. (ed.), *Catholicism and Anti-Catholicism in Early Modern English Texts* (New York: St. Martin's Press, 1999).

Critical Essays on John Donne (New York: G. K. Hall, 1994).

Marsden, J., *Fatal Desire: Women, Sexuality and the English Stage 1660–1720* (Ithaca, NY: Cornell University Press, 2006).

Marshall, P., *Religious Identities in Henry VIII's England* (London: Ashgate, 2006).

Martz, L., *The Poetry of Meditation: A Study in English Religious Literature of the Seventeenth Century* (New Haven: Yale University Press, 1954, revised edn. 1962).

Maus, K. E. and E. Harvey (eds.), *Soliciting Interpretation: Literary Theory and Renaissance Poetry* (University of Chicago Press, 1990).

May, S. W., *The Elizabethan Courtier Poets: The Poems and Their Contexts* (Columbia: University of Missouri Press, 1991).

Maycock, A., *Chronicles of Little Gidding* (London: SPCK, 1954).

McClendon, M., J. P. Ward, and M. MacDonald (eds.), *Protestant Identities: Religion, Society and Self-Fashioning in Post-Reformation England* (Stanford University Press, 1999).

McCoog, T. and P. Davidson, "Father Robert's Convert," *Times Literary Supplement* (Nov. 24, 2000), 16–17.

McCoog, T. (ed.), *The Reckoned Expense: Edmund Campion and the Early English Jesuits* (Woodbridge: Boydell Press, 1996).

Mehl, D. (ed.), *Plotting Early Modern London* (London: Ashgate, 2004).

Miller, J., *Popery and Politics in England, 1660–1688* (Cambridge University Press, 1973).

Milton, A., *Catholic and Reformed: The Roman and Protestant Churches in English Protestant Thought, 1600–1640* (Cambridge University Press, 1995).

Mintz, S., "The Crashavian Mother," *SEL* 39.1 (1999), 111–29.

Moore, T., "Donne's Use of Uncertainty as a Vital Force in *Satyre III*," *Modern Philology* 67 (1969), 41–9.

Morrison, K., *Conversion and Text* (Charlottesville: University of Virginia Press, 1992).

"I am You": The Hermeneutics of Empathy in Western Literature, Theology and Art (Princeton University Press, 1988).

Understanding Conversion (Charlottesville: University of Virginia Press, 1992).

Mueller, J., "Women among the Metaphysicals: A Case, Mostly, of being Donne For," *Modern Philology* 87 (1989), 142–58.

Murray, M., "'Now I ame a Catholique': William Alabaster and the Early Modern Catholic Conversion Narrative," in Corthell (ed.), *Catholic Culture*, 189–215.

"Performing Devotion in *The Masque of Blacknesse*," *SEL* 47.2 (Spring, 2007), 427–49.

Nock, A. D., *Conversion: The Old and the New in Religion from Alexander the Great to Augustine of Hippo* (Oxford: Clarendon, 1933).

Oberman, H., *Luther: Man Between God and the Devil*, trans. E. Walliser-Schwarzbart (New Haven: Yale University Press, 1989).

Ogg, D., *England in the Reign of Charles II*, 2nd edn. (Oxford: Clarendon, 1956, rpt. 1972).

Oliver, P. M., *Donne's Religious Writing* (London: Longmans, 1997).

Ovid, *Metamorphoses*, Books IX–XIV, ed. and trans. F. J. Miller, revised G. P. Goold, 2nd edn. (Cambridge, MA: Harvard University Press, 1984).

Papazian, M. A. (ed.), *John Donne and the Protestant Reformation* (Detroit: Wayne State University Press, 2003).

Parker, T. W. N., *Proportional Form in the Sonnets of the Sidney Circle* (Oxford: Clarendon, 1999).

Parrish, P., "The Feminizing of Power: Crashaw's Life and Art," in Summers and Pebworth (eds.), *The Muse's Common Weale*, 148–62.

    "O Sweet Contest: Gender and Value in 'The Weeper,'" in Roberts (ed.), *New Perspectives on the Life and Art of Richard Crashaw*, 127–39.

Parry, G., *Seventeenth-Century Poetry: The Social Context* (London: Hutchinson, 1985).

Patterson, A., *Censorship and Interpretation: The Conditions of Reading and Writing in Early Modern England* (Madison: University of Wisconsin Press, 1984).

    Fables of Power: Aesopian Writing and Political History (Durham, NC: Duke University Press, 1991).

    "A Man is to Himself a Dioclesian: Donne's Rectified Litany," *John Donne Journal* 21 (2002), 35–49.

Patterson, W. B., "The Peregrinations of Marco Antonio de Dominis, 1616–1624," *Studies in Church History* 15 (1978), 241–66.

Petti, A., "Unknown Sonnets by Toby Matthew," *RH* 9 (1967), 123–58.

Phillippy, P., *Love's Remedies: Recantation and Renaissance Lyric Poetry* (Lewisburg, PA: Bucknell University Press, 1995).

Pilarz, S. R., *Robert Southwell and the Mission of Literature, 1561–1595: Writing Reconciliation* (Aldershot: Ashgate, 2004).

Pincus, S., "From Butterboxes to Wooden Shoes: The Shift in English Popular Sentiment from Anti-Dutch to Anti-French in the 1670s," *HJ* 38 (1995), 333–61.

Piper, W. B., *The Heroic Couplet* (Cleveland: Case Western Reserve University Press, 1969).

Pollen, J. H., "The Politics of the English Catholics during the Reign of Queen Elizabeth," *The Month* 100 (1902), 176–83.

    "William Alabaster: A Newly Discovered Catholic Poet of the Elizabethan Age," *The Month* 103 (1904), 427–30.

Praz, M., *The Flaming Heart* (New York: Doubleday, 1958).

Price, M., *To the Palace of Wisdom: Studies in Order and Energy from Dryden to Blake* (New York: Doubleday, 1964).

Pritchard, A., *Catholic Loyalism in Elizabethan England* (Chapel Hill: University of North Carolina Press, 1979).

    "Donne's Mr. Tilman," *Review of English Studies* 24.93 (Feb. 1973), 38–42.

Questier, M., *Catholicism and Community in Early Modern England: Politics, Aristocratic Patronage, and Religion, c.1550–1640* (Cambridge University Press, 2006).

Conversion, Politics and Religion in England 1580–1625 (Cambridge University Press, 1996).

"Crypto-Catholicism, Anti-Calvinism and Conversion at the Jacobean Court: The Enigma of Benjamin Carier," *Journal of Ecclesiastical History* 47 (1996), 45–64.

"John Gee, Archbishop Abbot, and the Use of Converts from Rome in Jacobean Anti-Catholicism," *RH* 24 (1993), 347–60.

Rambuss, R., *Closet Devotions* (Durham, NC: Duke University Press, 1998).

Rasmussen, M. D. (ed.), *Renaissance Literature and Its Formal Engagements* (London: Palgrave, 2002).

Raspa, A., *The Emotive Image: Jesuit Poetics in the English Renaissance* (Fort Worth: Texas Christian University Press, 1983).

Reynolds, E. E., *Campion and Parsons: The Jesuit Mission of 1580* (London: Sheed and Ward, 1980).

Roberts, J. R. (ed.), *Essential Articles for the Study of John Donne* (Hamden, CT: Archon, 1975).

New Perspectives on the Life and Art of Richard Crashaw (Columbia: University of Missouri Press, 1990).

New Perspectives on the Seventeenth-Century English Religious Lyric (Columbia: University of Missouri Press, 1994).

Roche, T. P., *Petrarch and the English Sonnet Sequences* (New York: AMS Press, 1985).

Rose, E., *Cases of Conscience: Alternatives Open to Recusants and Puritans under Elizabeth I and James I* (Cambridge University Press, 1975).

Ross-Williamson, H., *Four Stuart Portraits* (London: Evans Brothers, 1949).

Sabine, M., *Feminine Engendered Faith: The Poetry of John Donne and Richard Crashaw* (Basingstoke: Macmillan, 1992).

Salvaggio, R., *Dryden's Dualities* (British Columbia: University of Victoria Press, 1983).

"Time, Space and the Couplet," *Philological Quarterly* 82 (1983), 95–108.

Schoeck, R. C. (ed.), *Acta Conventus Neo-Latini Bononiensis* (Binghamton: State University of New York Press, 1985).

Scott, J., *England's Troubles 1603–1702: Seventeenth-Century English Political Instability in European Context* (Cambridge University Press, 2000).

Seaward, P., *The Cavalier Parliament and the Reconstruction of the Old Regime 1661–1667* (Cambridge University Press, 1989).

Segal, A., *Paul the Convert: The Apostasy and Apostolate of Saul the Pharisee* (New Haven: Yale University Press, 1990).

Sellin, P., *So Doth, So Is Religion: John Donne and Diplomatic Contexts in the Reformed Netherlands, 1619–1620* (Columbia: University of Missouri Press, 1988).

Severance, S. L., "'To Shine in Union': Measure, Number and Harmony in Ben Jonson's 'Poems of Devotion,'" *Studies in Philology* 80.2 (Spring 1983), 183–99.

Shagan, E., *Popular Politics and the English Reformation* (Cambridge University Press, 2002).

Shagan, E. (ed.), *Catholics and the "Protestant Nation": Religious Politics and Identity in Early Modern England* (Manchester University Press, 2005).

Shami, J., "Donne on Discretion," *ELH* 47 (1980), 48–66.

John Donne and Conformity in Crisis in the Late Jacobean Pulpit (Woodbridge: D. S. Brewer, 2003).

Shapiro, J., *Shakespeare and the Jews* (New York: Columbia University Press, 1996).

Shell, A., *Catholicism, Controversy, and the English Literary Imagination, 1558–1660* (Cambridge University Press, 1999).

"Multiple Conversions and the Menippean Self," in Marotti (ed.), *Catholicism and Anti-Catholicism*, 154–97.

Shuger, D., *Habits of Thought in the English Renaissance: Religion, Politics and the Dominant Culture* (Berkeley: University of California Press, 1990).

Sloan, T. O., "A Renaissance Controversialist on Rhetoric: Thomas Wright's *Passions of the Mind in Generall*," *Speech Monographs* 36 (1969), 38–54.

Sloan, T. O. and R. Waddington (eds.), *The Rhetoric of Renaissance Poetry from Wyatt to Milton* (Berkeley: University of California Press, 1974).

Slights, C. W., *The Casuistical Tradition in Shakespeare, Donne, Milton and Herbert* (Princeton University Press, 1981).

Sloman, J., *Dryden: The Poetics of Translation* (University of Toronto Press, 1985).

Smith, A. J. (ed.), *John Donne: Essays in Celebration* (London: Methuen, 1972).

Smith, N., *Literature and Revolution 1640–1660* (New Haven: Yale University Press, 1994).

Perfection Proclaimed: Language and Literature in English Radical Religion 1640–1660 (Oxford: Clarendon, 1989).

Smuts, M., *Court Culture and the Origins of a Royalist Tradition in England* (Philadelphia: University of Pennsylvania Press, 1988).

Sorlien, R., "Apostasy Reversed: John Donne and Sir Toby Matthew," *John Donne Journal* 13 (1994), 101–12.

Spellman, W. M., *The Latitudinarians and the Church of England, 1660–1700* (Athens: University of Georgia Press, 1993).

Spurr, J., "'Latitudinarianism' and the Restoration Church," *HJ* 31 (1988), 61–82.

"'Rational Religion' in Restoration England," *Journal of the History of Ideas* (1988), 563–85.

The Restoration Church of England 1646–1689 (New Haven: Yale University Press, 1991).

Stachniewski, J., "John Donne and the Despair of the Holy Sonnets," *ELH* 48 (1981), 677–705.

Stewart, S., *Poetry and the Fate of the Senses* (University of Chicago Press, 2002).

Stock, B., *After Augustine: The Meditative Reader and the Text* (Philadelphia: University of Pennsylvania Press, 2001).

Augustine the Reader (Cambridge, MA: Harvard University Press, 1996).

Strier, R., "Crashaw's Other Voice," *SEL* 9 (1969), 135–51.

"John Donne Awry and Squint: The 'Holy Sonnets,' 1608–1610," *Modern Philology* 86 (1989), 357–84.

"How Formalism Became a Dirty Word, and Why We Can't Do Without It," in Rasmussen (ed.), *Renaissance Literature and Its Formal Engagements*, 107–15.

Love Known: Theology and Experience in George Herbert's Poetry (University of Chicago Press, 1983).

Resistant Structures: Particularity and Radicalism in Renaissance Texts (Berkeley: University of California Press, 1995).

Stroud, T. A., "Ben Jonson and Father Thomas Wright," *ELH* 14 (1947), 277–9.

Sullivan, C., *Dismembered Rhetoric: English Recusant Writing, 1580–1603* (London: Associated University Presses, 1995).

Summers, C. and T.-L. Pebworth (eds.), "Bright Shootes of Everlastingnesse": *The Seventeenth-Century Religious Lyric* (Columbia: University of Missouri Press, 1987).

The Eagle and the Dove: Reassessing John Donne (Columbia: University of Missouri Press, 1986).

The Muse's Common Weale: Poetry and Politics in the Seventeenth Century (Columbia: University of Missouri Press, 1988).

Representing Women in Renaissance England (Columbia: University of Missouri Press, 1997).

Swedenberg, H. T. (ed.), *Essential Articles for the Study of John Dryden* (Hamden, CT: Archon, 1966).

Sweeney, A., *Robert Southwell. Snow in Arcadia: Rewriting the English Lyric Landscape 1586–95* (Manchester University Press, 2006).

Targoff, R., *Common Prayer: The Language of Public Devotion in Early Modern England* (University of Chicago Press, 2001).

John Donne: Body and Soul (University of Chicago Press, 2008).

Tavard, G., *Holy Writ or Holy Church* (London: Burns and Oates, 1959).

Thurston, H., "Catholic Writers and Elizabethan Readers," *The Month* 82 (1894), 457–76; and 83 (1895), 231–45.

Townshend, D., *The Life and Letters of Endymion Porter* (London, 1897).

Trevor-Roper, H., *Archbishop Laud* (London: Macmillan, 1940).

"Toleration and Religion after 1688," in Grell (ed.), *From Persecution to Toleration*, 389–408.

Trimpi, W., *Ben Jonson's Poems* (Stanford University Press, 1962).

Tulloch, J., *Rational Theology and Christian Philosophy in the Seventeenth Century*, vol. 1 (Hildesheim: Georg Olms, 1966).

Tumbleson, R., "'Reason and Religion': The Science of Anglicanism," *Journal of the History of Ideas* 57 (1996), 131–56.

Turner, F. C., *James II* (London: Eyre and Spottiswoode, 1948).

Tyacke, N., *Anti-Calvinists: The Rise of English Arminianism c.1590–1640* (Oxford: Clarendon, 1987).

Tyacke, N. (ed.), *England's Long Reformation, 1500–1800* (London: University College Press, 1998).

Veevers, E., *Images of Love and Religion: Queen Henrietta Maria and Court Enter-tainments* (Cambridge University Press, 1989).

Walker, G., *Writing under Tyranny: English Literature and the Henrician Reformation* (Oxford University Press, 2005).

Walsham, A., *Church Papists: Catholicism, Conformity, and Confessional Polemic in Early Modern England* (Woodbridge: Boydell Press, 1993).

Warley, C., *Sonnet Sequences and Social Distinction in Renaissance England* (Cambridge University Press, 2005).

Warren, A., "The Reputation of Crashaw in the Seventeenth and Eighteenth Centuries," *Studies in Philology* 31 (1934), 385–407.

    Richard Crashaw: A Study in Baroque Sensibility (University: University of Louisiana Press, 1939).

Watt, T., *Cheap Print and Popular Piety 1550–1640* (Cambridge University Press, 1991).

Weiner, C. Z., "The Beleaguered Isle: A Study of Elizabethan and Early Jacobean Anti-Catholicism," *Past and Present* 51 (1971), 27–62.

Whigham, F., *Ambition and Privilege: The Social Tropes of Elizabethan Courtesy Theory* (Berkeley: University of California Press, 1984).

White, H., "John Donne and the Psychology of Spiritual Effort," in Jones (ed.), *The Seventeenth Century*, 355–68.

Whiting, R., *The Blind Devotion of the People: Popular Religion and the English Reformation* (Cambridge University Press 1989).

Williams, G. W., *Image and Symbol in the Poetry of Richard Crashaw* (Columbia: University of South Carolina Press, 1963).

Winn, J. A., *John Dryden and His World* (New Haven: Yale University Press, 1987).

Wolfe, H. (ed.), *The Literary Career and Legacy of Elizabeth Cary* (New York: Palgrave, 2007).

Wood, H. G., "The Conversion of Paul: Its Nature, Antecedents, and Consequences," *New Testament Studies* 1 (1955), 276–82.

Wooding, L., *Rethinking Catholicism in Reformation England* (Oxford University Press, 2000).

Young, R. V., *Doctrine and Devotion in Seventeenth-Century Poetry* (Cambridge: Brewer, 2000).

    Richard Crashaw and the Spanish Golden Age (New Haven: Yale University Press, 1982).

Zagorin, P., *Ways of Lying* (Cambridge, MA: Harvard University Press, 1990).

Zwicker, S., "The Paradoxes of Tender Conscience," *ELH* 63 (1996), 851–69.

    Politics and Language in Dryden's Poetry: The Arts of Disguise (Princeton University Press, 1984).

REFERENCE WORKS

Allison, A. and D. M. Rogers, *The Contemporary Printed Literature of the English Counter-Reformation Between 1558 and 1640*, 2 vols. (Aldershot: Scolar, 1989–94).

Clancy, T. H., *English Catholic Books, 1641–1700: A Bibliography* (Aldershot: Scolar, 1996).

Florén, C. (ed.), *John Donne: A Complete Concordance of the "Poems"* (New York: Olms-Weidman, 2004).

Foley, H. (ed.), *Records of The English Province of the Society of Jesus*, 7 vols. (London: Burns and Oates, 1875–83).

Gee, E. (ed.), *The Catalogue of all the Discourses Published Against Popery, During the Reign of King James II* (1689).

Gillow, J. (ed.), *Bibliographical Dictionary of the English Catholics*, 4 vols. (London: Burns and Oates, 1885–7).

Guiney, I. (ed.), *Recusant Poetry* (London: Sheed and Ward, 1938).

Jones, T. (ed.), *A Catalogue of the Discourses for and against Popery, in Two Volumes*, Chetham Society 48 and 64 (London: Chetham Society, 1859 and 1865).

Keynes, G., *A Bibliography of Dr. John Donne* (Oxford: Clarendon, 1973).

Milward, P., *Religious Controversies of the Elizabethan Age: A Survey of Printed Sources* (Lincoln: University of Nebraska Press, 1977).

Religious Controversies of the Jacobean Age: A Survey of Printed Sources (London: Scolar Press, 1978).

Miola, R. S., *Early Modern Catholicism: An Anthology of Primary Sources* (Oxford University Press, 2007).

Pollard, A. W. and G. R. Redgrave, *A Short-title Catalogue of Books Printed in England, Scotland, & Ireland and of English Books Printed Abroad 1475–1640*, 2nd edn., revised by W. A. Jackson, F. S. Ferguson, and K. F. Pantzer (London: Bibliographical Society, 1976–91).

Stephen, L. and S. Lee (eds.), *Dictionary of National Biography*, 22 vols. (London: Smith and Elder, 1885–1901).

The Term Catalogues, 1668–1709 A. D.: A Contemporary Bibliography of English Literature in the Reigns of Charles II, James II, William and Mary, and Anne (London, 1903–6).

Wing, D., *A Short-title Catalogue of Books Printed in England, Scotland, Ireland, Wales, and British America, and of English Books Printed in Other Countries, 1641–1700*, 2nd edn., revised by J. R. Morrison and C. Nelson, 3 vols. (New York: Modern Language Association of America, 1982–94).

Index

Abercrombie, Robert, 107
Alabaster, William, 5, 6, 22, 30, 36–68, 69, 72, 74,
    75–76, 84, 103, 119, 122, 135, 138, 159, 171
    Augustinian influence on, 31, 37, 47–51, 64
    autobiographical poetry of, 65–68
    Catholic conversion of, 42, 44–45
    and Earl of Essex, 36, 44, 84
    early literary productions of, 37–38
    at English College at Rome, 38–42
    Jesuit meditative techniques, in poetry of,
        52–53, 63, 64
    use of metaphor, 60–62, 63
    multiple conversions of, 36–37
    penitential poetry of, 58–61
    Spenser's praise of, 36, 37
    and Thomas Wright, 44, 53
    volta (turn), in sonnets of, 31, 55
    works
        Alabaster's Conversion (narrative), 43–51, 59
        Apparatus in Revelationem Iesu Christi, 36
        "Elisaeis," 38, 44
        Holy Sonnets, 51–68, 72
        Roxana, 37, 44
        Seven Motives, 43, 46, 75–76, 159
        Spiraculum Tubarum, 37
        "Upon a Conference in Religion between
            John Reynolds then a Papist and his
            Brother William, then a Protestant,"
            46–47
Allison, Anthony, 23, 117, 137
Alsup, Vincent, 159
Anderton, Hugh, 41
androgyny, conversion and, 121–126, 129–130,
    131–133, 134–135
    see also conversion, eroticized descriptions of;
        hermaphroditism
Anna of Denmark (wife of James I), 20, 107, 108,
    109, 146
Askew, Anne, 16, 33, 35
d'Aubigny, Lord, *see* Stuart, Charles, Lord
    d'Aubigny

Augustine, Saint, 42, 47–51, 104
    Confessions, 9–10, 25, 31, 47–51, 94
    early modern converts likened to, 17, 70
    influence of, on Alabaster, 31, 37, 47–51, 64
    quoted by Donne, 94
    use of, in early modern polemic, 25
Austin, John ("William Birchley"), 106
autobiographical writing, *see* conversion
    narratives; motives for conversion, first-
    person accounts of; *responsa scholarum*
Aveling, John, 109, 142

Bacon, Sir Francis, 101
Baker, Augustine, 113
Baker-Smith, Dominic, 85
Bald, R. C., 96
Bale, John, 16
Barlow, William, 159
Barnes, Barnabe, 52
Barnes, Robert, 16
Barroll, Leeds, 107
Bell, Ilona, 52
Bell, Thomas, 89
Bellarmine, Robert, 42
Benedict, Saint, 11
Benson, Donald, 140, 161
Bernard of Clairvaux, 11
Bilney, Thomas, 16
Birchley, William, *see* Austin, John
Birrell, T. A., 161
birth, as metaphor for conversion, 124, 130
Blackloists, 161
Blount, Mountjoy, Earl of Newport, 110
Boleyn, Anne, 156, 164
Boteler, Anne, Countess of Newport, 108, 110
Bossy, John, 1, 18, 19, 109
Breda, Declaration of (1660), 140
Bredvold, Louis, 85, 138
Breton, Nicholas, 56
Bristol, Earl of, 47–51
Broughton, Hugh, 72